HE RESTORES

by

Denise C. Herndon Harvey

Title: HE RESTORES

Author: Denise C. Herndon Harvey

Published by Pine Tree Press

www.pinetreepress.com

Printed in USA

Acknowledgement

I thank my Heavenly Father, for purposing in me the gifts and abilities to put into words what He had placed in my heart, for such a time as this.

I would also like to thank my family for their love and support for me as a wife, mother, grandmother, and ultimately daughter of the Most-High God.

Dedication

I dedicate this book to my family, and especially to my beautiful mother, who passed away in 2018. Her absence has made me acutely aware of the many aspects of her life that I never inquired about and never knew, and even now, I often reflect on the questions I wish I had asked.

This reflection on family has been deeply meaningful for me. I believe that understanding our family history and intentionally building strong foundations are crucial because a lack of knowledge about our roots can have lasting effects on future generations. My mother, much like the main character in this book, experienced a challenging childhood, a reality that resonates with many families.

True healing often begins with open and honest conversations about our beliefs and the traditions that have been passed down through generations. My hope is that families and especially my own will learn, grow, surrender, seek, and honor both each other and the Lord through this story.

CONTENTS

Acknowledgement 3

Dedication 4

The Virtuous Woman 9

(Proverbs 31:10-31, NKJV) 9

Reflections 11

Chapter 1. 12

AND SO IT BEGINS 12

Sweet Annabella 12

Essobella and Ezra 15

Looking from the Outside 15

Chapter 2. 22

Standing in the Gap for Family 22

Chapter 3. 30

Divided with discord 30

Who is Hezekiah 30

Life of Josiah 34

Roaring Life of Nelsa 43

Where Did He Come From 50

The Story of David 50

Chapter 4. 57

Fight for Those You Love 57

Chapter 5. 66

The Rising Dawn of a New Day 66

Double Dose of Faith 87

Michael's Fight to Live 92

Chapter 6. 96

The Gathering 96

The First Arrival 96

Nelly and Jennesis 111

Chapter 7. 123

The Gathering 123

About that Time 123

Chapter 8. 143

Breakthrough and Heal 143

Chapter 9. 189

Broken 189

Yet for Such a Time as This 189

Chapter 10. 204

Cleansing of Our Souls 204

Chapter 11. 219

Fire PIT Revelation 219

Chapter 12. 268

Truth Revealed 268

Chapter 13. 276

Healing Light of Forgiveness 276
Nelsa's Regret 278
Cleansing of Our Souls 285
Bella's Faith Walk 289
Chapter 14. 294
Power of Forgiveness 294
More Grace 294
Bonded with Love 304
Chapter 15. 311
Family Restoration 311
Chapter 16. 318
Hope arrived 318
Hearts Transformed 329
Chapter 17. 334
Sweet Day of Change 334
Chapter 18. 368
Bloodline Breakers 368
Chapter 19. 376
New Beginnings 376
Chapter 20. 382
Glory 382
Prayer of Salvation 384
About the Author 385

The Virtuous Woman

(Proverbs 31:10-31, NKJV)

"Who can find a virtuous wife? For her worth is far above rubies. The heart of her husband safely trusts her; So he will have no lack of gain. She does him good and not evil All the days of her life. She seeks wool and flax And willingly works with her hands. She is like the merchant ships, She brings her food from afar. She also rises while it is yet night, And provides food for her household, And a portion for her maidservants. She considers a field and buys it; From her profits she plants a vineyard. She girds herself with strength And strengthens her arms. She perceives that her merchandise is good, And her lamp does not go out by night. She stretches out her hands to the distaff, And her hand holds the spindle. She extends her hand to the poor, Yes, she reaches out her hands to the needy. She is not afraid of snow for her household, For all her household is clothed with scarlet. She makes tapestry for herself; Her clothing is fine linen and purple. Her husband is known in the gates, When he sits among the elders of the land. She makes linen garments and sells them And supplies sashes for the merchants. Strength and honor are her clothing; She shall rejoice in time to come. She opens her mouth with

wisdom, And on her tongue is the law of kindness. She watches over the ways of her household And does not eat the bread of idleness. Her children rise up and call her blessed; Her husband also, and he praises her: "Many daughters have done well, But you excel them all." Charm is deceitful and beauty is passing, But a woman who fears the Lord, she shall be praised. Give her of the fruit of her hands And let her own works praise her in the gates"

Reflections

Myra sat staring at the beautiful pond from the porch in her rocking chair. The air was chilly after all; it was fall, and the dew covered the foliage, and a damp chill hovered in the air.

Myra breathed deeply, exhaling with a soft sigh. She leaned her head back and began to wonder if this was even a good idea, let alone a great one.

This gathering now seems scary, she thought. Scared of the unexpected. Scared over the potential explosions just waiting to erupt, the hurt, the lies, the secrets, the unforgiveness, and the unhealed wounds.

It felt like ripping off an old bandage, exposing pain that never fully healed. The memories, the betrayals, and the things left unsaid; they all pressed in on her heart.

"Oh Lord, what on earth was I thinking?" She whispered aloud. Tears welled in her eyes as she tilted her head back against the chair. Then she said softly, "Well… no turning back now. It's time, it's past time."

"But as for me and my house, we will serve the Lord"

(Joshua 24:15)

Chapter 1.

AND SO IT BEGINS

Sweet Annabella

“What on earth was she thinking?” Bella shouted, pacing as she tossed clothes into her suitcase. “We may be family, but we are not the same kind! I love Mama, but this is a big mistake. What’s that saying about letting sleeping dogs lie?”

Daniel stood quietly, watching her. “You mean, let sleeping dogs lie?” He offered gently. “I get it, Bella, but if this is heavy on her heart, maybe it’s something she really needs. She’s getting older. She’s felt alone since your dad passed.”

He paused; his voice softened. “My grandma was like that too. She’d get sad and say she didn’t want to be here anymore, even though we were all around her. Sometimes people just start reflecting on their lives, their friends, and their siblings and wonder why they’re still here when others are gone. My Mama had to tell my grandma to stop asking God why she was still here. Not long after, she went to bed happy, had a great day, and just…slipped away peacefully. My Mama said that was her time. She was okay with it, even if the rest of us were devastated."

Bella stopped pacing. His words settled heavily in the room.

Daniel stepped closer. "So, I'm just saying, try to be there for your Mama this weekend. Love her. Don't give her a hard time. And try not to get into it with your sisters. I know it feels like they gang up on you, but just be cool. I'm here with you. If you need air, we'll step outside. Just… don't add to her stress. She's got enough to handle."

Bella stood with her back to him, arms crossed. After a long pause, she sighed. "Yeah, I guess it's time. There's a lot I don't know, but I know there's stuff nobody ever said. Sometimes I'd catch Mama just staring out the window, lost in thought. You'd call her name, and she wouldn't even answer. Grown folks always say, "Mind your business." That's how it was. Every family has secrets, but when it's your family, it hits different, especially when you've been kept in the dark for so long."

She looked down at the ring on her finger. She and Daniel hadn't even set a date yet, and once he found out what she was hiding, she wasn't sure they ever would.

"Well," she said quietly, "I guess we'll see how this goes."

"Therefore, if anyone is in Christ, he is a new creation; old things have passed away; behold, all things have become new."

(2 Corinthians 5:17, NKJV)

ESSOBELLA AND EZRA

Looking from the Outside

Essobella was in her bedroom packing her bags and getting everything ready when she heard the garage open and her husband pulling into the garage. As he came through the door, Essie hollered out to him, "Hey hon, is that you?" "I'm in the bedroom." He entered the room where his wife was organizing their clothes for the trip to Lake Misty.

Eza walked into the room and kissed his wife on her forehead. "Hey sweetheart, how's it going today? "Hey, my love, I'm well. How are you? How was your day? "It was good, good but long," he answered his wife.

How was your day?" he asked back. "It was fine, just running around here trying to get everything ready for our trip."

"Yeah, well, I'm just hoping that when we go to Lake Misty with our family, everything's going to be okay. I know how you feel about the entire situation; you don't even know everything, but at the same time, we know there are things that have been hidden. We know there are things that your Mama is still dealing with, so let's just hope that everything doesn't hit the fan hard and all your siblings don't get knocked down hard, especially Zek and Nelly; they can be hard.

Essie, still sitting on the bed, put her hand up in the air towards her husband. "Listen, that's my sister and brother, and I know how they are, and I love them, even with all their faults. I also know that you don't have anything nice to say concerning Nelly because of how she treated Samuel.

Samuel is your boy; he's like your best friend, so I get why you are extra hard on Nelly. My sister was really hurt. I know you don't like hearing all the things that she says about Samuel and how she treats him, but like I said, she's my sister, and I'm going to stand up for her."

Ezra spoke up, his head tilted slightly, staring at his wife. "Stand up for her? For what? You're telling me you agree with the filthy stuff she says out of her mouth and how she treats him. How about how she treats your mama? What in the world is wrong with you for saying that you stand behind that foolishness? Blood or not, I will not stand for unrighteousness, and that is all she displays, and you shouldn't either, especially when it concerns your mother.

"Listen sweetheart, yes, she is your sister, but she is as wrong as twenty left feet, not two. TWENTY. Your sister is a hard and bitter woman, and listen, Sam isn't perfect, and he isn't responsible for all that happened, and you know that, Essie. You know that. She didn't just break his heart; she broke his soul, and on top of that, she won't even let that man see his own daughter, and for what? Because he refused to stay around her bitterness? He wasn't wrong. I told you before how to help her!

You help her by praying for her; she needs to talk to someone. She is holding on to some really hard stuff, and it's jacked her up, but guess what? God still wants her to get better; we all do. You love her like that? Pray for her and try to get her to agree to get help; now that's how you can help her. Tell her you will even go with her; maybe she won't be so afraid to let that great big evil shield down."

He turns around and looks at his wife, puts his hands on her shoulders, and says very quietly and gently, "Look, she may be your sister, and she may be your blood, but she is not your kind. Your sister has a hard heart, and the things that she says and does have made Samuel's life miserable. It's ridiculous. She doesn't even realize that the things that she is saying are not only hurting Samuel, but they're also hurting their daughter too. Jennesis is one of the sweetest children you ever want to have, and yet Nelly is her mama. I'm just glad that Jennesis is more like her dad than she is her mama. Poor child, and how fair do you think it is that Samuel pays support and tries his best to take care of a daughter that she won't even let him be around just because he didn't want to be married to her anymore?"

Ez shakes his head in disbelief. "Man, who would want to be married to her? She has a lot of things going on in her life, for one, just not being a nice person. Man, I can't believe anybody would want her to be their attorney, because I wouldn't trust her because of how she comes off to people."

Essie breaks her silence. "Listen, I understand what you're saying. Nelly went through a lot, and I know for sure there are things that she is holding on to. More secrets, just like everybody else in the family. Can there be another family with more secrets than our family? I'm not saying it's all bad. I'm just saying these folks like they hide stuff! Why do people, especially older people, do this? They hide stuff, their sin, thinking that their life can look a different way if no one knows the dirt that they were doing when they were younger, and everybody has some type of sin from when they were younger, things that they aren't proud of and don't want anyone to know about." Ezra nodded in agreement with his wife. “Yeah, this family here, they want to keep it hidden. I get it, but as I said, let’s just try to get through this weekend and not only the weekend but the holiday too. This will be one holiday that we will never forget, but let’s just try to be there for each other and do what we need to do, and if it’s at all possible. I’m just trying to say stay neutral; no side-taking this weekend. Please don’t be siding with Nelly and Zek, because you know how they are, and especially if they get to cussing, fighting, and drinking, stay out of their way.

Love your mama; try to be there for your other brothers and Bella. Try to be the person that you need to be, whom I know you are. Sweetheart, you’re not like them. You’re not like Zek, and you’re darn sure not like Nelly, and I’m so glad about that. You’re my sweet boo! Essie smiled and gave her husband a great big hug. “You’re mine too! “Oh man, I think your aunt and uncle are coming as well.”

“Yeah, they’re coming. Listen, the fact that they’re coming tells you there’s some stuff about to go down.”

Ez rolls his eyes, putting his hands on his head. “Girl, I don’t know if we’re going to make it the entire weekend. We must be prayed up and oiled up for sure! “I agree with you there.” “Your

Aunt Ester," Ez shakes his head. "She and Nelly are so much alike in how they act and treat others."

"You are right again. That's my Mama's sister, and yes, she's nothing like Mama. But the crazy thing is that Mama and cousin Faith are really close, and Faith isn't like her Mama, thank goodness."

"Yeah, it's kind of crazy and hard to believe that your Aunt Ester is Faith's mother, the way she carries on too. Faith is an angel, and you know that Faith tries to do all she can for you; she opens her heart up sincerely for others. She doesn't just talk the Bible; she walks out her faith and beliefs."

Yeah, you're right, Essie adds. "Even with the things that Faith has experienced in her life, she is always trying to help people with her ministry, she and Mike both."

"Faith and Mike, they are the two anchors in our family. Calling on Jesus and praying for our family, that's how we all need to be."

"I'm telling you, sweetie," Ezra says, "we need to stay neutral and not be siding with the foolishness that I know is going to pop off this weekend. All right, my dear?

I love you, and I'm going to go and get a shower and start packing so that we can get ready and get up out of here early in the morning."

"For I know the thoughts that I think toward you, says the LORD, thoughts of peace and not of evil, to give you a future and a hope."
(Jeremiah 29:11, NKJV)

Chapter 2.

STANDING IN THE GAP FOR FAMILY

Michael could be heard singing as he stood in his bedroom packing his clothes, bellowing out the words to "What A God": "God, *what a God, what a God, what a God, yes, what a God, what a God."* While he is singing and praising the Lord, he thinks to himself, 'Man, this is going to be so wonderful to finally be able to get the family together. To finally be able to share the word of the Lord with our family, and finally to be able for Mama just to be able to clear her heart.

For everything to come to the surface that's hidden. How in the world do they ever think anyone's going to heal when everything stays so concealed, so closed off? Man, I'm so grateful to God that Faith and I can bring our mamas and bring our family together for such a time as this.

There's nothing like peace and love and forgiveness. There is so much that has happened that no one even knows about within our family. Let me call Faith real fast." Mike stops what he's doing, grabs his phone, and sends his cousin a text. Faith texts right back, then Mike calls, "Hey Sis how's it going?" Faith answers, "Hey, what's up, Mike-Mike?" "Good to hear from you."

"I can't wait to see you tomorrow. I know you said you were coming early, right? I know you told me, but I didn't want to keep asking you, and I was praying you wouldn't check out on me after putting this all together. You are so needed."

"Of course, Faith, I'm coming. I would never do that to you and Mama. This is very important for our family. The others may not understand, and they may not be happy about it, but man, I'm excited, Faith, because I can't wait to see what God is going to do."

Mike, says Faith, "I can't wait to see the restoration that's going to take place in our family. We've been waiting so long, so I'm excited. I know that it might be hard. I know that it might not be all good, and I understand that it's definitely not going to be pretty. There are going to be some things that are said that our family is not going to be pleased about.

I also know that there may be accusations and all kinds of evil information that may come out, but you know what? Even in all the bad stuff that comes out, it's necessary. "Amen, my cousin, I agree with you," replied Mike.

"I am so excited and happy that we are doing this, Mike. You don't have to tell me, Mike. We should have done this before Uncle Edward passed away, while he was still alive. The things that were hidden should have come out before your daddy passed away." Mike, hearing his cousin, didn't comment but nodded his head in agreement.

"Forgiveness should have been given; forgiveness should have been asked. Grace needs to be extended to everyone involved, and the secrets and lies should have been unearthed, but they weren't. But you know what? I'm telling you two things. Number one, I'm glad it's happening now, and I'm glad your Mama and Aunt Myra are still here, that she can be restored as well, and I say she's restored, yet we know this is a holy spirit restoration, and she, just like we are, is all obeying. All this to come together like it did, we know this is God, wanting restoration for this family that He loves."

"Man, Faith, I hear you, and you know what? I hope Aunt Ester and Uncle Ray make it too and don't flake out."

"Well listen," Faith says, "I asked them; they said they would think about it. Well, actually it was really my Mama who said she would think about it. I never really did say much to my dad, but my Mama said that she would think about it, so I'm going to call her when we get off the phone, just to see if she is coming. I didn't want to keep harping on the fact that she needed to come up here, because I believe that there's a lot between her and Aunt Myra that they need to get off their chests as well. They are both sisters, the only siblings to each other, and yet they act so distant to each other. That part I don't understand; if they were all that to each other and the only family growing up, then why are they not closer to each other? I believe that they too need to be up here. Mike, you know my dad is a whole trip himself, not to mention my brother and sister, Randall and Raynisa; I don't even know if they're coming." Mike just listened to Faith as she continued to speak, and he definitely understood where she was coming from.

As I said, I did put it out there to all of them, letting them know they are all welcome. Yet, when I say family, my siblings didn't answer me back either.

I'm sure that my dad talked to them, but I don't know what their answers are right now. It's more important to me to know that my cousins, your brothers and sisters, will be there for your mama, because more than anything, this is going to do a world of good for your aunt Myra, to have her whole family restored to the Lord and living in a way that God intended for families.

They don't understand Mike. They just don't understand generationally how things can change for us as a family.

Mike speaks up, "Yeah, Faith, you're right, and let me tell you why. Because they're not in the word of God, they are not serving the Lord, so there are a lot of things that they don't understand, nor do they care. If it's not about them or getting paid, they just don't care. It's a selfish attitude, rooted in the world. Unfortunately, a lot of families are like this. Messed up mindset, because it's a worldly mindset.

There are issues taking place in our family, and they think that it's just happening circumstantially or is a consequence because that's just how it is. They don't understand that even with the world that we live in today, a lot of the things that we see happening are because of generational issues and past traumas that occurred in our family that weren't right, and yet nobody was trying to break ungodly covenants or agreements. We all must have an understanding of the word of God. Consistently studying, learning, seeking, and asking the Holy Spirit—otherwise, how is it going to be uncovered and healed?"

"Yeah, Mike, you're right about that. Let me tell you, I've done the work. I know I've done the work, and there is still so much more that can be done. I've gone before the Lord, I've asked for forgiveness, and I've even asked for forgiveness concerning our ancestors. I have done what I know to do. I have been praying for salvation for the rest of the family. It's so important, and I pray that they'll come to understand for themselves, you know? I know what you want to say, and that you would hope and pray that they'll come to understand that we aren't just trying to push the Bible down their throat, the way they always look at us, 'like, *oh, here they go again, hitting us over the head with the Bible.'* No one is trying to do that to them; we just pray they understand that there are just two kingdoms, just two. The Kingdom of God and the kingdom of darkness: if you're not in the kingdom of God, and if you are living for the world and the things of the world, and if you are not a child of the Most High God, receiving Jesus as your Lord and Savior, then you are in the kingdom of darkness, point blank. You've been signed up for the other kingdom; by default, it's the easiest way I can explain it and make it plain."

"I get it, cousin," agreed Faith. "I understand that they don't understand, or maybe they just don't believe it and rather just spin the wheel, so to speak, and take their chance; after all, that is what's happening in the world. That serving God and salvation doesn't matter, but man, they got to know the truth, and the Truth is our Lord and Savior Jesus Christ."

"This weekend is about forgiveness. Understanding that secrets must be revealed, lies being canceled out, putting down whatever ungodly devices they were involved in, and the hatred and the way people feel about each other must change for the good. We're all family, yet we don't even love each other. This is crazy! This is how the world acts, and this is how the kingdom of darkness interacts with the world, and this is where we need to step out."

"Preach, Mike, preach!" That's exactly what I'm talking about! You know what's going to happen this weekend; we are not going up there and not coming back the same way. We are asking God, and we're seeking God for restoration; we know that He has restoration and reconciliation for our family. We know that He has for all that seek Him; that's what I'm talking about, babe. That's what I'm talking about. Let's thank Him already; it's already done!

"So, listen, I'll be up there in the morning, I'll be finishing things here, and then I'll be on my way, all right?" "All right, all right, much love to you." "Love to you, bye-bye, Mike." "Bye now," Mike says back to Faith.

"Trust in the Lord with all your heart and lean not on your own understanding; in all your ways submit to him, and He will make your paths straight."
(Proverbs 3:5-6, NKJV)

Chapter 3.

DIVIDED WITH DISCORD

Who is Hezekiah

Hezekiah, also known as Zek to his family and friends, already started off in a bad mood. Zek owned his own auto repair shop and a car lot selling used vehicles. Zek is terribly upset that he has to go up to the lake house at Lake Misty, even if it is for Thanksgiving. "Man, *I cannot believe that I had not only had to take off for Thanksgiving but the day after Thanksgiving too. That's the money-making day; heck, the entire weekend.*' He thought to himself.

I couldn't care less about what Pops did when he was married to Mama; he wasn't right! Did he treat any of us, right? How much time did he spend with me? How much time did he spend with any of us? Zek walks into the house and slams the door. Arrya calls out his name, "Zek, is that you?" Arrya says.

"Yes, it's me. Who else would it be?" "Hey, what's up? Why are you in such a bad mood? You just got home? I was just making sure it was you coming through the front door, because I knew I had left it unlocked."

"I tell you all the time," Zek says, "don't leave the door unlocked. I don't understand why you keep leaving the door unlocked, even if you're here. You need to do a better job at that: protecting yourself, protecting our home, and protecting our kids."

Arrya was used to his mood. She tried to keep the peace, especially since Myra, Zek's mother, was struggling after her husband's death. Arrya hadn't grown up with a father, and though she sometimes envied Zek for having one, even a flawed one, she still struggled to understand his deep resentment.

Zek had never told her the real reason for his bitterness, how he and his sister Nelly had discovered their father's secret a long time ago. They'd seen him with another woman and eventually realized he had a second family, a son. Zek and Nelly had sworn to keep it a secret, not even telling their mother.

Arrya, a nurse and a woman of faith, loved her husband despite his flaws. She had embraced Kai, Zek's son from a previous relationship, as her own, and together they had two sons, Matthew, who they called Matty, and Luca. The kids loved both parents but hated their fighting, especially Zek's harshness toward their mother.

Arrya sometimes questioned whether she should keep trying. She prayed for their marriage, believing that God didn't want them to divorce, but she also knew she deserved better than constant harshness, and she was coming to the end of her rope concerning their loveless marriage.

"Zek, I know you're unhappy about leaving the shop in your manager's hands, but you must trust the people you've trained. Your Mama spent a lot of money getting to this lake house so everyone could be together. It's important to her; she's been hurting since your father passed," Arrya said gently.

Zek cut her off. "I don't need you to tell me what to do with my family. Just promise me you won't nag me about drinking. Drinking is the only thing that calms me down and makes me feel good, and I don't want to hear about how it affects my attitude; I like it and I'm not stopping."

Arrya just shook her head. "I do believe you can heal if you're willing."

Zek muttered under his breath, "*Why is she always trying to fix me? Why does she think that there is something wrong with me? Why isn't she looking at her own life? She didn't even have a father in her house. She doesn't even know what it's like. Why can't I just come home and sit down and have some peace in the house as opposed to listening to all this BS? It's the last thing I want to listen to.* Instead, he said aloud, "Just get the kids ready so we can get this over with and leave on time. We can leave tonight or in the morning, whichever you want. I'm done talking about it." Arrya nodded and resigned. "We will all be ready in the morning."

"Therefore, if anyone is in Christ, he is a new creation; old things have passed away; behold, all things have become new." (2 Corinthians 5:17, NKJV)

Life of Josiah

"All right, later. Y'all have a good one! I'm out of here. Won't be back till next week!" Josiah hollered out to his coworkers as he walked out of the building, heading toward his car. He was ready to clock out from more than just work, ready to leave behind the noise, even if it meant walking into a different kind of storm, a family storm he wasn't ready for.

Josiah is the second-born son of Myra and Edward. Josiah looked up to his older brother, Zek, and besides him, the only other person he even remotely cared about speaking with was Nelly. As soon as he slid into his car, he grabbed his phone and called Zek. The line rang a few times before going to voicemail.

"Yoo, what's up? I can't come to the phone right now. Leave a message, and I'll call you back. Bye."

Josiah sighed, shaking his head. "Man, I've been trying to call you all day. It's your brother. What's going on? I just wanted to see if you're going this weekend to the lake, because if you aren't, I really don't want to go. I'm not trying to sit around and listen to folks talk about how you got out of the service or how you should've stayed in. I'm not trying to hear all that, man. Call me back. I'm heading home now. Peace out."

He hung up, tossed the phone in the passenger seat, and drove in silence. The thought of spending Thanksgiving at that lake house made his stomach twist. He could already hear the arguments, the fake apologies, the prayers he didn't want to join in on. He loved his family, but that didn't mean he liked being around them. He hadn't liked being around them for a long time, even before his father passed away. Now with him gone, he found every opportunity to stay away, and since he wasn't close with most of his siblings, that was a great reason to stay away.

Only Zek and Nelly, the two who understood him best. The rest, nothing; they didn't get him. He didn't really get them either. Still, he tried to be there for his Mama since their dad passed, but even the short visits with his Mama were too long for him. Plus, she felt a little distant anyway, like she was somewhere else or had a lot on her mind.

He thought, 'Yeah, she might still be in grief, but she's got to work that out for herself. I *can't do anything for her,'* he said to himself. Every time he looked in her eyes, she seemed lost, as her joy had died with his dad. And although Josiah loved her, he didn't know how to reach her. He didn't know what to say to offer her comfort.

He pulled into his apartment garage, went inside, and collapsed onto the sofa, then got right back up to go to the kitchen. "Glad to be off work," he muttered, reaching for a beer from the fridge. He popped the top, took a long drink, and walked back to the sofa.

The last thing he wanted to do was to start packing for a family weekend he didn't even believe in. As he sat there, sipping his beer, he thought about his dad, how he'd always wanted his father to come see him play ball, to show up, to show that he cares. But most of the time, his mother did come through, and so did Zek, even when his dad didn't. Myra never missed a game. Zek came when he could, and that meant something, but it wasn't the same as having his father there.

Josiah wanted his father to be proud of him and cheer for him. Instead, he'd been left chasing that approval in all the wrong places when he didn't receive it from the one who mattered.

He has had his own struggles now. A few years back, he'd been in the Air Force. Met a girl, things moved fast, and before he knew it, she was pregnant. Their daughter, little Lai-Joy, lived in another state. Josiah worked at the airport now, trying to visit whenever he could afford to fly out. He FaceTimed her when her mother let him speak with her, but it wasn't the same. He wanted to be a father who showed up, something he'd never had, even with a daddy in the home.

He grabbed his phone and called Zek again. This time, his brother answered.

"Hey man, what's up? Been trying to call you," Josiah said.

"I've been working. What do you think I've been doing?" Zek replied.

Josiah chuckled. "Yeah, I got it. Same here. But I just wanted to see if you're going to Mama's thing at the lake house."

"It's called Thanksgiving, in case you forgot," Zek teased.

"I know, I know," Josiah replied. "But you know it's more than that. It isn't just turkey and mac and cheese. It's…whatever Mama's planning. To be honest, I'd rather stay home and chill."

Zek sighed. "Looks like we don't get a choice, bro. The rest of them are going, so we must be there too. Nelly already said she thinks something's up; maybe Mama's hiding something. You know Faith's always in her ear. It could be about money. Maybe she found some old insurance policy or something."

Josiah laughed. "Now that would be nice. I could use a few extra coins myself."

"Yeah, me too," Zek said. "Could help me breathe a little easier."

"Still," Josiah said, "just because you all are going doesn't mean I have to go. You can fill me in when you get back."

"Man, look," said Zek, "if I gotta go, your butt's going too. Don't make me come back and drag you. We all need to be there."

Josiah laughed. "Fine, fine. But I'm not going tonight. If you all aren't leaving till morning, I'll go then too. There's no way I'm sitting up there all night with Mama and Faith talking about prayer and Jesus. I'll pass."

Zek chuckled. "Yeah, I get that. You talked to anybody else?"

"Who, me? Nah, I don't talk to anybody but you and Nelly. Mike sometimes, but not much anymore. But Mike's close with Faith, and you know how they are; they can't wait to preach to us about how we're all going to hell if we don't straighten up."

Zek laughed. "Yeah, he can try that mess with you, but he better not come at me with it."

"Exactly," Josiah said, grinning. "That's how they roll. And you know that's what Mama loves. Man, I remember she used to drag us to church every Sunday, choir rehearsal, Bible study, children's church, and even vacation Bible school. What was that club she had us in? Oh yeah, AWANAs! Man, we did everything."

Both brothers laughed hard, remembering their childhood. It wasn't all bad. Their mother really had tried to give them a strong foundation. But somewhere along the way, life had chipped away. What was imparted in them now appeared to be buried deep in their souls.

"I gotta go, man," Zek said finally. "Gotta finish packing and help Arrya get ready. We're leaving early tomorrow."

"Yeah, all right. I'll see you then." "Cool. Love you, bro." "Love you too, man."

As the call ended, Josiah leaned back on the couch, staring at the ceiling. "Lord," he whispered sarcastically, "If you're really up there, don't let this weekend be a hot mess."

Then, with a smirk, he muttered, "But you probably don't care anyway, at least not about me."

Josiah went and lay across his bed before getting up and grabbing his duffel bag from his closet. He sat slouched on the edge of his bed, staring at the half-packed duffel bag. He tossed in a few shirts, then kicked the bag shut. Packing wasn't what was on his mind, he figured. He'd just get up in the morning and finish. What he brings isn't important anyway. What weighed on him was the same thing that always did: how much he hated being dragged into all this family drama, and especially when his name came up.

He lit a cigarette, inhaled deeply, and muttered, "What's the point? Same drama, different day."

Josiah had always felt like the outsider, the middle boy, the one nobody really took seriously. His older brother and sisters had their own lives, their own successes, and their own scars. He'd stumbled and gotten into trouble when he was younger, and though he'd tried to climb out of the hole, no one seemed to notice. Not even his dad. Edward had promised to be there, but when it mattered, he wasn't. That wound never healed.

The only ones Joey felt understood him were Zek and Nelly. They didn't judge him, not really, but they were pissed off at him when he got in trouble, but he always believed they loved and cared for him. He knew they were bitter too, carrying the same anger that he carried. He looked up to Zek and admired how strong and outspoken he was, even if it came out harsh. And his sister, man, that one was tough too and fearless, and man, was she smart. She said what she wanted and never cared about who it hurt. Josiah figured out that was the only way to survive in this world and in his family.

Despite his bitterness, he loved his mama. Myra was the one person he couldn't bring himself to turn away from. She'd stood by him when he messed up and prayed for him even when he told her not to. Deep down, he knew she meant well. And that's why he was going to show up at the lake house. Definitely not for any of his siblings, but for Myra. Only his mother.

He picked his bag back up and decided to toss in a few more items. He zipped his bag open again, dug through it, and laughed to himself. "Mama *thinks this weekend about family bonding. Man, she's dreaming.'* He shook his head, grinding out the cigarette. *'I'll go for her. Only for her, but don't any of you try to preach to me. I'm not doing the church mess or the God thing. I've had enough of people shoving that holiness stuff down my throat.'*

He slung the bag over his shoulder, muttering under his breath. *'I'll go, but don't expect me to change. I'm not here for the family; I'm going to my mama.'*

With that, Josiah walked out of the bedroom and lay back on the sofa, bracing himself for a weekend. He already knew he hated it but couldn't avoid it.

"Call to Me, and I will answer you, and show you great and mighty things, which you do not know."

(Jeremiah 33, NKJV)

Roaring Life of Nelsa

Nelsa, Myra and Edward's oldest daughter, sat behind her desk facing the window. She dictated a list of duties to her secretary; things she wanted her to handle after the Thanksgiving holiday while she was away.

"Make sure you take care of everything I've given you," Nelly said firmly. "Contact our clients, and if there's anything you don't understand, text me or email me. But don't call me unless it's an absolute emergency. You got it?" "Yes, Miss Nelly, I got it," her assistant replied. "No worries at all, and I hope you have a wonderful vacation with your family."

"Girl, this is not a vacation!" Nelly scoffed. "Not the kind of vacation I'd choose. It's a situation I have no choice but to go to and do what I must do."

"All right, Miss Nelsa," the young woman said, smiling as she left.

"Shut the door! Sorry, I meant to say close it behind you, please!" Nelly hollered after her.

Nelly was sharp and commanding, but her life wasn't as polished as it appeared. On the outside, she was beautiful, tall, striking, wealthy, and educated. On the inside, though, she was broken and bitter. Pride and arrogance cloaked her like fine silk. She didn't like many people, least of all her own parents.

She suffered much rejection; at least that's how she framed the bitterness she sported around her neck, like a beautiful bow tie. Nelsa wanted everyone to play by her rules and pay for the soul wounds that still haunted her soul.

Nelly believes that no one appreciates her, and she set out to not only prove her worth to her family but to the world. Nelly wasn't just an attorney, and she was a great attorney. She was cutthroat and emotionless. Grace wasn't something she offered, not to clients, not to friends, not even to her family.

Nelly decided long ago that God didn't care about her; therefore, she didn't care either. In fact, she often spoke up against her upbringing in the world of faith, saying that it was a bunch of fantasy and emotional shows from a bunch of people foolishly conned by money-hungry preachers who don't know what they are talking about.

She had always felt she needed to earn her father's love, and the rejection she carried became a seed of bitterness she wore like a fine piece of jewelry. She wanted everyone to play by her rules, to pay for the pain she had suffered.

Long ago, Nelly decided that God didn't care about her, so she wouldn't care either. She often mocked the faith she was raised in, calling it "a fantasy for people fooled by money-hungry preachers." Her words had cut Myra deeply. Still, Myra had done her best to raise her children to know Jesus, to understand salvation and the sacrifice of Jesus Christ. But when Nelly went off to college, she stopped pretending. She didn't pray, didn't attend church, and didn't bother being kindhearted or sympathetic to anyone.

Now, her daughter Jennesis was the opposite. Quiet, gentle, and loving like her father, Samuel. Though still a preteen, Jennesis was wise beyond her years. She loved her grandmother, Myra, dearly and often sat with her, listening to her stories about Jesus, in person but mainly over the phone.

Jennesis carried a secret her mother didn't know. She had given her heart to Christ when she was ten, praying with her grandmother. Myra wept with joy. But they kept it hidden; Nelly would be livid if she knew.

Jennesis prayed every day for her mother, that God would soften her heart. She couldn't understand how someone so beautiful and smart could be so mean. It hurt her when her Mama spoke harshly about her grandparents.

She had once told Myra, "Grandma, I want to be loved. I want a husband like my daddy, who loves me and treats me right. When I have children, I want them to know how much Jesus loves them because He loved us first."

That simple, childlike faith touched Myra's heart. Jennesis also loved her father, Samuel. She often asked to visit him, but Nelly found ways to avoid it. Her bitterness toward Samuel ran deep. When he'd finally asked for a divorce, Nelly had told him, "If you don't want me, then you don't want your daughter either." And she had kept pulling the visitation strings with Sam ever since.

Now, Nelly gathered her things, left the office, and drove home, dreading the trip ahead. Spending a weekend at Lake Misty with people she barely tolerated wasn't her idea of peace. The only one she truly cared to see was her brother, Zek, because they understood each other. For years, they had carried a secret that bound them together: the truth about their father's affair and the son he had with another woman. They'd seen him that day, laughing and hugging the boy who called him Daddy. They both heard his voice clearly: '*Yeah, that's my boy!' How's my boy doing?'* They both heard their father say this to this little boy, and Zek had turned pale. Nelly thought he might pass out right there on the sidewalk. That image had never left her. The pain had rooted deep inside her soul.

She had made Zek promise never to tell anyone, not even their mother. Since then, the two of them had treated their parents with resentment and disrespect. They didn't serve God. They believed the world owed them something. Arrya, Zek's wife, was the only one among them who walked in faith, but even she couldn't persuade them to step inside a church, not Nelly, and certainly not her husband.

When Nelly got home, she pulled into her spacious garage and walked into her immaculate picture-perfect kitchen. Her house was as pristine as a showroom, a reflection of the image she worked hard to project to the world. But the reflection staring back at her in the window was a cold woman, full of pride, jealousy, and pain.

"Jennesis!" She called. "Hey, sweet girl, you here?" "Hi Mommy! Yes, I'm here!" Jennesis came skipping down the steps. "How are you? Did you have a good day?"

"I had a day," Nelly said flatly. "Good or bad doesn't matter. I did what I had to do to get what we needed. Are you packed for the lake house?"

"Yes, Mommy, I'm already packed! I can't wait to see Grandma Myra and all my cousins, aunts, and uncles! It's going to be so much fun! And it's Thanksgiving! And a house with a lake—oh my gosh, it's so beautiful there!"

Nelly said nothing, shuffling through the mail in her hands. Finally, she muttered, "Yeah, it's beautiful, all right. I just don't know how this trip's going to go. But… I guess it'll be nice for you to see your grandma. I know how much you love her. Anyway, make sure you have everything you need, so we don't have to go out and buy anything, okay? I'm going to lie down before I start packing. Did you eat yet, or do you want some pizza?" "Pizza would be great, Mommy! Do you want me to order it?" "Yes, honey. Go ahead and order the pizza here, and use my card to pay online. Let them deliver it; I don't feel like going anywhere tonight."

"Yes, Mommy, I'll take care of it right now." "Thank you, sweetheart," Nelly called as she walked down the hall to her bedroom, closing the door behind her.

Jennesis smiled softly, grabbed the laptop, and placed the order, whispering a quiet prayer as she did. "God," she said under her breath, "*please help my mommy. I love her and I love You.*"

"Do not sorrow, for the joy of the Lord is your strength."
(Nehemiah 8:10b, NKJV)

Where Did He Come From

The Story of David

David turned off his phone and sat in silence for a long while, staring down at his hands. "Yeah," he muttered under his breath, "I'll be there. Tomorrow."

The words felt strange, yet they were words that he waited all of his young life to hear. He'd waited his whole life to hear her voice, to be invited to finally belong to this family, a family that knows nothing about him, yet they are his family.

Now, that time had finally come, and fear and faith wrestled quietly in his chest. It should have come from his father, but instead it came from Myra, his father's wife, yet not his mother. He sat in silence, his head down, tears welling up in his eyes. He looked up with his eyes closed and began to pray silently. David leaned forward, elbows resting on his knees. "I don't even know if this is a good idea," he whispered. "But I know I have to go…. I need to go, at least this one time."

His apartment was still very sterile and very neat; it looked as if no one actually lived there. David kept it that way: no pictures, no warmth, yet the total opposite of what his heart desires, the love and warmth from a family. He could hear the faint hum of the refrigerator, along with the rhythmic ticking of an old grandfather's clock, one of his mother's family's gifts to him.

David walked to his bedroom and began to pack for the weekend. He'd bring enough clothes, just in case he decided to stay. Still, his head told him it may only be dinner, so pack the bag, but leave it in the car. In his bedroom as he packed, an old picture of his father lay face-up on the nightstand, beside a Bible marked with worn pages, still open from his earlier studying. He reached for it gently, tracing the image with his thumb, a man in a dark suit smiling beside a woman and several children who shared his eyes.

David loved it when his father came to see him. He loved looking at that picture. It's all so real now; it's all becoming real every minute now. "That's *them," he whispered. My brothers... my sisters.'* He swallowed hard. '*Do they even know I exist?'* He remembered the day he finally saw them, not at a family reunion, not in joy, but in grief. The day before the funeral. He'd almost turned around three times before walking through the doors of the funeral home. The flowery scent mingled with the heaviness of grief, filling the air.

From the door, he could see the casket. His father, his daddy, his hero, his lifeless body lying there. He was such a big man to David, but now, he seemed so very small, and yet in that instance, David felt like the little boy, the boy that loved his daddy so much, the boy that only wanted to be loved and protected by a father who loved him back. A father who would tell him how proud he was of him. A father who would come to his games would be cheering him on in the stands. A father, when he brought his report card home, would gush over how smart his smart boy was. When he went to the prom, the same father would be there to give him the car keys and tell him to be safe but have a good time. The dad, who, when he got accepted into college, would burst at the seams that his boy got a full ride; oh, how proud his dad would be! When he got baptized and accepted the Lord as his Savior, he would cry tears of joy and rejoice over his newfound relationship with Jesus, and the salvation he had in Jesus. That Father, who was now lying in a satin-lined casket, lifeless, void of his spirit, that he prayed was now with Jesus. The family, the friends, the neighbors, all gathered to mourn the passing of a man, a father, his father, and husband, and so much more. David gathered his strength, keeping his head down as he entered the viewing room and walked down towards the casket. David could feel the eyes on him, but he didn't look around, and he didn't stop walking until he got to the front of the casket. He stood, quiet, still, deep pain hurting, his heart beating so hard, he was quite certain others could hear it. His stomach held knots so tight he thought he was going to pass out. He hadn't seen his father in such a long time. Yet, seeing his face began to stir something deep inside him. Everything mixed together, the sorrow, love, and anger. He wanted to pass out, or better yet, that he'd wake up from this nightmare. David remained standing tall, with much dignity. His right hand reached out and touched his father's folded hand. He stared at his father's face, if only he could open his eyes. If only he could see his father smile, one last time, just one last time, *'Daddy, please open your eyes, daddy, I love you so very much, and I always will.'* Attempting to hold in the tears, he refused to blink as tears hovered on the brim of his eyes. As he turned to leave, he saw her. David knew immediately who she was, and their eyes locked. For what felt like a very long heartbeat, time stood still. Myra stood up and walked toward him, her steps steady, her expression gentle but knowing. He saw a faint smile across her face and her eyes; she looked at him with love in her eyes. Oh, how he wished he had been in her presence as a child. He'd never forget the way she said his name. There was peace behind her voice, laced with love. Not like towards an outsider, or stranger, no it was kind, it was with love, love for family. "Hello, David," she said softly, and she touched his arm, as he took her hand in his hand. "I'm glad you came. I'm sorry it had to be under these circumstances, but… he would have wanted you here." "David, son. I'm so sorry. I'm so sorry for so many things, but mainly that you didn't have the life with your earthly father, like you should have had. I want you to know he loved you, son. I know he didn't always show it, I know it had to be hard for you, it would have been for any child. Children don't ask to be born into such horrible situations; adults are supposed to know better and do better. I just wanted you to know that. Please come tomorrow if you can. You are welcome, son, you will always be welcome. David, standing speechless, tears rolling down his face, and his throat closed. He managed only a whisper that could come out. "Thank you, yes ma'am, yes ma'am. Thank you for telling me this." Myra leaned in and gave him a hug that melted the little pride he had left, as he collapsed in her arms, holding in the sobs, yet the tears flowed uncontrollably. "You don't have to hide anymore." Her words, soft, filled with love, yet loud enough to him, only for David to hear, lifted his spirit and touched his very soul. It was the first kindness he'd ever received from anyone, let alone his secret family.

David, graciously thanking her, broke away and quickly walked out of the room and down to the men's room. He needed to breathe; he needed to leave. But not everyone missed the moment. From across the room, Zek's eyes had narrowed. He recognized something, the resemblance, maybe, or the way his mother looked at the young man she'd just spoken to, as they embraced. He witnessed the love and kindness on his mother's face and wondered who this could be that received such a gracious response from his mother, at his father's viewing. Then it hit him; it was his father's son. Right on cue, and just behind him, Nelly froze, as she witnessed the same thing, just like when they were kids. She'd seen David, too, yet neither of them said a word. Myra returned quietly to her seat, her face calm, but her heart was already beginning to turn toward more forgiveness for her husband and love towards David, which she knew he had never received, yet deserved. Now, sitting alone in his apartment, that scene, that beautiful, yet sorrowful scene replayed over and over again.

The look of love in her eyes, yet deep pain, existed but was not demonstrated in her voice. That simple love and grace were given to nothing more than to a stranger. Wow, if only his own mother had that kind of resolve to love even a child that wasn't hers. That one act, that one encounter, he had never forgotten it. And now she has called him and invited him to Thanksgiving dinner with all of the family. David, now lying across his bed, still holding his father's picture, closed his eyes. A family dinner…my family, finally, finally...

"Beloved, do not avenge yourselves, but rather give place to wrath; for it is written, 'Vengeance is Mine, I will repay,' says the Lord."

(Romans 12:19, NKJV)

Chapter 4.

FIGHT FOR THOSE YOU LOVE

The air outside was crisp, the sun barely breaking through the horizon. Sun rays filtered through the blinds as she awoke. Myra rose early that morning. "This is the day the Lord has made, and I'm more than ready and able and never alone," she whispered, "and more importantly, I will rejoice and be glad in it." She wasn't sure if she was excited for the day to begin or more excited for the weekend to just be over with. Myra rose, turned to the side of her bed, and stretched her arms over her head. Lowering her arms, she bent her head, clasped her hands, and began to pray, giving God thanks for waking her up to see another day.

She didn't take it for granted. Edward hadn't made it as far as she had; there was no telling how much farther she would go, and that went for everyone. Sanctify it, Jesus, and let Your Spirit fill every corner of this house before my family walks through these doors. Heal, Jesus; bind up the pride, the rebellion, the selfishness, and the unforgiveness that've taken root in us, and cast them out in the Name of Jesus. Loose your love and peace in this family. Heal, Lord, like only you can heal."

After praying, Myra got up. Faith was going to arrive early to lend a helping hand, so Myra showered and got herself ready. She put on her favorite warm-up suit, a royal blue and gray one her son Michael had bought for her birthday. She smiled, thinking about him. "Boy, that boy sure knows what I like," she murmured. "And I do love this color. Yes, I look pretty good for my age, and it sure looks good on me," she said softly, patting the fine little lines around her eyes and smoothing her gray hair, pulling it back in a neat bun.

'*Well, let me go get this coffee started,*' she told herself. Myra walked down the hallway to the kitchen. The morning light poured gently through the blinds on the window, radiating on Myra's beautiful face. She started the coffee pot, then picked up her Bible from the table. Quietly sitting, she let the Word of God soak into her before the day began.

The sound of coffee brewing along with that wonderful aroma filled the kitchen air, while outside, that same light from the brilliant sun glistened on the water as the day was finally ready to launch. She prayed again, quietly, and when the coffee was ready, she poured herself a cup and went out to the front porch, settling into the rocking chair with her Bible on her lap. She sipped her coffee, thinking about how the day had finally come, all the preparation, all the tension, all the mean words she'd heard her family say about each other.

Sitting on the porch in the stillness of nature, she sipped and meditated on the Word. Her thoughts turned again to her family and what the weekend would bring. So much had transpired. So many secrets. So many unhealed wounds. So many things no one else knew. It's time for healing, it's time for honesty, and it's past time for doors to be closed and sealed up by the Blood of Jesus.

"Lord," she whispered, *"I waited all these years to come to this understanding that no matter what, You, Lord, are for me. Through all the dysfunction, the lies, the secrets, I know it's time. I understand Your Word about forgiveness. I understand Your Word about healing. But how do I help my family get there? I ask You, God, guide me. Guide me, Holy Spirit. I'm trying not to be afraid because Your Word tells us not to fear. Your Word tells me You love me and that You have me, and even at this age, I can still be used for Your purpose. Right now, the purpose You have for me is that my family needs healing. They need to learn to love You. They need to learn about Your love for them, and they need to learn how to love each other. They must learn that they can't keep seeking what the world offers believing it will satisfy them or please You"*

She took a breath and continued, "*'Father, I thank You for my family.' I thank You for my sweet Michael and Faith. They've both been through so much, yet people look at their lives and can't understand where the joy comes from how they're still here, functioning and fulfilling what You've called them to do. I'm grateful, Father."*

Her voice softened. *'Father, I believe there are things Nelly knows, maybe things she's gone through that she's never shared. There's never been much trust with Nelly, especially when she was a teenager. Lord, I see how mean-spirited she can be with her siblings, the same way she is with me. Except with Zek, sometimes it's almost as if Zek and Nelly have their own little secrets. And my Lord, he's the same way. He's a good man, but Zek has so much drama in his life. He doesn't know how to deal with it. I pray for Zek, oh God how I pray for Zek. I pray that he will stop being so mean. so verbally hard on Arrya. What a wonderful woman of God she is. She does all she can for her family, yet he treats her as if she's not worthy of being his wife or the woman of God You created her to be. I pray for her to stand strong, but I also pray for him that change will come to his heart. Just like Nelly Lord, I pray that the fire of the Holy Spirit will touch Zek's spirit. There's so much unforgiveness, so much repentance needed, touch them both Lord, touch them both, and change their stony heart."*

She blinked back her tears. *'Before Edward went to be with You, Lord, Zek treated Edward the same way as Nelly treats me.'* Myra shook her head as tears rolled down her face, showing the hurt and pain on her face, as she continued to speak to the Lord. *'To love your children, yet they don't love you back...oh the hurt she felt in her heart and in the pit of her stomach.*

He doesn't treat me well Lord, he doesn't treat me as if I were the Mama that birthed him, birthed them both. I didn't birth the bitter, Lord, the bitter can't come out of me Lord. Change their hearts, Lord. You see it all, Lord. They don't know it Lord, they don't understand. You see everything, and especially the hearts of men, Lord, you see it all. I pray for his soul. Do mighty work in him, in my family.

I always thought Edward and Zek, father and son, would do those father-son things, would want to be together. But that never happened. He grew up so distant from his father. It hurt Edward, it really did. But you know that, Lord. You know it all. It didn't help that Zek started hanging out with people he shouldn't have been with. His friends were a bad influence; they didn't love you, Lord, nor did they love and respect their parents. It really didn't need to rub off on Zek. He was already living that life on his own, yes, Lord, he and Nelly both.

I still remember the first time Zek got in trouble. Edward was furious. I was so worried. I didn't want Edward to hurt him. Kids get in trouble; they need guidance. As parents, that's what we're here for, to guide them. Nelly helped Zek a lot, and I'm grateful for that. She's so smart, always has been. We were proud of her for going off to college, getting scholarships, working hard, and becoming a lawyer. But I think Nelly does things for the wrong reasons. She doesn't do things as unto the Lord. Nelly wants to prove something to everyone. She believes she's better than everyone. She wants to show off, to be accepted. You see her hard heart too, Lord.'

Myra's voice grew faint, slightly shaking her head back and forth.

'I wanted to be accepted too. So much has happened in my life. So many times, I was left outside, always on the outside. But being on the outside taught me how to lean on You, Lord. If I didn't have a friend to talk to, I would talk to the Holy Spirit. The Holy Spirit has all the answers. You know my hurt, and my pain,

Lord. Faith and Michael's faith helped me come through that season.

The trials, the pain, the betrayals, the things I never could share with anyone, especially my children. I prayed Edward would be that father for his children; the father they loved running to the window to see coming home. I didn't have that in my life. Instead, we were afraid and carried that fear into adulthood. There was no joy, no laughter.

Especially after what happened to me as a teenager, all the things no one knows except Ester and Raymond. That night changed my life forever. Even then, I'm still grateful for what they did for me, although sometimes Ester's looks towards me aren't looks of love but pity and shame. Oh, poor Myra,' they think. She just doesn't know any better. Poor stupid Myra, she can't do it for herself. She's got nobody now.'

She wiped her eyes. *But You know, Lord. They don't understand; I do have someone. I got you Lord, and You got me; that I'm quite sure about. Oh, no worries there. You got me Lord, through it all, and I thank you, Lord; I thank you. I'm going to make it because I have You. It's not my time yet, but when it is, I'll be ready.'*

Myra paused as her warm tears gently traveled down her face.

'Sometimes, Lord, I think I'm already ready. I get so tired, God, Lord, so tired. I try my best not to be weary because Your Word tells us not to grow weary in well-doing. So, I keep trying to do well, to think right, to protect my thoughts, my eyes, and especially my mouth. Oh yes, Lord, I do my best not to let foolishness come out of my mouth. No meanness, no hatred—it's not pleasing to You. Talk like that opens doors; it hurts us; it hurts our families, our spirits, and you, Lord.

People don't realize what they're building with their meanness and hateful words. They let the enemy into their heads. They need to stop listening to evil, watching evil. So much evil. Lord... Lord, they don't understand what they are building. Help my family, Jesus. Help them! I know that's why. You've got us here, your children. We're supposed to do the work, right? We're supposed to do the work of the Lord. Lord, I keep trying to do the work and do it well. All glory to You. All praise to You. Amen, amen.'

She took a deep breath, then said aloud, "Well, I better get in here and at least get a little breakfast ready for Faith. I know she'll be here early to help me. Yes, my sweet Faith. She was always my sweet Faith. And one day soon, even Faith is going to know the truth of what she's never known before. I hope even Faith will still see me as Aunt Myra who loves her with her whole heart. Yes, she's going to come to know the truth as they all are."

"So I will restore to you the years that the swarming locust has eaten, the crawling locust, the consuming locust, and the chewing locust, my great army which I sent among you." (Joel 2:25, NKJV)

Chapter 5.

The Rising Dawn of a New Day

The smell of fresh-brewed coffee filled the air, mingling with the hum of Myra's gentle praise. Eggs, sausage, bacon, and potatoes soon covered the counter. Myra cooked not just out of routine but out of love, preparing for everyone, even those she wasn't sure she would eat or even show up. The rhythm of cooking steadied her heart. She always started the day before the holiday with the pies and cakes, and then all the food that she could prep and cook in the morning. She had Thanksgiving preparations down to a fine-tuned science, so she was never overworked, and never stressed out.

A little later, a familiar voice called out, "Aunt Myra! Where are you? It's me, Faith!" "Oh, my dear Faith!" Myra laughed, her voice warming the air. "Come on in here, honey bunny, I'm in the kitchen!"

Faith came running in, grinning wide. "Oh, Aunt Myra, it smells so good in here! You cooked this much for breakfast when we still have pies and a whole Thanksgiving feast to make?

You're gonna have me gaining five pounds before dinner tonight!"

They both laughed, and Myra waved her off. "Hush now. You know I can't let you help me on an empty stomach. You've done so much, baby. Least I can do is feed you."

Faith smiled, sitting down at the kitchen table. "I'm grateful for you, Aunt Myra. This… all of this, it's long overdue. It should've happened when Uncle Edward was still alive."

Myra nodded, her eyes glistening. "You're right. But God's timing is perfect, even when we don't understand it."

Faith reached across the table and took Myra's hand in her hand. "The biggest joy in my life was knowing that before Uncle Edward passed, the Lord blessed me to sit and talk with him, and he rededicated his life to Jesus."

He didn't know he had only a month left, but the Lord did. Aunt Myra, he's resting now, truly resting. And I believe this weekend, that same restoration is coming for the rest of the family. Destruction isn't what God has for us; restoration and healing are."

Tears welled in Myra's eyes. "Oh, Faith… that meant more to me than you'll ever know."

Faith squeezed her hand. "Forgiveness is the key, Aunt Myra. That's what this weekend is about forgiving, even when others won't take responsibility.

"Letting go and forgiving so we can finally heal."

Faith smiled knowingly. "You are always loving on us and making sure we all have enough to eat."

Honey, serving and coffee are my second language. Jesus is my first, coffee is definitely my second, and Aunt Myra I would love some coffee, I didn't even have time to make any before leaving the house. I wanted to make sure I had everything you needed.

"No worries, dear; I have everything here. I cannot have people bringing things that we all want, like macaroni and cheese, and they mess it up. No, I just like to make everything myself, that way, I know we're good."

Faith chuckled to herself, thinking about the time they had no rolls, and the little they did have, were left in the oven by mistake, by aunt Myra and they came out black and smoking. "I asked Bella to bring extra rolls, just in case, because you remember what happened, Myra looked at her serious, knowing she was to blame for the fiasco."

"Aunt Myra, I was just thinking about that. Oh, it was too funny. Remember that time you left the lemon pie in the oven, and the meringue caught fire?" "Yes, I remember. Heck, I was only trying to brown the peaks, I turned my back for a minute, one minute, I'm telling you, and the entire top is on fire."

Myra couldn't help but to laugh. "I'm so glad all the family wasn't here when that happened, I know they would never let me forget, and I've not done that since. What a lesson I had to learn: not to take my own cooking for granted; therefore, I now buy lemon meringue pies, no stress required.

Faith by now is laughing and crying at the memory of her aunt screaming for the fire extinguisher and her cousins laughing and grabbing their phones to take pictures and not helping one bit, as Myra took the flaming pie out of the oven, setting it on the stove.

"Aunt Myra, that is one of those great memories that we will always have when we need a good belly laugh." "Well yes, I guess you're right, but at my expense."

"I'm sitting here we're talking your ear off and ain't even let you go put your stuff up. You know the rooms, go pick yourself a room out there I believe you're going to have a room to yourself, but if not, you can always stay with me in my room.

"Okay and Aunt Myra, no problem at all. I'll stay wherever you have me, I'm not trying to be a problem to anybody this weekend I'm trying to be a blessing, and definitely a help to you, so that you're able to get this over with, and do what finally needs to be done for our family."

Myra just kind of nodded her head and didn't say anything. She understood exactly what Faith was saying. She knew she was so right, it is such a time as this, and there's no turning back now.

"Aunt Myra did you already do all the food prepping?

"Honey, since when have I not? I started yesterday; that's why I wanted to make sure I got up here nice and early. We just need to finish cooking all the food, and it's a blessing this place is so big that it even has an extra refrigerator, just enough room for everything."

"Well, it's for multiple families to stay there, so it's definitely equipped with everything that we need."

"Aunt Myra, I want you to know, I'm here for you no matter what, I'm here for you and Mike is too! He loves you and we want this for you, for our entire family. We want the family restoration to take place it's been way too long, and so many things have taken place, gone unsaid, unforgiven, people just let it be, let things go unsaid, not talk about issues as if they will go away because it's hidden."

"I agree, Faith, I agree, and you know I was a little bit apprehensive—I hate to say the word 'fearful,' but I was feeling that way because I'm going to be honest with you, it is somewhat easier to just let it go and not say anything. You know, we've gotten used to living life the way we live: you deal with who you want to and leave the rest alone and just stay in peace and in your own lane, but nothing is resolved, just hidden. Not making it right, not making it better, and it's also not forgotten."

"Yea, Aunt Myra, how is that healing? "It's not dear, it's just surviving." God loves the family structure. He didn't create family to survive in their dysfunction; He created family to be here and to love one another the way He loves us.

To minister to the needs of each other and our community, that's what we're here to do. Not to be selfish and live a life as if we're our own island and can care less about what happens in this world, and what happens to each other. Unfortunately, that's how it was when Edward was here.

He was full of guilt, and remorse about how he lived his life. Of course, with him transitioning on, it's all water under the bridge, yet no healing for our family. I'm still here to do the part that I'm supposed to do, and if I am a true believer of the Word of God, I've got to stand on faith and the Word, knowing God wants us to be restored and healed, and that's what's going to happen this weekend, and especially when we're open and honest with one another. Forgiving and offer the grace necessary."

Faith nodded her head in agreement, "Aunt Myra I think we should go pray before we get anything started. "Faith honey, I was already praying and have been talking to Jesus from the time I got out of my bed, and sipping coffee on the front porch, so yes dear, I don't mind praying again, this is going to be a weekend where that's probably what we are going to need more of, to stay in prayer, Let me have your hands my dear."

> *"Father, we come before You humbly, thanking You for blessing us to see this day, for blessing us to come together, blessing our family. Father, thank You for blessing us to be healthy, blessing us to be able to have our limbs in our full faculties in our temples. Lord, we repent of our sins, and we ask for forgiveness. Search our hearts Lord, and use us Lord, as Your willing vessels.*

Let every thought, word, deed that we have represent Your heart, and Lord, as this weekend is about to really start when everyone arrives.

Holy Spirit, prepare our hearts, our thoughts, our hands to be your hands and feet to everyone this weekend. Let us sow love, and let everyone see you Lord, and come to understand just how much you love them, and you have good for them Lord.

Oh, Holy Spirit, we pray for every one of our family members. We pray that they are well, and we ask You to cover them as they each travel here this weekend. We pray their journey is one of peace, and we thank you for this time together.

We ask for Your will and Your guidance and Your words and Your wisdom and all that you've given us to do. We are obedient to Your word, and we will not back down. We love You, and we thank You in Jesus' name, Amen and amen."

"Amen, Aunt Myra. I'm going to go ahead and start pulling everything out, getting it going. I'll be back shortly, says Faith."
"Take your time honey, take your time.

Myra went back into the kitchen checking her rather long list, making sure she had everything in order and timed. She wanted this meal to bless her family. She wanted her family to at least enjoy the food even if they didn't really enjoy each other's company.

Over the years, the hurts, betrayals, bitter words have stacked up higher than a deck of cards. Myra wanted the meal to be one that the kids would look back on, the one that would change generations to come, if they do what they are supposed to do, and that is love and forgive each other.

Myra wanted her family to learn how to love and support each other. Instead of always having so much contempt towards one another. Always pointing out mistakes and criticizing their faults. They have got to do better. It's imperative for their children and their children's children to get it right and begin to live as God has called and created them to. His glory, His purpose, not their selfishness, hatred, thinking they're always owed something.

Yep, she thought, the clock on jealousy and foolishness had run out! It must happen this weekend, it must, and she is standing on her faith that it will.

Faith walks back down the hall to where the kitchen was to find her aunt, busy preparing everything, and getting everything in order.

"Aunt Myra, this is a pretty nice house with some really nice rooms. "We did very well, Mike and I finding this for the family, and it's perfect. So big and beautiful. It's going to be quite comfortable for everyone.

"I know Faith, even the rooms downstairs are what you call bunk rooms because all the rooms have bunk beds, so they're able to fit multiple families. A large-sized family up here, this is great so we'll be able to house everybody I thought my sweet girls would love to stay there, Jennesis and Elianna."

"Yes, Aunt Myra, that'll be perfect for them too, since they're the only girls in the family, so they won't have to be worried about the boys and their games, and their bothersome tendencies.

"I agree," said Myra. "Plus, them being girls, it will be nice to have them up here with the adult women, so we can keep an eye on them as well."

Mike and Daniel and will be able to stay downstairs and keep an eye on the boys, so no one's sneaking out, cause I'm not really trusting those boys alone down there." "You're right about that."

Myra turned and walked towards the front door. "I just heard a car. I think Mike is here."

"Yeah, I think you're right. Because he said he was coming early."

Before Myra could reply, the front door opened. A deep voice called out, and Mike came through the door, "Hey, what's up, what's up!" What's all that smell? You cooking breakfast too?"

"Michael!" Faith laughed. "Your ears must've been burning, we were just talking about you!"

Mike stepped into the kitchen, grinning. "Talking about me, huh? Hope it was all good." "It was," Myra chuckled. "Well, you're right on time, come eat some breakfast. There's plenty."

Michael grabbed a plate, shaking his head. "I can't believe you cooked all this, Mama. You know we've got a mountain of food to make."

After giving his mother and cousin big hugs, he grabbed a plate and started filling it up with food. "While you're eating, I'm going to find my room. I've decided that I'm bunking with Aunt Myra."

Faith went down the hall and found her room, finding what she believed was her bed and sat down for a minute to think and quietly talk to God.

'*Man, and she thought to herself, I'm happy to be here for Aunt Myra, but Father, I ask you to keep me, let me be able to be an effective witness, standing on Your Word. Let me show love to everyone here, even if they're not showing me love. I'm not here to be a stumbling block, but I'm here to be a stepping stone to help them raise a leg up, to help them take a step forward, in their walk with you. To help them understand, surrender and submission to the word of God. I'm here to give hugs and love. I'm here to give smiles and laughter, and more importantly, I'm here to share Your Word. Allow me to be that person God, that I can be for Aunt Myra, and that I can be for all of my cousins this weekend, and maybe even my sister and brother, and my own parents, if they show up.*'

Walking back down the hall to the kitchen, she could hear the laughter of Mike with his mama.

"Michael, I'm so glad you were able to get up here early to help Aunt Myra out." "Of course, we did all this work, all hands on deck for this weekend, that's why we're here, to get our family back the way a family is supposed to be."

"Son" Myra said, "I could not agree with you more and let me share with you this, your father would be so happy about how you have stepped up, how you are such an awesome man of God, how you are doing those things that God has given you to do, and how you're not backing down. I'm so proud of you. You may be the youngest son, but you function as a wise son, one that we can trust and one that I know I can trust in and lean on, and I appreciate you so much, son.

Mike stood hugging his mother, not wanting to let her go. "If I've not told you how much I love and appreciate you, please know I love you, and I appreciate all you've been doing over this last year; you were helping me before your father transitioned. Faith, I appreciate you and Mike for showing up and being the sunshine and silver lining that God has called you to be."

"Mama, I love you, and there is not one thing I would not do for you. You deserve to be happy. Mama, you deserve to have peace in your life. You've been through so much, and I know there are things that I don't know, none of us know, but it's ok. You're still my mother, and I love and honor you, with all of my heart."

"You know Mama," Mike went on to say, "I was so embarrassed to tell anyone what I experienced, I had so much shame, believing for a long time that I opened the doors, and allowed that awful assault to happen. I didn't want to share with anyone, but in order to heal, you have to reveal, you have to be transparent, and you have to allow the Holy Spirit to do the work in you."

Mike, now holding his mother's hands, while tears rolled down his face, with Faith beside him holding his arm, "I was lost Mama, I was so lost I was living a life that was not pleasing to God, there's things Mama that I got into that I never should have opened the door, but because I opened that door, there were things that had to be undone in my life, and I thank God for you and Dad. Because you are a woman of God, I know you were praying for me.

The word of God speaks about the prayers of the righteous, and I knew that you were praying for me, and that's why I did not stay stuck in a lifestyle that is not pleasing to God. A lot of people, men and women, get lost…they lose themselves, and our culture today adds to the confusion, the judgment, and the shame. I get it, and I know so many don't. But we cannot come into agreement with a lifestyle that's displeasing to God.

It's desiring them to want to know the love of God and the truth from a good Father, who knows the consequences and what opening demonic doors will lead to. We have to love our family and friends to share the truth with them, the truth of God's love. And still pray for them, and that Holy Spirit will do the work in them." "Amen, Mike, unfortunately, people like to twist and turn your words or your actions, and the fact that we're standing on our convictions and the Word of God. If we don't stand for this, if we don't stand for the word of God, then man, we open up the doors to the enemy and stand for nothing."

"Thank you, cousin," Mike says to Faith, "you were there with me too, and yeah, I agree with you."

Myra was so taken aback by her son's words and testimony, one that she already knew, one she lived out with him, she and Edward, were blessed to help Michael pick up his life, and live the life God had called him to, right into ministry, helping save lost souls, leading back to the Lord. Even with mistakes, it's never too late for us all to turn our lives around for good. "It's interesting how both Faith and I have been through some tumultuous issues, that happened in our lives, but yet when we were seeking, searching, surrendering, and turning to the Lord Jesus Christ, when you give up the world, and accept who you are, and who God has called you to be, accept Jesus Christ, as your personal savior, things will begin to turn around for you, and that's what happened with me and Faith.

It absolutely doesn't mean life is perfect, and things still don't happen, but we're both submitted, and we're also covered by the Blood of Jesus. We know who and what we are. "Son, I could never be prouder of you, and more pleased at how God is using you, for such a time as this, you and Faith, are what the world needs, you're who our family needs. For you to be living, speaking, breathing and being a blessing to others, who need to hear the word of God, for their lives. I can also say, I believe a lot of what you both went through was planted by our ancestors, and unfortunately, those doors had cracks; they didn't even have to be open all the way, but just enough, that when exposure to sin occurred, they were blown wide open, and we walked right in."

"Mama, that's why we're here, because we have to start with our own family. You tried your best, and Dad tried to give us a firm foundation, but Mama, the firm foundation is on the Lord Jesus Christ. God has got to be our foundation. He has to be the foundation for all families, and that is what we're going to do on this weekend."

"I love you son. I love you Faith, thank you both for coming here, being here, and standing here with me. "Well, all right!

Let's get the festivities going. We got a lot of work to do." "Yes ma'am, Mike your room's going to be downstairs I'm not sure who you're going to bunk with, probably should be Josiah or Daniel. Michael went downstairs to find the room he wanted to claim for himself. Michael put his bag on his bed, and sat down, putting his head in his hands, he thought to himself.

'*Man, this day is finally here. I'm so grateful for my Mama still being here and for her obedience to the Lord. I'm grateful for the woman of God that she is, and especially when I was a kid growing up. I love going to church with Mama. I love being that boy singing in the church choir. It wasn't a lot of boys in the choir, so I would sing as loud as I could. Mama always said, she could tell her boy was singing that song because I wasn't afraid to sing to the Lord, it was a good time I always believed.*

But man, did I mess up! 'Going off to college, thinking I was grown, but making horrible decisions. My Mama knew all about the assault and the situation that followed, however getting mixed up with people that I should not have gotten mixed up with was definitely bad. I probably tried just as much as Zek and Josiah, drugs, getting high, and I did way more. I'm so thankful, God pulled me out before I went even deeper into a lifestyle that God disapproves of.' Michael continued pondering on just how his life had turned out despite all the horrible things that had happened to him. Unfortunately, these same situations can easily engulf our kids today, and it does. It can easily confuse them about who they are and their purpose in life.

Mike's thoughts took him to the bible, the Word says, in the book of Mark "For what will it profit a man if he gains the whole world, and loses his own soul" (Mark 8:36, NKJV).

"There was no profit in what I fell into, only misery, and me sinking in my sin,' he thought. Mike lay back on the bed, with is arm covering his eyes, he said out loud, "*Father I cover my entire family in prayer and especially my nieces and nephews. This is a hard and cruel world with a lot of evil trying to take our youth out. Trying to confuse our children, and the parents don't know which way to turn. "Cover us Father, in the Name of Jesus, and reveal your truth to us, In Jesus' Name, I pray."*

Back upstairs, Faith was helping Myra get everything ready. Michael entered back in the room, picking up right with Faith, whatever needed to be taken care of.

"Mike, is your room good?" "Yes, ma'am, it will work for us. This is a beautiful home; we are truly blessed to have been able to book it." "I definitely agree with you," Myra said as she began to load the oven with casserole dishes in the oven. While they bustled around the kitchen helping Myra prepare the food, set up the table and do whatever she asked them to do, their laughter and warmth filled the room. For a moment, it truly felt like family again, peaceful, definitely loving. They talked about travel plans and sleeping arrangements. Michael, sharing a room with Josiah, Myra hoped it would give her a chance to reach him.

"Joey's heart is hard," Myra said quietly. "He's angry at the world! Angry at himself. I just keep praying God will soften him." Michael came walking in right on cue, it seemed.

Michael nodded. "He doesn't even wanna talk to me anymore. If I mention Jesus, he shuts down." Faith's eyes were steady. "That's why we're here, not to push, but to pray. The Holy Spirit can reach him when our words don't." They joined hands right there in the kitchen. Myra led the prayer, her voice trembling yet strong.

> *"Father, touch every heart that will walk through this door. Let this house be a place of peace, not of the hurt and the pain my family leads with. This weekend, take over Lord, and you are in charge, you always are, even with those that don't realize it and honor you. But we do Lord, and we know Lord we*

will do Your Will, Lord and we will lead our conversation with love and grace. Heal the years of hurt, Lord. Make it like it never happened Lord. This weekend is easy for you Lord, all power and love are from our gracious Father. Love wins! Your love wins forever Lord."

When they finished, Michael whispered, "Amen." Faith nodded, eyes bright. "Amen."

As Myra turned back to start getting Thanksgiving dinner prepared, some food she had already cooked would only need to be heated tomorrow. She stirred the gravy and she smiled softly to herself.

"Well," she said, "if nothing else, we're gonna eat good this weekend." They laughed again, the kind of laughter that in times like this is all you can do because it is too late to turn back now, and yet their hope and trust are in the Lord and they honestly couldn't wait to see what God was going to do. Oh yes, it was going to be really good and good for everyone.

He Restores

"So I will restore to you the years that the swarming locust has eaten, the crawling locust, the consuming locust, and the chewing locust, my great army which I sent among you."

(Joel 2:25, NKJV)

Double Dose of Faith

"What a morning it had already been!" Taking a break from the family dinner prepping, Michael and Faith walked slowly along the path that led down to the lake, their shoes brushing against fallen leaves as the evening wind stirred the water into soft ripples, and the sun gently began to shine over the sky. "You know, Michael," Faith said, "I know we planned this, and I know it's necessary. But man, I pray that it all goes well. At this time, there's no turning back now."

"Yeah," Michael replied. "Faith, you are so right. I know this has to happen. I know it's necessary. All the talks, all the evenings, all the times we spent with Mama, especially after my Pops died—she's changed so much. She's grown so much. She's gotten so much stronger." "Yeah, Mike," Faith said. "You know, getting all that stuff out of her soul, unveiling things, and allowing the Holy Spirit to work through it, that will do it. She's looking for peace in her life, and peace in our lives."

Faith and Mike took a seat on the bench. "It is such a beautiful location here," Faith said softly. "The house, the lake, the grounds—nothing but beauty and peace. Look at all that God has blessed here, and we are getting to experience it."

"You know," Faith continued, "I've had some really hard times. Even growing up. Even those times I never shared with anyone at all. Often, I feel so much closer to your Mama, Aunt Myra, than I ever did to my own mother."

"Yeah, I get it," Michael said. "Because, you know what, Faith? You are so much more like my Mama. And it's interesting; my sister Nelly seems so much like your Aunt Ester. Some of the things she says and does…"

"Yeah, Mike, you're right," Faith replied. "Your sister can be a piece of work at times. But absolutely, we're going to continue to pray for her, just like we've been praying for everyone else.

We pray for breakthroughs for them all. We pray they'll set aside their flesh, their desires, and the way the world works and surrender it all over to Jesus. To live the life God wants for them. And how much better will life be? Even for your Mama."

Faith paused. "You know, I don't know if I ever shared this with you. I think I did when we were talking to your mama about what really happened to me growing up…the molestation. For a minute there, just like what happened to you, it led me down another path. I was so insecure. I didn't want anyone to find out. I was embarrassed. I thought it was my fault. I thought maybe it was something I did or said, or that I didn't fight enough or fight them off. She took a breath. "I was afraid to speak up; afraid it would look like it was my fault. I blamed God. Why wasn't He protecting me? When you're young, you think, 'If God is so good, why do these bad things happen? Why did it happen to me?'" Michael listened quietly. "I got into some bad stuff," Faith continued. "A lot of us, when we go away to college, fall into the wrong crowd.

Even in Christian schools, it can happen. You have to discern who's who. Even knowing right from wrong isn't always enough; we need the discernment of God, especially as children of God." She looked at him. "I fell in and out of relationships, thinking these boys liked me. But all they wanted was to put me in a position where I would submit it to them and not in a good way. And it happened. I ended up pregnant. I was terrified. I didn't tell anyone. I had no money. I was in my first year of college and completely naive."

Faith shook her head. "You know how my Mama is. She's harsh, rash, and not very nice most of the time. I always have to stop and pray before talking to her. She had this whole plan for me to be a doctor, to make money, to have status. She's all about looking good in front of other people." "So," she whispered, "I had an abortion. I thought it was the only thing I could do. I didn't even allow myself to understand if it was a sin. I didn't know. There was so much I didn't know." Michael stayed silent as she continued.

"But now, going to the Lord, repenting, asking forgiveness, and then breaking the covenant I didn't even know I made, I mean, my goodness, how did I make a covenant and come into something evil? It was a lot of learning. People don't understand that what happens in the spirit, the spiritual realm, is more real than this natural life. When women have abortions, they're creating a blood covenant.

Once I learned that, I realized God forgave me, but I still had to break that covenant that was made." "Man, Faith," Michael said quietly, "I remember learning about covenants and curses too. The world makes it seem like you can do whatever you want, but it's a trick. It's the subtle lies of the enemy. Even the children of God get tripped up by that subtlety." "Yes," Faith agreed. "And when you don't repent, when you don't forgive, when you don't break these things, the enemy keeps attacking.

First, it looks like freedom. Then it looks like guilt, shame, and condemnation." She sighed. "But true repentance that's what we need. And that's what we need to talk about this weekend. There are things in our family that need to be broken. Things we don't even understand yet. God is and has always been against idol worship. Anything we put before Him is an idol."

Faith looked at Michael. "I pray our family is open to hearing us. We need to stay prayed up. We can even come back here before dinner and pray and concerning the conversations to be had, including concerns not spoken.

In God's time, not ours." Michael nodded. "I hear you, babe. And I love you. I think when we talk to our family, we need to share our stories. They look at where we are and think we've always had it together. They don't know what happened to me in school."

"Love suffers long and is kind; love does not envy; love does not parade itself, is not puffed up; does not behave rudely, does not seek its own, is not provoked, thinks no evil; does not rejoice in iniquity, but rejoices in the truth; bears all things, believes all things, hopes all things, endures all things."

(1Corinthians 13:4-7, NKJV)

Michael's Fight to Live

Faith and Mike, sitting quietly staring at the moving water of Lake Misty, Mike took a breath. Cousin let me share my story with you, "I was sexually assaulted, and my life took a turn." That is why I had dropped out of college when I did. I fell into the wrong crowd.

But God's grace, His mercy changed everything. I forgave. I repented. I surrendered. I can't change what happened, but I can change how I respond, and how I see myself." He took a deep breath. "But God… He never stopped chasing me. I remember Mama praying for me. She'd hold my hands, crying, pleading the blood of Jesus over my life. And something broke that night. I confessed everything to her about what happened, what I'd become. She didn't judge me. She prayed. Then she took me to the pastor the next morning."

A smile crossed his face. "The pastor told me something I'll never forget: 'The devil may have marked you, but God already claimed you.' After that, I went through deliverance, then inner healing sessions, and finally therapy. I learned that real healing doesn't come from pretending the pain never happened it comes from surrendering it." Surrendering it all to the Lord.

Faith reached over and took his hand. "Mike, that's why you're here. That's why we're here. Our testimony is the key to the healing of this family."

Michael exhaled deeply, looking toward the house on the hill. "Yeah. Mama's done her part. Now it's on us. These conversations… they're not going to be easy. But this family's been bound up in hurt and secrets for too long."

Faith nodded. "And we're going to pray before everything, before every meal, every talk, every revelation. Because we're not just talking about the natural, Mike. We're dealing with the spiritual."

"Exactly," he said. "This weekend isn't just about Thanksgiving it's about deliverance and healing, the healing of our family and their souls."

The two of them rose from the bench, the sun fully shining brightly over the lake, as nature is heard singing across the waters. Faith looked back once more at the lake, as Michael smiled softly. Mama did an amazing job. Aunt Myra has to be exhausted." Faith laughed lightly. "She'll still push through, though." "You know she is tired, regardless of what she says."

Michael smiled, steady and sure. "Yeah. Let's go help Mama get ready. We've got a family to fight for." "This is what we've been praying for," she said. "Let's be here for one another."

"Always," Michael replied. And together, they walked back toward the house. "This day is really about to get started in a few more hours."

Michael and Faith continued to laugh and share childhood family tales, as they walked back toward the house.

Across the miles, in a small, dimly lit and very sterile apartment, a man sat on the edge of his bed, still thinking about the phone call with Myra. This wasn't a dream, as he closed his eyes, thinking about what it felt like after answering the phone, his heart pounding, the echo of a woman's gentle voice still in his ear "David, I'm glad you're coming."

He stared at the half empty packed bag by his feet, then lifted his gaze toward the window. The same dawn that was breaking everything open in his world. He whispered to no one in particular.

'God... I don't know why now, but if this is You and if this is my time, I will listen because I know you have me, you have always had me.'

The wind outside sighed softly, and his unspoken prayers that he had for so many years, were not shaping his life, just as God promised. Just like in the Bible, he too will have a life and has been called for such a time as this.

"And whenever you stand praying, if you have anything against anyone, forgive him, that your Father in heaven may also forgive you your trespasses."
(Mark 11:25, NKJV)

Chapter 6.

THE GATHERING

The First Arrival

Myra watched as Michael and Faith walked back towards the house. Myra breathed. *'The still water reminds me of the washing of the Word. Clean, pure, and peaceful.'* She looked around, taking in the serenity. "You and Michael blessed me with this place, Faith. I couldn't have done it without you two." Faith smiled, as she sat down next to her aunt.

"Aunt Myra, you've done everything for all of us. This was the least we could do." Myra grew quiet. "It's been hard since Edward passed," she said softly. "Too quiet. Too many hours alone with my thoughts." Faith reached for her hand.

"I kept hearing those little whispers," Myra continued, her eyes misting. "You weren't a good wife. You weren't a good mother. Look at your children, none of them serving God the way they should… what kind of parent are you?" She shook her head. "The enemy loves to lie in the silence. But I rebuke that thought in the name of Jesus! God's been too good to me." Faith squeezed her hand. "Amen, Aunt Myra." Michael, settling into a chair beside them, said, "I see you had to take a break too, and I'm so glad you did. I made some more coffee to keep us going. Please help yourself. Family will begin to arrive soon." "Mike, I'll grab a cup for you. Stay here with Aunt Myra. Faith rose to go back into the house and retrieve the coffee for her and her cousin. As they sipped their coffee in companionable quietness before Michael spoke again. "Mama, Faith and I were talking. I think it's best we wait until after dinner to have the discussion. Let everyone eat, laugh, and breathe first." Myra nodded slowly. "You're right. A full stomach helps the truth go down easier." Faith laughed softly. "That's wisdom right there." "Besides," Myra added, "the kids will probably be downstairs playing. They'll hear some things, I'm sure, but maybe it's time they do. We've hidden enough in this family. If you walk in truth, there's nothing to fear from being known." Faith whispered, "Amen to that."

Michael took another sip, thoughtfully. "I wonder who's going to get here first." Faith smiled knowingly. "Bella. You know how she is on schedule, bossing Daniel around. He won't ever have to worry about that one making him late ever, and I'm sure he already knows that" Myra chuckled. "You're probably right about that; we love our Bella. You mark my words, they will both be here shortly and first, you can take that to the bank." Michael and Faith both burst out in laughter, as Myra, smiled and nodded her head in assurance of Faith's prediction.

Approximately an hour later, tires crunched on the gravel drive, and Bella burst through the door, all sunshine and perfume, and beautiful as ever. She was a presence of love and grace wherever she went.

"Happy Thanksgiving, Mama!" her voice sang out. "Praise God, come on in, baby!" Myra answered. "Faith and I are in the kitchen, trying to get everything together."

Faith stood and hugged her. "Hey, Bella. How are you doing, cousin?" Bella walks over, kisses her cousin and wraps Myra in the biggest hug and gives her a kiss on her cheek.

Bella instantly took in the vastness of the room she was standing in. "Oh, my goodness, this place is beautiful! Simply beautiful! I'm not even gonna ask how much it cost you. You outdid yourself."

“Don’t worry about all that,” Myra said with a smile. “I just needed space for all my babies.” “Well,” Bella said, “if you ever do need help paying for this, count me in. After all you’ve done for us, it’s the least I can do.”

“My sweet Bella,” Myra said, touching her cheek. “You always have such a giving heart. I love you so much. Thank you so much for even offering, but you know what? It’ll be okay.”

“All right Mama I just want to let you know I’m here for you, and whatever you need me to do, all right?”

“Well honey this is what I need you to do, I need you to be open, and I need you to be ready to participate in a conversation that we’re going to have today, about what our family needs to do, because we know it’s going to be really hard for everyone. It’s not going to be easy for everyone, but it’s necessary. I would like you to do that.”

“Mama,” Bella said, “I’m going to do whatever you need me to do. This is so important, and I understand, and I know there are a lot of things that haven’t been said, but they need to be said, and I’m here to do that for you. After all, I am the youngest daughter, and everybody knows, I’m like “the favorite” right Mama? It’s ok to say it, they all know already.” Faith snorted, and Michael nearly choked on his coffee.

Bella grinned. “I know, Mama, as she winked at her mother “I appreciate that absolutely, Mama. That’s what I said, I’m your favorite girl! And it’s ok, you don’t have to tell the rest of them, because you know that there is already enough jealousy going around in this family anyway.” Myra rolled her eyes. “Girl, stop it, please; you are too much, Myra laughed. You’ve been saying that since you were five. I’m your favorite, right?”

“Well, it’s true!” Bella turned, walking down the hall laughing.

“Well,” Myra said, “before you go exploring, I need to let you know rooms are shared this weekend. You’ll be with Nelly sweetheart, as Myra said to Bella.”

Bella froze mid-step. “With Nelly?” “It’s only for a couple of nights,” Myra said gently. “We’re short on space once everyone is here.”

Bella sighed, then smiled. “This big house, short on space…. It’s ok, Mama. I just gotta sleep there, not live there.” She kissed Myra’s cheek, “but I’m picking the side with the best bed!”

As she took a quick peek towards the room and then came back, Faith and Michael looked at each other and whispered, “Thank You, Jesus.” Daniel stepped in carrying grocery bags.

"Morning, Miss Myra," he said with a grin. "Smells like heaven in here. Thanks for having me." "Boy, you know you're family," Myra said, hugging him. "And now that you and Bella are engaged, you're one foot closer to being officially ours. You are always welcome." She gestured down the hall. "Faith, go check on Bella and help her with her room choice, please. Daniel, sweetheart, I hate to tell you this… actually no, I don't," she teased. "You'll be downstairs with the other fellas. You're in with Michael and Josiah, or with Samuel, until you and Bella are married, that's how it's going to be." Daniel laughed. "Yes, ma'am, no problem at all. That's why we haven't moved in together. We want to do this God's way." Bella smiled and bumped his shoulder. "It's all good. Faith, show me where we're staying."

"Upstairs with me, I'm rooming with Aunt Myra" Faith said. "But we'll have some girl time."

Michael stepped in, clapping Daniel on the shoulder. "Come on, let me help you with those bags, and then show you the downstairs rooms. That's where the guys are staying."

"Perfect," Daniel said. "And hey, Bella, and I want to help with the cost of the weekend. Food, cabin, whatever. Please don't say no." Daniel missing the entire previous conversation, smiled as Myra just nodded her head and blew him a kiss. Michael hesitated, then smiled. “Man, that means a lot. Faith and I pulled this together for Mama. But yeah, it wasn’t easy. I’ll let you know how to bless her quietly.”

As they walked downstairs, Daniel looked around, admiring the space. “This place is amazing. You and Faith did great, brother. Really great.”

In the downstairs hallway, their voices lowered. “Mike,” Daniel said, “I heard about David. Bella told me. Man, that had to be tough.”

Michael nodded slowly. “Yeah. Mama handled it with more grace than any of us knew how to. Even invited him this weekend.”

Daniel shook his head in disbelief. “Wow. That’s big.” “Yeah,” Michael said softly. “Zek and Nelly saw him at the funeral talking to Mama. But no one else knew who he was, or if they did, they didn’t say a word.”

Quietness took over. “You know,” Daniel said finally, “it’s always the kids who pay for the parents’ sins. But he’s still family. God knew he’d be here.”

Michael smiled faintly. "That's exactly right!" Their laughter drifted upstairs just as Bella called down the hall, "Are y'all done bonding yet? We got work to do!" "See," Michael whispered, "that right there is why she isn't my favorite." Bella swatted him playfully as they all laughed. "Okay," Daniel said, "Bella and I discussed this on the way up here, and we even said we would like to donate to help with the cost of this entire weekend the food, the stay, everything. We don't want anything heavy on Miss Myra, nor you and Faith, because all this weekend entails. I don't know how everybody else is going to feel about it, but I'm just saying we don't mind." "Man, thank you so much," Michael replied. "Even planning the weekend, Faith and I were determined to pull our funds together and do this for Mama. We didn't even want her to have to come out of pocket for anything. But you know Mama insisted on buying all the food and getting everything herself. We still tried to help her with that as well. We kept asking her, 'Give us the list, give us the list,' and she was like, "I'll go pick it out myself." Michael chuckled softly. "It's kind of like she didn't really trust us, that's what I believe, and that's fine. She has her ways, and she's been doing this for so long. Not only that, but she's always told us that Thanksgiving is her favorite meal to cook. Even when it was just her and my dad, she still loved cooking and being a blessing to anyone who needed a place to go.

That's just how my Mama has always been." "Yeah," Daniel said. "Your Mama is the best. She really is. I'm praying that everything she has planned for this weekend works out for her. She deserves it after all she's done for everyone else." "You're right," Michael agreed. "It's been hard on her all these years. It hasn't been easy, and it wasn't easy with my dad. But my Mama stayed the course. Even after she found out about David, she never let it affect how she treated us growing up, and of course, we kids knew nothing about the dynamics of marriage. She never let us see her sadness about what my dad did." Michael paused. "I even heard her say one time that she wished David could come over. But at the same time, she knew his Mama wouldn't let him. A lot of people don't realize David's Mama used to be friends with my Mama. That's how she was able to get close to my dad. My dad knew her, too. It's sad all the way around." He sighed. "And it's sad for David. There were many times, especially after I came out of my own situation, when I wanted to reach out to him. But then I found out he had joined the army. I guess he just needed to get away. He did turn up, though. I don't think he realizes we all saw him when he came to the funeral home." "Yeah," Daniel said. "I remember. I saw him, but I didn't know who he was. Later, Bella told me she saw a young man talking to your Mama. At the same time, she noticed Zek and Nelly huddled in a corner staring at him, thick as thieves. She wondered who he was and later asked your Mama. And your Mama told her." Daniel shook his head. "Just like the rest of us, we heard stories never straight from your Mama or dad. Just whispers. You know, 'He's like this,' or 'He's like that.' We knew something was up." He leaned back. "But can you imagine how hard life must have been? Kids don't ask to come into the world. They come the way he did, because of the irresponsibility of adults. But nonetheless, they're here and God knew they would be. So, we pray that David had not only a decent life, but a good life. He might even be married." "I don't think so," Michael said. "I don't think he's married, but I do think he's engaged, or maybe he just has a girlfriend. That's all I really know. Mama reached out to him first about coming to dinner, and he accepted." "Oh man, that is great." Daniel said. "I was a little apprehensive when she told me. We didn't know if he'd want to be around us, considering no one ever reached out to him growing up. But we didn't know about him then, not until we were adults. Even so, the fact that he came to the viewing and maybe even the funeral is important. I think he stayed in the back alone, he didn't come up front with the family." "You know what," Michael said, shaking his head, "funerals are when a lot of stuff comes out. That's when people find all kinds of stuff out, not to mention secret kids showing up that nobody ever knew about." Daniel laughed. "You're right. All kinds of things come out of the woodwork." "But you know what I'm learning," Michael continued, "especially being in ministry? There's always someone who knows something even if they never say it. My Mama's generation was big on hiding secrets. Saving face. Not talking about things. As if hiding it makes it go away." He paused. "It doesn't go away. It always comes out. People want to cover up sin like Adam and Eve hid from God, as if He didn't already know. But covering it up doesn't remove it. Only the blood of Jesus does. That's why He went to the cross." Daniel smiled. "Come on now Mike, Preacher Man." Michael laughed. "I love hearing you talk about the Word," Daniel added. "I say that in Bible study too. Half the time you're quiet, and I need you to chime in and back me up." "Nobody needs to back you up," Michael replied. "The Holy Spirit is right there with you. You've got the Word in you. I'm just here because I need to be. I need to be where you are. I need to be open to what God has for me, for Bella, and for the life we're building together. We're trying to do things the right way." Michael nodded. "And you are. Daniel, I applaud you and my sister. You love each other. You're doing well together, and you're doing things the right way. That matters." "It really does," Daniel said. "But I'm concerned about your sister. I feel like there's something she's not sharing with me. There are times when she is just staring and it looks like she may have been crying, but she always says, she's ok. Maybe this weekend, when everyone's being open and honest, she'll be open with me too."

He took a breath. "She needs to know I'm behind her that I support her and love her no matter what. I want her to trust me with her whole heart. I'm trying to be the man God has called me to be for her, and for her as my wife." "Amen," Michael said. "Pray about it. Be honest with her. Let her know you've got her back. She might be afraid.

People leave so quickly nowadays at the first sign of trouble instead of working things out." Michael sighed. "She's seen Mama and Dad stay married, but she's also seen their struggles. And she sees our siblings too, she sees how things really are." Bella sees how Zek treats Arrya. He treats Arrya horribly. And just like Nelly treated Samuel horribly. Man, Samuel's a good guy. You know he's one of our buddies, and the way Nelly treated him was really bad.

"But you know what?" Michael said. "That's because of what Nelly is dealing with herself, Daniel. That's why this weekend is so important. This foolishness needs to stop. It all needs to stop. We are not the family we're supposed to be. And if we're not the family, we're supposed to be for each other, then we're not the family we're supposed to be for the generations to come. There are things that need to be broken off from us, and it needs to happen this weekend. Enough of that mess."

Just then, Bella came bouncing down the steps. "Daniel! Hey, man, you've been down here for a while with Mike. What are y'all up to? What are you talking about? I could hear y'all, but I couldn't really make out what you were saying." Mike spoke up. "That's probably because you weren't supposed to be listening to what we were saying.

Sounds like you were eavesdropping. This is a conversation between two fellas." "Not two fellas and I'm your little sister," Bella shot back. "Number one, Mike, I'm not your little sister, I'm your older sister, in case you forgot, and I would have to eavesdrop if you just spoke a little louder for me to hear." "All right, all right," Michael laughed. "You got a point. I forgot for a hot minute, all about a year. But either way it goes, it's still a conversation between two brothers and not a sister snooping."

They all started laughing. "Okay, yeah, whatever," Bella said. "Anyway, we need to get upstairs and help Mama, see if there's anything else she needs."

Then Daniel spoke up. "Bella, before you go, I just told Mike about you and I helping out financially with this weekend what we discussed about pitching in." "Hey, not a problem at all," Bella said. "And on top of that, I mentioned it to Mama before I went down to the room. I told both her and Faith that I would love to give something to help out with this week. This weekend is for all of us, so I don't see the problem with being a blessing to Mama, to Faith, and to you, Mike." "I understand," Michael replied. "But Mama said she really didn't need anything." "Listen," Bella said firmly, "Daniel and I would still like to give you and Faith something. You can find a way to give it to Mama, pay something, do something with it, okay? Even if she said everything's taken care of, make a deposit or something." "All right." Michael nodded. "I hear you. And I'm not going to turn you down, sis. Even though we pulled things together, I can't say it was easy. We just knew we had to do what we needed to do."

He smiled. "And on top of that, Faith did even more than I did. I didn't ask any questions. I just knew that no matter what we found or needed to do, Faith was always saying, "Yes, Aunt

Myra, whatever you need, we've got this. We've got this together.' We're here for one another." "So absolutely," he continued. "We'll help out." "All right, not a problem," Daniel said. "All right, y'all," Bella said, turning toward the stairs. "Let's go upstairs and get this party started." "You got that," Michael replied.

Faith, Bella, and Daniel headed back upstairs, and just as they reached the top of the stairs … when the door opened again.

"For God so loved the world that He gave His only begotten Son, that whoever believes in Him should not perish but have everlasting life."
(John 3:16, NKJV)

Nelly and Jennesis

"Hello? Where is everybody at?" Nelly called, ushering Jennesis into the house beside her.

"We're in here!" Myra said. "Jenny, baby, come here my sweet girl, and give Grandma some sugar. Look at you, so tall and beautiful, all that curly hair, just a gorgeous model!"

Jennesis giggled. "Grandma Myra, I just love you. You're always so sweet to me." "There is no other way to be. You are truly a blessing, and I always will be sweet to you, my sweet girl." Myra said, hugging her tightly. "It's been a while. You doing okay, sweetheart?"

"I am. I'm really glad I can be here with you, with everyone. Maybe… maybe some weekends I can come stay with you? If it's okay with Mama." Nelly came back from the car with another bag, catching the last words. Hands on her hips, she asked, "What's okay with me?" Myra kept her tone gentle.

"Well, Jenny was asking if she could come and stay with me on some weekends. Only if you're okay with it." Nelly's jaw tightened. "We'll talk about it after this weekend." "Of course,"

Myra said, letting it rest. "Jenny, your room is upstairs. You and Elianna will have a big room, just you, girls. The boys have their own, and the men have theirs. All right?" "Yes, ma'am. Is there a lock on the door?" Jennesis asked, half-serious. "There is. Use it if you need some privacy," Myra said with a wink. "Go pick your room before your cousins get here. Breakfast is in the oven pancakes, biscuits, sausage, bacon, and potatoes. Come back up and make a plate." "Thank you, Grandma!" Jennesis ran off. Nelly glanced around the kitchen. "I see you and Faith are getting things together. Where is she?" "She's in her room, I believe, chatting with your sister." "Daniel will be downstairs with Michael and Josiah." "Good. I'll find my room, get some coffee, and something to eat."

Nelly said, already turning down the hall. In the corridor, she nearly bumped into Faith and Bella. "Nelly! I didn't see you sorry!" Faith said, "It's fine," Nelly said coolly. "I'm finding a room. Preferably by myself." Faith and Bella quickly looked at each other, then Bella looked down at the floor, without saying anything. "You should be fine," Faith replied. "Jennesis will also be upstairs with her cousin. If you need anything, I'm running to the store later to grab a few more things." "I don't need anything special." "Which room am I in?" Bella slid in smoothly and quietly, staring at her sister, waiting for the smart response that she knew would be coming. "With me." Nelly stopped in her tracks. "With you?" "We're short on rooms if you can believe it with the size of this house," Myra said, firm but kind. "We're all doubling up. Bella kindly agreed, and you shouldn't have a problem doing the same thing." Nelly's eyes cooled another degree, but she said nothing just turned and followed Bella down the hall. Nelly mumbled under her breath, "Do your thing sis." Bella exhaled when she returned from showing Nelly the room they would be sharing. "Man, that was… awkward. Her attitude is just too much, all the time. Y'all better pray for me, better yet, anoint my room, please. " Oil, Oil who has the oil?" Myra, shook her head. "Ok, Bella, not necessary, alright?" Faith bowed her head as if to pray. Faith gave a small, sad smile. "We grew up like sisters, and it is hard to believe our relationship is this far apart now." "Nelly only enjoys talking to Zek and Essie," Bella said. "Which is wild, since Ezra is still friends with Samuel, and you know how Nelly feels about him." Faith hesitated, then said, "It'd be good for Jennesis if Samuel could at least come for dinner. Even if he doesn't stay the night." Bella nodded. "Let's ask Mama if he confirmed. Plus, I don't know if Mama had already spoken with Nelly about it. "I believe she did, but nothing was finalized, so prepare for the Nelly storm," Faith said. "I'm girded up in the Word," Bella replied, half joking, half not, and OIL, more oil." "Girl, you are a nut," Faith said. Both ladies burst into laughter as they walked to find Myra. "Let's go."

Back in the kitchen, they found Myra talking quietly with Daniel. "Mama," Bella began, "we know the situation between Nelly and Samuel is rough. But Samuel was part of this family. When you invited him, what did he say? Did he give you an answer about whether we were coming or not? At least if he comes, even just to dinner, he'll get Jennesis?" Myra closed her eyes for a long moment, then nodded. "I know it's been hardest on Jennesis. And on Samuel too. Nelly has made it difficult for everyone. It's time to try to make something right." She straightened. "I'll go let her know that I asked him to come. Even though I had already spoken to her about it, I'm sure she is thinking I didn't go through with it, or he turned me down." "Thank you, Mama," Faith said softly. "We'll pray." They joined hands and prayed in low voices as Myra walked down the hall. Suddenly, a shout cracked through the house, Nelly's voice boiling over. "Why does everyone always take his side? He didn't want to be family! He didn't want either! All anybody says is 'Poor Samuel!' What about me? I'm raising my daughter alone! I'm the one doing everything!" Myra waited until Nelly ran out of words. Then, steady but firm, she spoke. "Nelly, listen to me. This is not always about you. You're not thinking about your daughter. Do you know how many times Jennesis cried with me on the phone, because she couldn't see her father? Can you imagine how he feels about not being allowed to see her? Let it be about your daughter this time." Nelly's chin lifted. "If you want him to come, then fine, he can come, but I don't have to stay. Jennesis can stay here and he can come, but I'm not doing this." "This weekend is important for all of us," Myra said. "But if you choose to leave, that's your choice. Jennesis will stay. And yes, he was invited, and my prayers are that he WILL show up." Myra returned to the kitchen, breathing out slowly. Daniel shook his head. "Ms. Myra, I can call Samuel if you want and check to see if he's coming. He did tell me that you invited him, but he wasn't sure if it would be a good idea for him to come with Nelly here." "No, sweetheart," she said gently. "Let me." She checked the number against Daniel's phone and then dialed.

"Samuel? This is Mama Myra." He answered in a hurry. "Ms. Myra, is everything okay? Is Jennesis okay? Are you okay?" "Calm down, son. I'm calling to check and make sure you are still coming. Now listen, your family and I want you to be here with us for Thanksgiving dinner, and the weekend if you're able. Jennesis is already here, and she'd love to see you. Samuel's voice cracked with relief. "I… I'd love to come. Did you run this by Nelly? I don't want to make things worse." "I did," Myra said.

"She's aware. She isn't thrilled, but this is the right thing to do. For your daughter." We can keep it a surprise, or we can tell her that you're coming, it's your call." Samuel thought for a moment and said, "Please tell her. As much as I want to surprise her, I think just the fact that she knows I'm coming means that Nelly can't change your mind, if you know what I mean. Myra laughed a little. "Samuel, you are a little bit smart, that's why you're such a wonderful teacher, and you are absolutely right. I'll go ahead and tell Jennesis, and give her a head up right now, so that she can be anticipating the fact that she's going to get to spend the entire weekend with her daddy. What a joy it will be for her." He exhaled. "Then I'll be there in time for dinner. And…thank you for still considering me family." "You always were," Myra said. "There's room here if you want to stay. The men are downstairs in a bunk room." Samuel laughed softly. "Yes, ma'am. I'll bring a bag, as long as Jennesis is there, I will be there."

When Myra hung up, Bella clapped a hand over her mouth. "Praise God. Jennesis is going to be so happy."

As if on cue, Jennesis skipped into the kitchen. "What am I going to be so happy about?" Myra opened her arms. "How would you feel if your daddy came for Thanksgiving dinner?"

Jennesis froze, eyes shining. "Grandma… did you talk to him?" "I did, and he's coming. Your Mama knows, too. I've already talked to her, and I just hung up the phone with your daddy. And he is so happy to see you.

Now as much as we wanted to surprise you, your daddy thought it better if we told you that he was coming, just so your Mama would know that you're aware, and she can't back down or change her mind about him coming.

"I will tell you, sweetheart, your mommy was not happy with the fact that we all wanted to invite Samuel up here, but it will all work out, God will make sure it does, we just have to believe." Jennesis hugged her tightly.

"Thank you, Grandma! I miss him so much. I love my daddy so much, and I miss him so much. I wish we could still be a family, even if Mommy and Daddy aren't married. I just wish we could be a better family, you know, talk to each other, and do things for each other, instead of just saying nasty things about each other. "My dad never says anything bad about my Mama to me. He knows how she talks badly and treats him, and says mean things, and I see the difference, Grandma, I can tell the difference, when people are not being nice, and like how you teach me about God.

They have meanness inside of them, that must come out." Bella and Daniel were standing by quietly listening to their brave and oh, so smart niece speak from a place of deep love in her heart, tears of love welling up in Bella's eyes.

Bella thought to herself, "How do we adults not lead our families from a place of love? When we know who God is, how is it that this child, whose own mother isn't even serving God…but just look, look at what our gracious God is doing right here in front of us all. Jennesis went on to say, "I also know that my daddy loves God, and I think that helps him to be nice to my mommy no matter what she says, my daddy loves God. I think that's why he stays kind."

That did it for Bella; she couldn't hold her joy in any longer. "Oh, my goodness. Oh, praise God, praise the Lord." Her voice got louder, and her tears began to fall, as she raised her arms up in praise to the Lord. Daniel stood there with her, head bowed, thanking God for His goodness. "Jenny, I love you so much. I love you, sweet girl, you're it. You are the change maker for your generation and for our family."

Myra now had tears running down her face as well, as Faith walked in to witness such a precious scene unfolding right there in the middle of the room. "You know, sweetheart, Myra said.

"You're absolutely right. Your father understands the love of God, and just how much Jesus loves us; he also understands that even though he's being mistreated, he's being talked about, he's being blamed for things that he didn't do, he's not holding anything against her; instead, he's praying for her soul. He's forgiving her, like we are supposed to do. We're all praying that one day she'll come around, that Jesus will touch your mommy's heart." Everyone in the room got quiet, as they pondered what they had just witnessed and spoken. Jennesis went over and hugged her grandmother again, Myra softly kissing the top of her head. Holding her beautiful granddaughter. Then Jennesis went over to Bella and hugged her as well. "Aunt Bella, I love you totally, you are my sweetest auntie, and Uncle Daniel, I love you too."

Aww, sweetheart, you are our sunshine, and you always will be. We all love you so very much, Bella tells her niece." "I ditto that, my Jenny-bean." "Girl got us all crying up here," as they all burst out in laughter.

"Ok, I'm going back to my room to get on my phone and listen to some music for a little bit, if that's okay. Plus, Grandma, I brought my schoolwork with me, because when I go back to school on Monday, I'm going to have a paper due, but I don't understand why the teachers have to give homework over Thanksgiving break. I sure hope Dad doesn't give his classes homework like my teachers give me." They all started laughing. Girl, you are so smart, a little paper is nothing for you to complete." "Thank you, Aunt Bella," Jennesis giggled and replied. "You're right, baby," Myra said, kissing her forehead. "Now go get unpacked while you're listening to your music and get ready for your cousin to come." Jennesis ran down to her room.

"I can't thank you, Faith and Bella, enough, for thinking about Jennesis and thinking about Samuel, and how much better this family is with Samuel in it."

When the hallway finally quieted, Bella glanced around. "We're almost all here." "Josiah's still on his way, I hope," Myra said. She exhaled and pressed a hand to her heart. "And… our guest as well." Faith met her eyes. She knew. For now, they would clear as much air as they could, in preparation for their special guest, but there was no telling what was going to happen, and it was too late to even worry about that.

A few minutes later, they again heard tires turning into the driveway. Faith peeked through the window. "They're here," she said softly. Myra went to open the door and waited for her family to enter. Zek strode in first, whistling. “This place is huge, Ma. You hit the lottery?” “You can hush that foolishness,” Myra said, smiling despite herself. “We just needed room for everybody to be comfortable.” Myra called to Arrya, “Arrya, are you alright or do you need some help?” Right then, Arrya popped her head up from under the car seat. “No, ma’am, I’m good.” Gathering her bags and the boy’s backpack and walking up to the house with Matty and Luca close behind. “Hey, family!” She called. “Sorry, Matty dropped his game figure under the seat.”

“Come say hi to your grandma,” Zek said, ushering the kids inside into the living room to greet their grandmother. “My babies!” Myra said, kneeling to hug them. “You’re getting so big.” Arrya hugged Myra tightly. “I’m so glad to see you.” “How have you been, Zek?” Bella asked, hugging him. “I’m good. Where’s everybody? Arrya asked,” Michael and Daniel are downstairs. Nelly’s here. Jennesis is in her room as well,” Faith said. “Rooms are first-come, first-served.” “You two go ahead and take the boys downstairs and get them settled in. Eliana will be staying in the room with Jennesis,” Myra suggested. “The boys are going to love having a room to themselves, I don’t know if they’ll ever come out, except to eat, exclaimed Arrya. Zek, please grab the boys’ bags and let’s go find them a room.”

"Trust in the Lord with all your heart, And lean not on your own understanding; In all your ways acknowledge Him, And He shall direct your paths."

(Proverbs 3:5-6, NKJV)

Chapter 7.

THE GATHERING

About that Time

Myra moved throughout the kitchen, stirring, and putting food in casserole dishes, covering and taking it all in with a quiet steadiness, yet her eyes kept drifting to the window, as she waited patiently, inwardly praying for the arrival of the rest of her family.

Headlights swept across the glass as Essie's SUV rolled in. "Praise God," Myra breathed, then called over her shoulder, "They're here!" Not a moment later, Essie and Ezra stepped in with Eli and Elianna, right behind them, arms full of bags and buzzing with holiday anticipation energy. "Anybody home?"

"Where are y'all at?" Essie joyfully sang out. "Come on in!" Voices could be heard from all directions. "Hello everyone!" Essie sang out again, then turned to her mother. "Hey, Mama. How are you doing?" "We're good, baby. Not everyone's here yet, but we're close." Myra pulled her into a long hug. "I'm so glad you came." Ezra leaned in respectfully. "Mama Myra, thank you for having us. We're glad to be here with everybody."

Myra beamed, giving him a big hug, then bending down to the children. "Eli! Elianna! Come here and love on Grandma!" She squeezed them both. "Your cousins, Matty and Luca, are downstairs. Eli, you boys get a whole room for yourselves! And my sweet Elianna," she smiled, "you're upstairs with Jennesis. Just the girls." "Sweet!" Elianna grinned. "Daddy said I could bring some games as long as we eat first and don't play all day," chirped in. "You can explore and play," Myra said gently to her grandsons, "but only outside with an adult. There's a big lake in the back, and Grandma wants zero accidents this weekend, do you hear me?" "Yes, ma'am!" Eli said, already bolting for the stairs. The house was alive, voices bouncing down the hallways, laughter spilling from room to room, and down to the basement, as the cousins all greeted each other with much love and joy over seeing each other, just like a family should.

More hugs, more hellos, more directions about rooms and bunkbeds and locks on doors. The house was filled with footsteps, laughter, and the clatter of suitcase wheels on hardwood. “Faith,” Myra called, “show Essie and Ezra to their room, and Elianna too.”

Couples and us ladies are up here; the fellas and the younger boys have the bunk rooms downstairs.” She looked around with quiet satisfaction. “We should’ve done this years ago instead of squeezing into our small houses. A big place like this… maybe it’s the start of something we do every year.”

“Yes, Mama,” Essie said, her eyes softened as she looked around. “It’s beautiful. And it’s time. Let me go and put our things in the room and get the kids situated, then I will be back to help you.” “Now,” Myra closed her eyes as she was deeply thinking through her mental list, “we’re still waiting on Josiah, and Samuel is coming later. And my sister and Raymond, no clue if they’re staying; they didn’t say.” Essie exhaled a small sigh. “That’s…never mind, ok, Mama.” “Uh-uh,” Myra warned gently. “No starting please, I’m doing my best and all I can do. Can’t make anyone stay where they don’t want to be.” “I’m just stating the obvious,” Essie muttered, then smiled to soften it. “I’ll behave.” “Yes, please do, my dear Essie, I will definitely need you this weekend,” Myra said. “We’ve got plenty to discuss this weekend, and not everything’s going to be easy.” She glanced toward the oven. “I just took the macaroni and cheese out.” “Mac and cheese?" Ezra perked up. "How many pans?" "Two big ones," Myra said, chin tilted, proud. "And I made extra of everything, and brought plenty of containers for leftovers." Everyone laughed. "Ain't no running out of food on Thanksgiving," Essie said. "We don't ever want that to happen!" They all started laughing at the thought, a couple of years ago when the rolls burned, and the top of the Meringue on the pie caught fire. What a site, and a wonderful memory to still have in the back of their minds, happy times. "Tomorrow, if y'all want the madness," she added, "there's an outlet not far for Black Friday." "Whew," Faith laughed. "That's a crowd. I'll be shopping right here at this table, on my laptop." "Ya'll do what you want," Myra said, smiling. "I'm doing coffee and leftovers." The chatter began to thin slightly as folks drifted to rooms and the basement bunk area. Myra and her crew of helpers bustled back and forth from the kitchen to the dining room making sure everything was in place, and all was moving smoothly. Zek emerged from the hallway, jaw tight. Arrya followed, quiet, eyes red-rimmed.

"My family," Myra asked softly, shaking her head with it still down, "everything alright?" "We're fine," Zek snapped. "Everything's fine." Arrya stared at the floor. "Yes, ma'am. It's… the same as always." "What's that supposed to mean?"

Zek shot back. "I just said… It's how it always is. It would sure be nice if something changed," she said gently. "But right now, it is what it is." "I am not doing this up here," Zek barked. "You know what, Array, I'm not trying to be up here listening to your BS!" I don't know how much more I can take. I have not said anything to you; that wasn't true.

"Not today." Myra's chest tightened. "Enough," she said, more to the air than anyone. "Lord, help." Myra turned and walked away. "I'm going to take a walk," Arrya whispered to Myra. "If that's alright." "Of course," Myra said, touching her arm. "Breathe and spend the time with the Lord, ok?" Arrya nodded, affirming Myra's directions, as a lone tear traveled down her face. Arrya went back to the room, grabbed her jacket, slipped on a jacket, and left through the back door, just as the bedroom door slammed, which Zek would be sharing.

Silence followed, with no words added, just stares and silence. A knock came at the door. Myra turned, walked over, and opened it. David stood there. "Happy Thanksgiving." "David, I am so happy to see you. Come on in, come on in." A very nervous David stepped into the house. "Miss Myra, thank you so much for having me come up this weekend. I'm a little nervous. I didn't know what to expect, and I didn't know what to bring. I bought some sparkling apple cider, if that's okay. You didn't tell me I needed to bring anything, but I never wanted to show up empty-handed. "That is quite fine," Myra said warmly. "And no, there was absolutely nothing you needed to bring but yourself. I'm just so happy that you came. Please, let me show you your room." "Mama?" Michael called out as he came up the stairs. "Hey, Ma. Everything okay?" He stopped in his tracks when he saw David. "What's up? Hey," "Hey," David replied. "I'm David." David reached out his hand to shake Michael's, but Michael pulled him into a big manly hug. "No, man. You don't shake my hands. You hug me. Come on. You're my brother, I'm your brother Michael. I'm so glad to finally meet you, and I'm glad Mama invited you. You are more than welcome here. You're family." David chuckled nervously. Michael's greeting was warm and inviting, just like Myra's. David silently prayed that the rest of the family would welcome him the same way.

All he had ever wanted was to feel like he belonged somewhere. "Come on in, man," Michael said. "Have a seat. Can I get you something to drink? You got your bags in the car?"

"Yeah," David replied. "My bag is still out in the car." "We'll go get it and bring it in. I'll show you where you're staying. You'll be downstairs with Samuel when he arrives. I'll introduce you to him. He used to be married to our sister Nelly. They're divorced now, but we invited him for the weekend so he can spend time with his daughter, Jennesis."

David smiled slightly. "Oh, okay. I see. That's fine. You just tell me where to go." "You'll stay downstairs with the fellas. Go get your stuff and bring it back in. Don't try to leave or anything," Michael said, laughing. David nervously laughed, too. "All right, man. No problem." David turned to head back out to the car for his suitcase. Just as he reached it, another car pulled up and parked slightly sideways, since space was getting tight. It was Samuel. They didn't know each other, but they exchanged greetings. "What's up?" "Hey, how are you doing?" "I'm David." "Oh. I just heard about you," Samuel said. "I'm Samuel." "Nice to meet you. Miss Myra invited me up. I was told we'd be sharing a room." "Oh, okay," Samuel said. "That's news to me, but I don't have a problem with it. Glad to meet you." David and Samuel walked back into the house together. As Samuel entered, Myra turned around. "Sam, I'm glad you showed up. Come on in and get settled. I see you've met David. That's good. You two will be sharing a room this weekend." She continued, "Samuel, David is Edward's son. That makes him my stepson and a stepbrother to the rest of the kids." Samuel was caught off guard. He looked at David, trying to calculate his age.

David looked to be around Michael's age, maybe a little younger. Samuel didn't know what to say.

David noticed and spoke up. "It's okay. I'm not only illegitimate. I'm the son my dad had with my Mama while he was still married to Miss Myra. I'm that son." Samuel took a step back. He had heard about David from Nelly. She often complained about her father and the secrets he and her mother had hidden. She even admitted that she and Zek had seen David when they were younger. She had watched her father go to David's mother's house and saw David run out and jump into his father's arms. That was when everything changed for her. Samuel cleared his throat. "Well, David, it's nice to finally meet you. Just so you know, Nelly and I are divorced. I'm here because we share a daughter, Jennesis. Our divorce was heavy and nasty, and I haven't always been able to spend time with Jennesis the way I want to. Nelly still hasn't forgiven me for asking for the divorce." Myra spoke gently.

"All right, young men. I know this is going to be a hard weekend. Samuel, David, I want to ask you both to be there for each other. Samuel, I know this isn't easy for you. David, everyone here is new to you except for Michael and me. Faith is still downstairs with the boys, and she's here for you, too." She looked at David. “I want you to know you are welcome. You are not an outsider. You are family. Do you understand?” “Yes, ma’am,” David replied. “I understand, and I appreciate it. You don’t have to worry. Thank you for making me feel welcome.” “Michael, please show David and Samuel where their room is and help them get situated. And do me a favor. Ask Faith and Bella to come back up here, please.” “Come on, fellas. Let’s go down here, and I’ll show you where you’ll be bunking for the weekend. Samuel, Jennesis should be in her room. Do you want to wait and surprise her? She’s been waiting for you, man.” “Yeah,” Samuel replied. “I’ve been waiting to see my little girl as well.” Michael called out, “Hey, my sisters. Ma’am needs your help, but first let me introduce you to David.” The girls turned their attention to their brother, with Samuel and David right behind him, and jumped to their feet. “David, this is our sister Bella and our cousin Faith.” “David, it is so nice to meet you,” Bella said as she walked over and hugged him. “Cousin David, it is truly a blessing to meet you said Faith. We’re so glad you came. Aunt Myra is really over the moon. It means so much to her, and to all of us, that you’re here with your family finally.” David was stunned by such a heartfelt welcome. “I’m glad to be here, too,” David said. “And I must admit, I had second thoughts, but I'm glad I didn't back down and came anyway, even with the fear that tried to come over me."

"Oh, Samuel, we didn't mean to ignore you," Bella added. As they all started laughing, Samuel said, "It's fine. It's fine. I know y'all still love me." Putting his hand in the air and waving them off as if it didn't matter. "Yes, we do," Bella shouted, and the group continued laughing. "Well, let me put my stuff down and go find Jenny," Samuel said. "Wait until you see the whole house. There's even a sitting room down here. The kids are going to love our time together this weekend.

How awesome would it be if we all came together up here every year so we could spend more quality time together?" Bella and Faith ran upstairs to see how they could help, just as Nelly and Jennesis came out of their rooms. "Aunt Myra," Bella said, "Michael said you needed us up here." "I did, my dear," Myra replied. "I just needed to run a few things by you ladies." She noticed Nelly was within earshot and didn't want to leave her out. "Nelly, I wasn't trying to leave you out of the planning," Myra continued. "I've just been talking with Faith the whole time while planning everything, but I'm glad you and Bella are here. Everything is ready, and we can begin putting the food out." "Aunt Myra," Faith said, "the house looks beautiful. The setting is beautiful. The food smells delicious, and I know it's going to taste even better than it looks. We're all just waiting."

As they were talking, Ezra entered the room. "Boy, we are loving this already, and we are hungry. Like, starving. I hope Josiah is on his way." Myra grinned. "He'd better be, because as soon as my sister and Raymond arrive, we can eat." There was a slow, firm knock on the door. It opened to reveal Ester standing in the doorway, almost as if she had been asked to strike a pose. Ester walked over to greet her sister and brother-in-law. "Hello, Ester." "Well, hello back to you, my sister." "Myra, you are looking good. Better than I expected," Ester said, in a tone that made everyone within earshot look startled by the expressive comment and the innuendo behind it. "I'm good," Myra replied calmly. "I'm doing the best I can, and I trust God for the rest." "Hello, Raymond. How are you?" "I'm fine, Myra. Just fine." "You're looking very well yourself, both of you." Faith walked over and gave her parents a quick kiss on the cheek. "Hey, Mama. Hey, Daddy. Glad you finally got here. We're about to have dinner. Cousin Josiah is the only one missing." "Come on in and have a seat," Myra said. "Would you like something to drink?" "Yeah, I'd like something strong. What you got?" Raymond asked. Myra turned toward the kitchen and said over her shoulder, "The only strong thing we have is coffee. If you want some, I can do it for you. Other than that, we have sweet tea or my citrus holiday punch." Raymond grunted. "That's fine. Tea will have to work. I've got something in the car I can tap into later." Myra sucked in her teeth and pressed her lips together. "Daddy, please," Faith said as she grabbed his arm and pulled him toward the living room. "This is not the time. We all want a nice family dinner today. After all, it's Thanksgiving."

Ester glanced around the massive living room and decor. "Myra, I must say, this is a beautiful home." Her gaze landed on Nelly sitting on a stool in the kitchen. "Good to see you, Nelly. Looking as beautiful and striking as always. It's sure good to have an attorney in the family." "Hi, Aunt Ester. Hi, Uncle Raymond," Nelly replied. Raymond nodded his head toward his niece but said nothing. "I do what I do," Nelly added. "I know who I am, and I get the job done." Jennesis walked into the kitchen. "Grand mommy, is the food ready yet? I'm getting really hungry." "Well, hello there, Jenny." "Oh, hi, Aunt Ester. Hi, Uncle Raymond." "Hey, Scooter," Raymond said. "Look at you, growing like a weed." Jennesis giggled, and Nelly rolled her eyes. "Jennesis, we have a surprise for you," Myra said, shooting a look at Nelly that clearly said not to start anything. At that moment, Samuel quietly walked up behind his daughter and tickled her waist. Jennesis screamed and laughed at the same time. “Daddy!” “Oh, baby girl,” Samuel said, holding her tightly. “Ain’t nobody happier to see you than me. I miss you so much.”

“Hello, Nelly,” Samuel said. “Hello, Sammy,” she replied coolly. Samuel turned his attention back to Jennesis, refusing to let Nelly spoil the moment. He realized then that he needed to make sure Jennesis spent more time with her grandmother, so he could be around her without the tension. “I’m so glad you’re here, Daddy,” Jennesis said. “And I’m glad I’m here too,” Samuel replied.

“Your grandmother called and invited me for Thanksgiving, especially since you’d be here. There’s nothing in the world that would’ve stopped me from coming to spend time with you.” “Daddy, I love and miss you so much. I really want to see you more. Can we spend more time together?” “We absolutely can. And hopefully after this weekend, we’ll be able to spend more time together.” “Jenny, I’ll be staying downstairs with one of your uncles, okay? There are game tables and a TV. Maybe we can walk down to the lake too. “Dinner is almost ready, Myra informed all in earshot. “All right, Daddy. I’ll be right down later. I’m so happy.” Samuel walked over and hugged Myra tightly. “Ma’am Myra, thank you so much. I really appreciate you inviting me so I could spend time with Jennesis.” He glanced at Nelly. "Nelly, thank you for agreeing to let me come this weekend as well," Nelly said nothing. She turned and walked back to her room. "Ma'am, let me know when it's time for dinner, please," Samuel said. "I have a headache, so I'm going to lie down." Shooting an icy glance at Samuel as she walked back to her room. "I'll text Josiah one more time and see if he's on his way," Faith said. "I'll let you know what I find out." "All right," Myra replied. "We won't wait longer than thirty minutes. It wouldn't be fair to everyone else." Everyone went their separate ways to get ready for dinner, preparing to come back together once again.

When it was time for dinner, everyone began gathering around, pulling chairs together at the large table. There was also the kitchen table, where the kids were seated. The family helped bring food to the table, with plenty of oohs and aahs over all the goodness Myra, Faith, and Michael had prepared as a blessing. "Mama, everything looks and smells so good," Bella said. Samuel spoke up. "Oh my gosh, Miss Myra, I am so happy. I definitely wasn't going to get a meal like this at Golden Corral. I'm so thankful you invited me to come to dinner today." David walked into the room with Samuel. The room grew quiet. Myra walked over, took David's hand, and said, "Everybody, I would like to introduce you. This is David." She turned to David.

"David, this is my sister Ester and her husband Raymond. This is my daughter Essie and her husband Ezra. This is my daughter Nelly, my son Zek, and his wife Arrya. And you already know Samuel." She smiled gently. "Now, let me introduce you to the little ones. This is Jennesis. She is Samuel and Nelly's daughter. This is Matty and Luca. They belong to Zek and Arrya. And Essie and Ezra have these two babies over here, Eli and Eliana. Last is Bella and her fiancée Daniel." "Great to meet you, David," and Bella waved at David, "we already met," replied Bella. "The only one we're missing is Josiah. He's my second son after Zek. Zek's full name is Hezekiah." Myra took a breath. "Everyone, this is David. David is your half-brother. Your daddy is also his father or was his father." Everyone sat in silence except Faith, Michael, and Bella. Bella was the first to speak. "David and I met downstairs. And again, David, we are so glad to have you here with us. We're your family." Her words made both Myra and Faith smile. Next, Essie stood up. "Hey, David. I'm Essie. My name is Essobella, but everyone calls me Essie." "Hey," David replied. "Nice to meet you. I'm really happy to meet all of you." Arrya waved. "Hey, David. I'm Arrya, Zek's wife. Welcome to the family." "Nice to meet you," David said. "Thank you so much." The kids chimed in. "Hi. Are you our uncle too? What do we call you?" David smiled. "You can call me whatever you want. I'm glad to be an uncle. I've never been an uncle before." "Well, nice to meet you, Uncle Davey," one of them said, as all the kids broke out in laughter. David chuckled, too. Their laughter eased his nerves and made him feel welcomed in a way he wasn't sure he deserved. Ester spoke next. "Well, David, it is good to meet you. I've heard about you. Raymond raised his hand in a small salute. "I'm your Uncle Raymond. Folks call me Uncle Ray. If you need anything, let me know." "Raymond," Ester said sharply, "you need to settle down and drink that strong coffee. And I hope you didn't put anything in it that wasn't supposed to be in this house." Raymond ignored her. A few people laughed under their breath. David lowered his head slightly. "Nice to meet you, ma'am." "Don't call me ma'am," Ester corrected him. "Call me Aunt Ester. You're my nephew." "I'm sorry," David said. "Ain't nothing to be sorry about. Just get it right," she replied. "You'll be all right." David nodded, while everyone else signed and rolled their eyes, they knew how Ester treated everyone in her life. The only two who hadn't said much were Nelly and Zek. Finally, Nelly spoke. "David, I'm Nelly. My name is Nelsa. This is my brother Zek." David nodded. "Nice to meet you." Nelly's expression was cold, and everyone noticed it. "Yeah," she said flatly. "I'm sure you are." Myra quickly intervened. "All right, everyone. Let's go ahead and get ready to eat. The food isn't going to wait all night, and we're hungry." Everyone agreed and began finding seats. Myra pulled out a chair next to her for David. Faith sat nearby with her parents, and everyone filled in wherever there was room. "Let's bless the food," Myra said. "Michael, will you do the honors?" "Absolutely," Michael replied. Everyone bowed their heads. Right as Michael began to pray, the door opened, and Josiah walked in with an angry look on his face as he noticed everyone already sitting. Everyone turned and looked at him. "Well, about time!" Came falling out of Bella's mouth. "Oh, so y'all weren't thinking about waiting for me? You already started eating? Ain't nobody care about waiting for me?" Josiah snapped. Michael stood up. "Man, we waited for you. How are you going to come in here fussing and complaining?" Then Myra spoke firmly. "Josiah, go wash up and come sit down. We waited as long as we possibly could. We're ready to eat now." As Josiah turned away, he glanced at David, studying him. The face looked familiar. Then it hit him. David was the guy he had seen at the funeral home when his father passed away. Josiah looked over at his brother Zek, then walked down the hall to wash up. Turning, he stopped between the kitchen and the dining room. "Where am I supposed to sit?" he asked. "Wherever you can find a seat," Bella replied. "You may have to sit in the living room or in the kitchen with the kids; it's all open, we can see you."

Josiah scoffed, turned away, and walked into the living room. He dropped into a chair, ignoring everyone else. Michael began to pray again.

"Father God, we come together in Your name, and we thank You. Thank You for this day You've given us. Thank you for blessing our family to come together. Lord, we don't know if this will be our last time together, but since we are here, we are grateful. We thank You for this food that nourishes our bodies. Bless the hands that prepared it. Bless my Mama and give her strength not only for today, but for this entire weekend. In Jesus' name, we pray. Amen." "Amen," everyone said.

"All right," Raymond said. "Who's cutting the turkey?" Zek stood up at the same time. "I got this, Uncle Ray." "No, you go ahead," Raymond said. "Nah, I changed my mind," Zek replied, sitting back down. Arrya nodded approvingly. Raymond grabbed the knife and began slicing. "Who wants a leg?" he asked. The kids shouted and laughed. "Dark meat? White meat?" Raymond continued. Myra added, "I also made a turkey breast, all white meat, so we don't run out. And we've got ham too for the pork eaters." "Zek, why don't you slice the ham?" "All right," Zek said, jumping to his feet and going over to the buffet table to start slicing the ham. "Line up and start fixing your plates." Everyone grabbed plates, lined up, and filled them with food. "Mama, you put your foot in this like you always do," someone said. "This food is so good." "Thank you," Myra replied. "There's plenty. And don't forget dessert. Sweet potato pie, our famous store brought lemon meringue pie, pound cake, spice cake, and ice cream. Leave room." "Yes, ma'am," the kids answered in unison. As they ate and enjoyed one another's company, David fit right in. Michael, Faith, Bella, Daniel, and Myra made sure he felt welcome.

Now, Ester and Raymond were not saying much to David, but it did not matter, as long as David felt comfortable with the family that was happy to have him in their presence. At the end of dinner, everyone began helping clean up the kitchen, well, at least some of the adults did. Ester, Raymond, Zek, and Josiah all retired to the living room. Josiah asked where he was supposed to be staying, and Michael directed him downstairs, telling him that he would be rooming with him. Michael then took Josiah downstairs to put his things in the room and get him settled. Afterward, he came back upstairs.

"Being confident of this very thing, that He who has begun a good work in you will complete it until the day of Jesus Christ."
(Philippians 1:6, NKJV)

Chapter 8.

Breakthrough and Heal

Once the kitchen was clean and the adults were gathered in the living room, the kids were all downstairs having a great time. Michael cleared his throat, catching everyone's attention in the room. "I want to thank you all for coming this weekend. Mama, this weekend was very important to you. There are some things you want to share, and there are some things we all need to open up about if we're ever going to be the family we're supposed to be." Nelly immediately spoke up. "Exactly what are you talking about, Michael? We're here just for Thanksgiving. Ain't nobody trying to re-live our upbringing or talk about things we don't want to talk about."

Samuel spoke up. "You know what, Nelly, let your brother speak. The reason I'm here is that I hope you and I can clear the air so we can do a better job co-parenting our daughter, Jennesis." Nelly looked at him and said, "Our discussion about co-parenting our daughter is nothing that needs to be had in front of the whole family. Number one, it ain't none of their business." Samuel responded, "Yes, it is their business, because the things you say haven't been true, therefore, you have made it their business. Not to mention the fact that Jennesis is my daughter, too, and you're making it very difficult for me to be in her life. That's wrong, simply wrong." "Sammy, do you know what? Fine. Just whatever," Nelly snapped.

Myra sat quietly in her chair, listening to everyone present. "Ma'am, do you want to go ahead and start?" Michael asked. "I do," Myra said. "I never thought this would ever happen or even be possible after Edward passed away. I was a little lost, and it wasn't that I didn't know what to do or how my life would continue. But when Edward passed, and David came to the funeral home, I knew at that moment. This is what I've been praying for." She looked around the room. "You all are just meeting David tonight. I'm sure you've heard things and maybe even speculated about what happened in my marriage to your daddy, things we never talked about out loud. One of those things is David. See, David is sitting here, and because he is here, I need you all to know that what happened is no fault of his. He was an innocent child. A child does not ask to be brought into this world. When children are here, it is the responsibility of the adults to do their best to care for them and raise them in the fear of the Lord, the way they should be raised."

She paused. "Did everything go the way it was supposed to with David's birth and existence? No, it didn't. Was God surprised or unprepared? No. Our sovereign Lord was not. God knew about it all, the good, the bad, and the ugly." She took a deep breath. "Edward seeing someone else while we were married was wrong. It was sin. It could have ended our marriage. His betrayal hurt me deep in my soul, pain so deep that I didn't know which way to go. I asked myself, how could he do this to me? How could he be so evil? How could he not see that his actions would hurt me and eventually affect all of you, including David?"

"I know I was a good wife. I'm far from perfect, but I was faithful. I was loving and caring. I did what I believed I was supposed to do for him and for our family. My mind could not wrap around how selfish he was for allowing himself to be seduced into a relationship he never should have been in. Yes, it was very wrong." She looked at David. "Nonetheless, David had nothing to do with that. David deserves a family. He deserves love, kindness, and respect. Can you imagine growing up knowing your father had another family, knowing you had siblings whose lives you would never be a part of?" "David is a part of your daddy, just like all of you are. Yes, he has another mother, but he is still part of you. I expect you to treat him as another brother and another sister would." Everyone nodded except Zek, Nelly, and Josiah. "This weekend, I want you to treat him like the brother he is to you, because that's who you are to him. This one weekend won't make up for everything he lost, but we are together now." Zek, Nelly, and Josiah sat with their heads down, while the others listened closely. "Now there are other issues we need to discuss," Myra continued. "This family must start acting like a family. No one is perfect. Every family has ups and downs, yet you don't show love and care to one another. You hold faults against each other. You withhold forgiveness toward each other, and unforgiveness is wrong." She glanced at Ester and Raymond, who exchanged looks. "I prayed for you. I taught you the Word of God. I tried to demonstrate godly living, regardless of your daddy's drinking, partying, and violations of our vows. Yet he was still a good daddy to you. There was nothing you lacked. You had food, clothes, your own beds, and a roof over your head." "I did my best, but I see now it wasn't enough. You can have both parents in the home, but when they are not serving God together, you still grow up in brokenness." Her voice softened. "The things that happened to me as a child, being left on my aunt's doorstep and later being violated, those traumas were never healed. I thought loving Jesus was enough, but I was still unhealed." She continued, "Your daddy sinned badly. He committed adultery, and he paid for it every day of his life. We made peace before he passed. I forgave him long ago, but forgiveness didn't heal the wound. That betrayal left rejection in my heart that I didn't even realize I carried." "The therapy and inner healing this past year have taught me so much. I learned where Jesus was in all of it. I learned about open doors that needed to be repented of and shut for good. That is why we are here today. Those open spiritual doors must be shut by all of us." No one spoke. Heads nodded. Tears rolled. "There is not one of you who can say you are perfect," Myra said, looking directly at Nelly and then at Ester. Ester rolled her eyes. Nelly turned her head away. "There is only one perfect Savior. Our perfect Savior." "Yes, Mama," Bella, turning towards David, said, "David, you are my brother. I'm glad you're here. I pray you continue to come around and be part of our family. I hope nothing scares you away. Please know you belong." Michael added, "I ditto that. You're another brother, man. What my Pops did was wrong, but he loved all of us, and I know he loved you, too." David finally spoke. "I'm very happy to be here this weekend. Miss Myra, thank you for having me, and thank you for allowing me to come to my dad's viewing. It hurt that he passed away and that I didn't get to talk to him or see him before he died. I do know he loved me, and I loved him too." "There was a time when I was angry at him. Miss Myra, I'm sorry if anything I say hurts you. I just want to explain how I grew up." "As a little boy, I didn't understand why he didn't live with us or why he was always leaving. My Mama was always angry; she still is." David hesitated, but continued. "As I grew older, I heard the things she said to your dad. She tried to make him feel guilty because of me. She tried to force him to leave you by using me, but he wouldn't." "She promised him that life together with her would be like heaven. All the money and material things she'd make sure he'd have it, but it never worked. When it didn't, she used me to manipulate him, by trying to make him feel guilty." Samuel glanced at Nelly. "For a long time, I was angry with my mother. She doesn't even know I'm here this weekend. She didn't care that my father died. She didn't comfort me." David lowered his head, voice shaking. "I was so happy whenever my dad came to see me. I wouldn't wish this life on any child. I cried myself to sleep so many nights, just wanting to be loved." Myra and Faith wrapped their arms around him, praying softly.

"You are loved," Myra said. "God sees you." "I felt unworthy," David continued. "I felt rejected. My mother even told me she wished I were dead. What kind of person says that to a child?" Zek stood and stared out the window. "I knew I had siblings," David said. "I wanted a big brother, as he gazed over to Zek, while his back was turned I wanted a little brother too. But I had nobody. I felt like I wasn't supposed to be here." "When kids asked where my daddy was, it hurt so much. I thought if I wasn't here, maybe everyone would be happier." He swallowed hard. "I'm glad I never did it." As David continued speaking, Samuel shook his head as he imagined what David must have endured. "One of our neighbors went to church," David said. "They asked my Mama if they could take me with their family. She didn't care. As long as she didn't have to go by herself, she was fine with me going. Anyway, I went to church, and that's when I started learning who I am, who God is, and just how much He loved me. I knew my daddy loved me, but I learned that God loved me even more. That understanding alone changed everything for me." He paused. "I started learning that I was worthy, and that I was supposed to be here. I learned that all the bad things that were happening around me were not because of me. That belief, that you're not good enough or accepted, makes you perform. You try to live up to the world's standards. You do things just to fit in, and it's dangerous. That's where our kids and our families are today."

Michael walked over and put his arm around David's shoulder. "It's okay, man. It's okay. I see you, and I understand," Michael said.

"David, because you haven't been a part of this family, you've never heard my story. I can relate, because I wanted to commit suicide too. Some bad things happened." He took a breath. "The man you see today, I was not always this man." The others, including Myra, listened quietly. Most of them knew parts of Michael's story, and some of them were ashamed because of their own stories they were hiding and didn't want to share.

"When I was in college," Michael continued, "I decided I wanted to pledge. Yeah, I wanted to be that guy. I wanted to be accepted. I wanted to do what everyone else was doing. One night, when they had us out in the woods, I got separated from the other guys. Some older guys in the fraternity that didn't like me, jumped me and I got assaulted badly." As Michael spoke, Myra stood and walked over to him, wrapping her arm around his waist. David had sat down by then, his hands covering his face, listening. Michael continued to rest his arm on David's shoulder, and now Myra had her arm around Michael. Tears were not only running down Michael's face, but also down the faces of David, Faith, and Bella. Oh Father, Myra thought, as she witnessed the pain in her children's faces. They were hurt. Their hearts hurt so deeply for their brother and all that he went through. The pain, loneliness, the silence. He didn't share any of this with anyone, and they felt as if they had abandoned him because they weren't there for him.

"I was so ashamed," Michael said. "After that, I dropped out of school. I couldn't even go back right away. I was wrecked. I started drinking. I started doing drugs, smoking weed. Anything to numb the pain and the memories. The thoughts in my head and the thoughts in my heart kept telling me to kill myself. The voice told me I was nothing." He swallowed hard. "I kept thinking, what are my parents going to think? What is everybody going to think of me? So, I stayed away from my family. My parents didn't even know I had dropped out of college. I wouldn't come around. I wouldn't answer the calls. I was just partying, not doing what I should have been doing, and partying with anyone that wanted to be with me, that was until Cousin Faith." Michael looked toward her. "I truly believe God sent Faith to find me and help me. I was so messed up, and she allowed me to come stay with her and helped me get cleaned up. I told her what happened. She prayed with me. She helped me understand that what happened to me was not my fault. She helped me understand that the enemy wanted to take me out, just like he tried to take her out." Faith nodded through her tears. "She helped me understand there was a purpose for my life, even when I couldn't see it or believe it. She helped me understand that I needed to pray, repent, and forgive. Forgiveness is hard. It's not easy, and you can't do it alone." Michael continued. "I recommitted my life to God.

When I surrendered my life to the Lord, everything began to change. The more I sought God, the more I found who I was. The more I surrendered things to Him, the more those strongholds began to break off me." "Faith helped me, and so did my parents," he said. "She helped me not be afraid to go to them by reminding me of their love. I knew they loved me, but it was the shame of the enemy and my faulty thoughts that I didn't know how to capture." "When I finally went to Mama and Daddy and told them what happened, they were upset. Not at me, but because I kept it from them. My dad was furious at the ones who hurt me. He wanted to kill them. My Mama's heart was broken because I got hurt and didn't come to her. I ran and hid because of shame." He looked directly at David. "I felt unworthy, just like you. That's a trick of the enemy. When he can silence us and isolate us from those who love us, making us believe we're worthless, that no one cares, that we're damaged goods, he wins. And yes, there are people who will say those things to you, but they are being used by the enemy." Michael's voice steadied. "But when you surrender to God and allow the Holy Spirit to work, the scales fall from your eyes. You begin to see yourself the way God sees you. Through prayer, forgiveness, repentance, and deliverance, God did it for me. I committed my life to the purpose God created me for." Faith spoke up. "The enemy knew God had a purpose for Mike's life, just like He has for mine, for all of us. He wanted to stop him by making him doubt his identity and calling. Running from it. Doing things to avoid what God called him to do.

I did the same thing, David." She looked around the room. "All of us have a story, a testimony. We've all had battles. Unfortunately, we haven't always been there to support each other."

Nelly stood up. "You know, this is all fine and good," she said sharply, "but if this is going to be a whole evening talking about Jesus, surrendering, and being happy and satisfied, I think I can turn in for the night. I've had enough."

"Nelly!" Myra spoke firmly to her daughter. "Nelly, there is no place for you to go but right here. All of us need to sit here and hear each other out. We need to hear what happened in our lives so God can guide us to this point as a family. Why don't we support one another, the way that we should? Why don't we love one another the way we should? Why we would rather do for others than for each other." She looked around the room. "That is not pleasing to God. We are going to stay right here, discuss this, and get through it together."

Nelly sat back down in her seat, and right at that moment, that's when Raymond spoke up. "You know, it's all well and good, Myra, that you think you want to hear everyone else's sorrows and secrets and unveil everything, but you have a whole secret here that you ain't never told anybody."

Myra spoke very fast, knowing Raymond was about to expose, attempting to stop him. "Raymond and Ester, this is not the time, and this is not the place. I think we should speak with her alone first."

All the kids looked at each other, trying to figure out what their Mama, uncle, and aunt could be secretly talking about without actually saying it. Raymond said, "It's exactly the time, and it's exactly the place." Ester said to Raymond, "It is not your place to bring that up right now.

Raymond responded, "It is your sister, and all the hell you put me through because of what I did, because of my personal business. Heck, we weren't even married yet, not like what

Edward did. I'm not going to call my kids a mistake. I'm just calling it something that happened." Ester looked around the room at each person, as they all began to look at each other, wide-eyed wondering what he was getting at, yet knowing it had to do with Myra.

"Ya'll want to know what's going on here? You want to know how this family really is. I'll tell you how it is, Raymond spits out, as his voice began to get even louder." Myra went back to her chair. Michael looked at his mother. David looked bewildered. Everyone else stared at Raymond, trying to figure out what he was about to expose. Raymond said, "Well, it's about a young teenager named Myra. Oh yeah, sweet little Myra could do no wrong." "Right before Ester and I got married, Myra got knocked up." "Raymond, stop it now," Ester hollered. "No, no, no," Raymond continued. "I'm going to go ahead, because this is going to be everybody's business. Everybody loves sweet Myra, right? Well, let me tell you what happened. She got knocked up. That's right. Myra was pregnant by an older dude she was flirting with, one who used to come over to her Aunt Ruth's house. Oh yeah, I know all about it, Myra." "And what did she do? Let me tell you what they both planned." Raymond is pointing at both Ester and Myra. "Ester told Myra, 'Give me the baby and I'll get Raymond to marry me, and we can raise the baby, because you're too young. Plus, Ester can't have kids."

Everyone looked from Myra to Raymond and back to Ester, mouths hanging open, unable to hide the shock on their faces. Myra and Ester both stood up at the same time, "Raymond, you need to be quiet! This is not your story to tell; Myra sputters out to Raymon!" Raymond continued, slurring his words, his coffee was a little stronger than regular coffee, and he didn't even try to stop all his secrets from streaming out of his mouth. "Heck, what's the problem? I still married her," pointing at Ester. A woman who couldn't have kids, and I knew didn't even love me, and married her anyway." Shaking his head. His voice became lower and his head hung even lower, tilting sideways, eyes closed. Raymond opened his eyes, squinting as if he was replaying in his head what took place, as he continued to speak, "She knew I met somebody else, right after her and I became an item, and yeah, I made a mistake, got her knocked up before Ester, and I even got serious, so I thought. Now, I have two kids, Raynisa and Randall, just like that, twins. Raymond lifted his head a little as he continued speaking.

"And I'm still trying to figure out why Ester still wanted to marry me, and that part confused me for a little while, that is. So,

I married her, the twins' mother didn't want me, so yep, I went ahead and married Ester." He looked around at everyone in the room, he had everyone's attention. "Ester convinced Myra to give her the baby. Ester wanted her own kid. Don't get me wrong, Ester loved her little sister, and she felt responsible for her. She wanted Myra out of that evil house, and this was how it was going to happen."

At that point, everyone at the table was trying to figure out what Raymond was talking about. "I was a good daddy to Faith. Yeah, Ester made sure she didn't want for anything. Ester wanted Faith to always know she was her Mama, that there would never be any question to it."

Raymond chuckled, sounding evil and sour and very intentional about what he was saying, and not caring who he was hurting. Now, everyone was staring at Myra, then directly at Faith. "WHAT?" blurted out Nelly, "Faith, are you saying Faith is really Mamma's baby?"

"Raymond, I told you this was not the place for this discussion," Myra said. "We owed Faith more respect and love than what you just showed her." Faith sat there as tears rolled down her face, staring straight ahead. Myra had her head down, shaking it from side to side. Ester stood up and screamed at

Raymond, "You always resented my baby. Always! You never loved her like a daddy is supposed to love their child. I'm her mother." Raymond chuckled. "You can say whatever you want. That girl was born by Myra, and you can't take that away from her. She looks like Myra. She acts like Myra. What more needs to be said?" "Oh, my goodness," Myra said, putting her hands on her head.

She sighed deeply. "Let me explain. I never wanted Faith to find out like this. Raymond, how could you do this to the daughter you raised? How could you hurt her like this?" Faith finally spoke. "Stop it, stop it, please. I can't believe this is happening to me." She looked at Raymond, Ester, and Myra, and before Myra could speak, Ester jumped up from her chair. "I'm your mother," Ester said. She looked around at the rest of the family. "I raised her. Just because I didn't give birth to her doesn't mean I didn't raise her. I'm your mother, Faith, you hear me, I'm your mother." Ester screamed, collapsing to the floor in a heap of tears and sobs. "Myra is not her mother. I don't care how much she loves Myra. She will never be her mother. I raised Faith, and she is mine."

No one spoke a word. The silence of the shocking words that exploded into the room took over. Myra sat silently in her chair, eyes closed, tears running down her face. I'm so sorry, so very sorry for all the lies, the secrets. This was not the way to tell Faith, to tell any of you. Ester and I had a horrible and hard upbringing. Myra tried to continue speaking, but every word cut the breath from her voice, and nothing came out but whimpers. The whimper of the hurt and pain from the memories that came flooding back into her mind.

"Yes," Ester continued. "Raymond is telling the truth. Myra got pregnant. She was taken advantage of, and I knew she couldn't stay in that house; I had to get her out, but I also knew that if I asked, I had to ask her if I could raise Faith as my own. I couldn't have kids…Ester, swallowed hard. Now still sitting on the floor, leaning on the chair she had been sitting in. I was abused as a child; I was taken advantage of…I was raped when I was still a young girl, just blossoming and becoming a teenager. No one spoke a word, but the room echoed the sounds of gasp in the room from all. Let me just say, our aunt found out and didn't say a word, or even report what happened to the authorities. She told me to keep my mouth shut. Our aunt was an evil woman, and she hated us and our father dropped us off for her to raise and take care of my sister and me, after our mother died. So, after it happened and when she found out I had become pregnant, Ester stopped speaking, lifted her head to the ceiling and closed her eyes. Myra rose up and went and sat in the chair behind Ester and put her arms around her sister's neck, burying her face in her sister's neck. "Ssshhhh, it's ok my sister, it's ok." Ester went on to speak. "Let's just say our aunt was very angry, and said she'd handle it, not one more child is coming into her house for her to raise and not receive a cent from it.

When I got the infection, the doctor said I would never be able to have children. I was a child! I was a child, a child who just wanted to be loved. She had no love in her, she hated us, she hated me and Myra, evil, just pure evil. So, this is the reason why or how I became sterile and couldn't have children of my own. Then there is your uncle, Ester stood and gestured, pointing at Raymond across the room.

Yes, your uncle Raymond and his side lady were expecting. He got someone else pregnant, shortly after we began dating" shaking her head as she spoke. The anger, the pity, and yet, I still knew that I had to be married to him, not just for me, but for Myra too. Faith, along with everyone in the room, sat stunned over what they all just learned. Faith sat quietly, then spoke. "I'm going to say this, and I hope you all hear me." Faith cleared her throat and began. "I had a feeling that Aunt Myra was not my aunt. I remember hearing my parents argue one night, and some of the things they said didn't make sense to me. I heard my dad say to my Mama, that I was more like Aunt Myra because she gave birth to me. And my mother became so angry with him. "I never said a word because I wanted it to be true. I was so young, I wanted to be Aunt Myra's daughter." Faith finally turned and looked at her mother, "Mama, it's not that I don't love you, but you didn't treat me like the daughter you wanted. You looked at me with disdain, like I wasn't good enough, and it's how you've always treated me, like I needed fixing or wasn't good enough to be your daughter.

Aunt Myra, when she looked at me, I could see love in her eyes. When she hugged me, I could feel love oozing out of her towards me. I could truly feel that she loved me. She would tell me that I was so beautiful, smart, and wanted. She always said I was wanted, and I never questioned it because it made me feel so good. The love and calmness of her voice told me beyond any doubt that I was all those things. What hurt was that it was my aunt telling me this, and not my mother, and I guess that is why... It's why when I heard the argument, I said within myself, let it be so." Ester rose and went over to her daughter, tears continuing to stream down her face, hugging Faith. "I love you, Faith, I always have. I wanted my own child so badly. I saw Myra in you, her mannerisms, her love for the Lord, and I resented it. I resented it more and more, because I knew that it was true and made sense. You are so loving, just like her, and even I couldn't deny it.

Myra spoke up. She looked at Faith. "You were always wanted. I loved you so much before you were born. Ester allowed me to name you, and I will ever be grateful for that. I wanted your name to reflect who you are in God. Ester, "I never acted like I was better than anyone. You're my sister. We were dealt a bad hand by our earthly parents and relatives, but you were always there for me, and especially back then, and for all you did for me, by loving and caring for Faith. You gave her a great life, and you allowed me to be there for her, helping to take care of her and nurse her sweet little body. How can I ever resent you? I love you, I thank you. So many women would never have had the opportunity to do for their birth child as you allowed me to do, and to be there for her. Faith rose from her mother's arms, walking over to her aunt. She hugged Myra tightly. "Aunt Myra, I love you. I understand." Faith then spoke. "I got pregnant too, and I didn't do what you did. I had an abortion." Gasps filled the room. Only Michael and Myra knew Faith's secret; not even her own parents knew everything that had occurred when she went away to college. "Yes," Faith continued. "That's what I did after

I was taken advantage of by someone who I thought cared about me. I repented. I broke the covenant. I am forgiven."

Josiah muttered, "Man, this is getting deep." Bella replied, "You got stuff too Josiah." Myra finally said, "It's been a lot. Let's try to get some rest." Good nights were exchanged. Before Ester and Raymond left for the hotel, Faith called her father. "Daddy," Raymond turned and looked at Faith. "I forgive you." Forgive me for what Raymond said. "You had malice in your heart when you did what you did tonight. You lashed out and tried to hurt Aunt Myra, and you tried to embarrass my mother, both of them. Why would you do something like that? Why do you only think about yourself? You didn't even consider that what you were saying would tell their secrets before they were ready to share them with the family, and it would bring me pain. I thank God for covering me, despite all you did tonight, I still love you and I forgive you and I pray for you. You need to ask for forgiveness, you need to repent for the things in your heart that are not good, not of God and that unforgiveness causes you to want to bring pain, even to the ones you are supposed to love. You should never ever want to hurt my mother like that. She isn't perfect, no one is, but she doesn't deserve to be treated like you often treat her, and how you did just that tonight, and in front of all of our family."

Faith's voice rose a pitch, and Raymond stood silent, not looking at his daughter or his wife. Ester listened to Faith. She stood in place with her back turned towards Raymond, not saying a word. "Mama, I love you with all of my heart and I always will." Faith, baby, I love you too, always have, and I always will," said Ester. She began to walk to the door, opened it into the cool dark night. Raymond murmured a good night and followed after his wife into the night. Faith closed the door, standing against it with her back leaning against it.

Michael, who had been waiting and listening nearby, said, "Faith, hey sis, are you ok?" "Mike, right now, I just need to go and sit quietly, cry, pray, throw her hands up in the air, and shake her head. "Tonight was a lot, and I didn't see this coming. I thought tonight was going to be the healing and revealing from your brother and sisters, yet here I find myself right in the middle of it all."

Michael wrapped his arms around his cousin, as she buried her face in his chest and cried. "My cousin…my sister, you are so loved, so very loved, it had to come out, and in it all, you remember the Lord loves you, and He has you, and even in the pain of what happened, He had and still does, and He always will." Let's go sit outside on the porch, just for a little bit, and we don't even have to talk. Faith nodded her head, grabbed a throw over her shoulders and headed outside with her cousin, now the brother she always wanted. 'The Lord answers even in ways we don't expect she thought to herself, my best friend Michael was my cousin, but is really my little brother, just look at God." Arrya turned to Zek and said, "Zek, we need to have a conversation." Essie and Ezra were standing near the door when they overheard the exchange. They shrugged their shoulders and walked to the front porch and down to the bench facing the lake.

"Is this something that has to be done now? I don't understand why it can't wait until the morning." "No, it's past time, just like what today was about with your mom and all of the family." "I'm tired," Zek responded. "I'd rather go to bed. So if you want to talk in the bedroom, fine, but I don't want to talk out here." "All right, that's fine," Arrya replied. "We can talk in the room. But talking is what I would like to do, not screaming and hollering. You got that?"

Zek glared at his wife as she turned and walked away, and he followed. Once in the room, Arrya turned to face her husband. "Zek, what happened? You never really shared it all with me, and now I see, the reason you are the way you are stems from your childhood, you and Nelly, are you kidding me? I knew there were hidden secrets, but man, you allowed that incident about your dad to taint your life, our life. I'm actually a little angry, man…you have the nerve to have hated your father, your own father, to disrespect him, to not allow him in your life, and yet, what your dad did, the mistake he made, oh, and a mistake that your mother, the woman of God she is, actually forgave him for, but you, you did the same thing to me, in our marriage. What a hypocrite you are, pathetic, just pathetic, yet here you are acting as if you're are a righteous man loving me your wife, treating me with love and kindness, you know, like you love me, like you love our life and our family, yet you stepped out in the very same manner, then continued to ridicule and treat me like crap all of the time Zek." Zek finally looked up at his wife. He could see the disgusted look on her face as he slightly tilted his head to the side and squinted his eyes. "Look, I know I made my mistakes, I was young, and what my dad did has nothing to do with my life, do you hear me?"

"Obviously, you are delusional! shouted Arrya. You my dear are a very misguided and delusional man, who needs Jesus. I guess you can't see it, but honey, I'm living it, so I know that's where it's stemming from, and it's not fair to our sons or me. Heck, you have another child as well, one that no one in the family even really knows or has a relationship with, , not to mention, you're not even involved in his life, totally unfair to him.

Zek, this is it. After this weekend, if you're not willing to do better, to seek help, to speak with someone, to decide to choose God and live a life that is pleasing to him, then this marriage is over. I don't deserve to live a life in misery, with someone that can't bring himself to care about our children or me, and they certainly don't deserve to have a parent, a father in the home, yet so far away from them emotionally and spiritually." Arrya looked at her husband, seeing no response, she threw her hands up in the air and walked out. Zek lay back on the bed, covering his eyes with his arms, remaining there until sleep took over his body.

As Ezra and Essie, rested in front of the lake, quietly thinking about everything that had just taken place, Ezra let out a sigh. Ezra turned to his wife, "You know this weekend is turning out to be one big revelation for your family, and it's only the first night" Ezra said. Essie nodded. "Families don't know how to love anymore, if they ever did in the first place, but I'm still glad you're here to support your Mama." "Yea, I couldn't agree more, and I'm glad we are both here, for her and together, geeze, I just never really knew that so much drama existed in my family, so many hurt feeling and just things that are so wrong, but they don't want to let them go, don't want to forgive, and aren't even thinking about their kids. We're not perfect, far from it, but you have got to have, and show love to each other, for others and definitely for our children and family. That is where the biggest problem lies. Unfortunately, a lot of families don't know what that looks like." Ezra continued to speak, "so many have been raised to not have it demonstrated in front of them or given to them.

Love for many in our culture, in our families, broken or together, back then it was believing that if you have food in your stomach, a roof over your head, what do you have to complain about. I mean, listen, that's how it was in my family. I loved my Pops, but it was if he was always tired, and always mad at the world. We didn't really see him, and my sweet Mama, as kids, we would be laughing, and kidding around with each other and my Mama, that was until Pops got home. The atmosphere would change, and don't let it be anything that had to do with money, or something that he thought she did wrong. All you know what, broke loose.

This is the life, the family that I didn't want to have, I didn't want to have a wife and kids and take them through that kind of life, hard, full of anger and pain. Essie, I'm grateful to be married to a woman like you. You are nothing like Nelly, nothing." Essie nodded her head and went and put her arms around her husband.

"I appreciate the man you are, my sweet hubby. We are nowhere near perfect, this is not a perfect marriage, and yeah, we've had our ups and downs, and right now my heart's a little heavy after hearing Michael, Faith and David speak, and my mother, my own mother and Aunt Ester.

"You know, I actually feel a little bit sorry for Faith. She's been doing her best to be the woman of God for all of us and in this family. She's been standing on faith, and she herself has had so much happen to her, and especially tonight. Oh my God, can you even believe this? Faith is not Cousin Faith. Faith is actually my big sister. Heck, Faith is Mama's firstborn. That's why Mama goes to her so much. That's why Mama loves her and shows her so much love, and Faith loves Mama." "Can you believe that Faith actually overheard your Aunt Esther and Uncle Raymond, talking about this when she was younger, and she never said anything to them? She never said anything to anyone. She kept this all hidden." More secrets that had to be revealed.

"Yeah," Ezra replied, "that's pretty hard to realize, that she actually kept all this inside her all these years, knowing how her

Mama is. I mean, think about it. Faith really is more like Miss Myra, your mom, than she is her mom. Because her mom…maybe this is… I don't know, this is kind of funny. Well, it's kind of interesting. Maybe they switched the kids. Maybe Nelly is really Aunt Esther's daughter, because boy, oh boy, they sure are alike, like twin walking attitudes."

"You know what, Ez, you need to stop now. You know good and well Nelly is not Aunt Esther's daughter." All right, they both kind of chuckled and looked at each other. "All right, we're not even going to go there. But I was just saying, you know we just found out that Faith is Myra's, and now I'm just wondering. Maybe they did a swappo or something like that." "Why do you have to make jokes out of such a serious situation?" "Hey, I'm just trying to make it a little bit light. Today has been nothing but a heavy load for all of us. So, just a thought. It was just kind of funny that possibly could be." "Right now, I am not surprised by anything that comes up out of this family anymore. Honey, a little bit of everything came up tonight. It makes a TV so-called "reality show" situations look like a piece of cake." "Oh, no, there is no way we are on that level of bad and worldly living. Let me just say, my sister Nelly and Aunt Ester, they don't like each other…just too much alike, and with a lot of bottled pain." Essie got serious with her Ezra, "We never knew everything about anyone's life, even if we are in their life. I still have questions about my parents, but I'm a little afraid to even ask. I definitely don't want to be the one to bring up all those horrible memories. It's not like a lot of people who can look back on their upbringing, and you know, reminisce about how much fun they had, and the joy their home brought to them, just all that stuff we see sometimes on television. Everyone does not have great memories about the house or neighborhood they grew up in. Even me, I didn't have a bad life, but nothing in my childhood stood out that I wanted to look back on as if it was a wonderful life, it's one we all survived, we survived."

Essie lowered and shook her head at the same time, as Ez pulled the arm, he had around his wife even closer, as she closed her eyes, allowing tears of pain to trickle down her face. "Ez how, just how can so much bad blood happen in our family? Especially when we love the Lord, like my mom and Faith, and just look at what happened to them, it hurts my heart, and now my head hurts. I can feel the pain of my family, it's not good. Yet I know in my heart, our family and our love for one another can be restored, I know we can be reconciled back for the good, for our children and generations to come." Ez leaned his head on his wife's head as they both sat quietly and pondered the thoughts bouncing through their minds.

"It makes me just think about how I've acted, how I've treated others without knowing their story, and especially Nelly. I know how my sister is, I still love her and I try to be a good sister to her and encourage her even though she can be so hard and mean to everybody else. So, I pray this weekend will unleash something in her that will soften her, convict her, and maybe it will start by forgiving Samuel for doing what he believed he had to do for his life and family." "I hope everything works out but you know what, I'm tired too. Let's go check on the kids and make sure they're okay and get their pjs on, and get them into bed, and then after that we can go ahead and turn in, said Ez.

"Sure, my dear, it's going to be kind of hard to get them in bed if they haven't already fallen asleep with all the games. The boys are probably having so much fun with their cousins, but either way it goes, it's getting kind of late." Ezra and Essie walked back up to the house and downstairs to send Elianna back upstairs to bed and help their son get ready as well.

Faith was sitting on the front porch. She could see the glistening lake and her cousins resting on the bench. Her face was still wet with tears, her mouth moving, but her words were not really audible to others. *"Lord, I knew this was going to be a hard weekend, but my gosh, Father, I pray that I'm doing the right thing. Lord, right now my heart is hurting. I never thought that revealing the truth in the family, and also the things that were going to happen with my own parents and me, would turn out like this. I already knew, but I never knew it was going to come out to the rest of the family like this. I wasn't ready for everyone to know."* Faith continued staring out into the night when she heard a voice behind her.

"Well, you sure did cause a whole lot of things and issues that did not need to be talked about to come up, and all the way out today." Faith turned around at the voice, but she already knew who it was. It was Nelly of all people. "Come join me, Nelly. There are things that you and I have to get clear, too." Nelly crossed her arms and said, "You know what, it's been a long time, and I don't think there's anything we need to clear up. But I'll tell you what I don't like. I don't like how you have always manipulated my Mama. I don't like how you've gotten so close to her that I always thought it was as if you were her daughter. Now what do I find out? You really are her daughter. You're her first daughter. I'm no longer the 'first' daughter. But then again, I'm not like her anyway." Faith looked at her and said, "You know what, Nelly? One thing I've never understood is how you can be so mean and evil to your own mother." You're mad at a woman that you have just found out what happened in her life, and all you can say is that you're not her firstborn, and yet you treat her so badly, so very bad, as if you couldn't care less if you're her daughter at all. Nelly started at the porch floor, saying nothing back to Faith. "And Aunt Myra loves you so very much. She loves you and has always been so proud of you. It hurts her when you all treat her badly, and yet, I don't understand how you don't really know her, and see her heart, and yet still treat her so badly. She continued, "So, your Mama is my Mama. I overheard my parents arguing about it one night, and I kept it to myself. I was a kid, I heard what I heard, but no one ever told me anything, so I just kept it on the inside. I was filled with joy knowing that Aunt Myra, whom I knew loved me and treated me like she loved me, really was my Mama. "Even though I didn't understand the circumstances around her giving me up and allowing my mother Ester to raise me, she was still my Mama. She still carried me. She still sacrificed. She had me even when she wasn't married." Faith paused.

"You know what, Nelly raises her voice to Faith, I don't even want to get into how children are seen before they're born, how they're already alive and not just cells." She looked directly at Nelly. "Listen, Nelly, I know what you did. And what you did is no different than what a lot of women do. It doesn't make you a bad person, but it does mean that if that was a decision that was made by any woman, especially a child of God, then they, just like me, need to ask God for forgiveness, just like I did. Sister, God loves you so much. Women are told, and many believe it's their only choice, without recognizing they have more choices than they think. You made a choice, but you made that choice alone. You were married to Samuel, and you still made that choice alone." Nelly spoke up. "I did what I thought was the best decision for me. Nobody was looking out for me. I had to look out for myself. All y'all want to do is put Sammy on this big pedestal like he's some perfect man. How perfect is he? After everything, he went out and found somebody else." Faith shook her head. "No, my dear. He didn't just go find someone else." Samuel was fighting for his marriage. He was fighting for his family. He was fighting for his daughter, Jennesis, and he was fighting for you, his wife.

You gave up on him. You put your career, your status, and your image above everything else. Those things became idols in your life." Do you even think God is pleased with the fact that these idols were above Him? Everything that mattered to you was how you looked and how having another child would affect you in climbing the corporate ladder. No, my dear, you did that. You pushed him right out of the way and into someone else's arms, someone who was waiting.

Do you know there is always somebody waiting in the wings? When you don't appreciate what you have, there is always someone ready to step into your shoes and do what you won't do."

Nelly snapped back, "You know what, Faith? The last thing I need is to hear you preach to me about my sins, wrong living, and the decisions I make. I got more money than all of you put together in this family, and I am proud of the status and place I've made in my life." Yes, Samuel's gone, and you know what? I don't need anything from him to take care of me. So keep me out of your mouth." Faith shook her head. "Nelly, I'm not trying to argue with you. I was sitting here praying and thinking about everything that happened today. I was thinking about the forgiveness that hasn't been given, shared, or even tried." "That's what has to happen. You have to understand that forgiveness is the most important thing."

Nelly responded sharply, "I'm not trying to have this conversation with you, Faith. On top of that, it ain't none of your business what I do with my life or my marriage. It's nobody's business in this family how I live my life, what it looks like now, or what it looked like then." "If Samuel wants to tell you all everything, that's his business. I'm living my life for myself and nobody else, except Jennesis. Other than that, all of you can kick rocks."

Faith looked at her in disbelief. "I can't believe you're taking that posture, Nelly. But then again, that's what you do. You only think about yourself, and you don't care how others feel." "Even your Mama. Your own mother sits around wondering what she did wrong to make you treat her the way you do. I know I already asked this, but why do you look at her with such contempt in your eyes?" Nelly folded her arms. "Faith, as I said before, I'm going in. I'm not having this discussion with you or anyone else. Good night."

She turned and walked away from Faith, throwing her hand up as if to say goodbye, or maybe just "later," and kept walking. Faith continued sitting there in silence, staring out into the darkness. Right when Nelly walked inside, she almost bumped right into Samuel. "Nelly, can I talk to you for a minute?" he asked. She sighed. "You know what? I just got done talking with Faith. What is it that you want to talk about? I'm ready to go to bed." "It won't take long. Maybe we can go into your room and have a chat," Samuel said. "Well, unless somebody's in there," Nelly replied. "If she's in there, then we can just stay out here." "Fine. Whatever works."

They walked down the hallway and into the room. Of course, no one was in there. Samuel took a deep breath. "Listen, I'm grateful that your Mama allowed me to come here this weekend, especially because Jennesis was going to be here. I was able to see my baby and literally spend time with her for a whole weekend, something I haven't been able to do since you and I broke up." Nelly crossed her arms. "Samuel, I'm not trying to go into this right now. You may be happy that you're here this weekend, but I absolutely was not. Number one, I didn't want to be here with all these people anyway." Samuel looked at her. "What are you talking about, 'these people'? You're acting like this isn't your family. These people are your family. These people love you. These people will be here for you when no one else is."

"Let's get this straight. You don't have anybody else. You treat everybody like crap. You treat the people you work with like crap. You don't go to church. The only person who puts up with your mess is Essie, and I don't even know why she does it, because she is such a sweet woman, just like Bella." "How did it turn out where Bella, Essie, and Faith are such kind souls, and then there's you? Nelly rolled her eyes so hard at Samuel, raising her hand as if she wanted to hurt him for the truth he said out of his mouth. And then there's you." "Well, at least we found out tonight that Faith is really your Mama's child, and we can all see that. Maybe that's the problem. You're jealous because you see the goodness in Faith. She's just like your mother, just like her." Nelly snapped, "You know what? That ain't none of your business, how my Mama is or how Faith is. You ain't nothing but a loser anyway. You can't even take care of my kid and me, much less anything else." Samuel stared at her. "Nelly, what are you talking about? I went to school, I'm a teacher, I'm educated. I do what God called me to do. Just because it wasn't enough money for you doesn't mean it wasn't enough to take care of our family." "I don't know what kind of man you're looking for, but I am a God-fearing, God-loving man. I'm grateful to be who God created me to be. And more than anything, I'm grateful to have a sweet little girl in my life, a beautiful daughter with a heart of gold." "I'm grateful she doesn't have a heart of stone, or should I say a black hole, like yours." Nelly gasped.

"What happened to you, Nelly? What changed in you? You're not the woman I met. You're not the woman I thought I fell in love with and wanted to spend my life with." "You're more concerned with your job, with trying to make partner, with trying to take over the world, and look good doing it than you are about your family, your daughter, and even about me and our marriage." Nelly rubbed her forehead. "Samuel, I'm tired. I'm not trying to have this conversation." "This conversation is past due," he replied. "I just want one thing. I want us to try to get along for Jennesis' sake. I know we're not a family anymore, and I'm not trying to be one with you, but I want to be in her life. There is absolutely no reason for me not to be." "All right, fine," Nelly said. "You want to be in her life? We can get an arbitrator and come up with something for visitation and all that. If that's what you want." "Because frankly, I'm tired of all of you all. I'm tired of everybody pointing their finger at me like I'm the bad guy."

Samuel shook his head. "You're not a bad person, but your values are, and your morals are wrong. You see everything through the world's view. You follow what the world puts up and puts down." "The world will take you straight to hell, and if that's where you're trying to go, it's not hard when you follow its ways. Your heart needs to be renewed. Your faith needs to be found. You need to be rooted in the Lord."

Nelly snapped, "You're trying to talk Bible to me? I grew up in church. There ain't nothing about the Bible, you can teach me." "I'm not trying to teach you," Samuel replied. "I'm trying to share what's on my heart. It's important. But until you submit to the Lord, until you change how you think, the thoughts in your mind, and the words out of your mouth, nothing will change." "Nothing will ever change with you." "Where is your love? How do you represent people when you have no love for anybody but yourself? You need a serious heart change. I don't understand where life went wrong for you that you see everything half-full and only cut people down instead of being a blessing." Nelly grew quiet. She lowered her head. Finally, she said, "Samuel, we'll have to talk about this another day. Right now, I'm going to bed. You can stay here and keep talking if you want, but I'm going to bed. Good night." She turned and walked into the bathroom, leaving Samuel standing there. Samuel lowered his head, then walked down the hall to Jennesis's room and knocked on the door to say good night to his daughter.

Just as Nelly was walking out of the bathroom, Bella came into the room, humming a little tune to herself. "Oh, hey, I didn't know you were in here." "Yeah, I'm in here getting ready for bed." "Oh, okay. Cool. Yeah, let me go ahead and use the bathroom and get ready myself." "All right, that's fine." "Are you okay?" Bella asked. Nelly sighed. "I'm good. I'm fine. I'm just a little bit tired of all this family drama today. I think I've had about as much family drama today as I could for the last five years." "Well, it has been a bit challenging today," Bella said, "but you know Daniel, and I believe that a lot of it needed to come out. A lot of things needed to be said. And yeah, it may be hard to listen to. It may be hard to hear, but there are a lot of changes that really need to take place for the good." Nelly spoke up. "Not you too. I just had it out with Samuel and Faith, and now you. And we've got to share a room, so please, no lectures tonight."

"That's fine," Bella replied. "I'm just trying to let you know that even though it was a hard day, it was still necessary. It was really necessary for Mama, and it looks like it was necessary for the rest of us as well. You know Mama has been doing the best she can since Dad died, and there's so much that needed to be said when he was still alive, but it wasn't.

And unfortunately, now it's just Mama here. She really wants to clear the air, so we really should listen to her. We really should lean into what's best for our family." "You know what, Bella, I hear you," Nelly said, "and it's not that I want bad for our family, but I'm living my own life. I'm living life the way I want to live it. However, you all want to do it, y'all do it. But you can definitely keep me out of any decisions and all this 'Lordy, Lordy' and 'praise the Lord' type conversations. I'm really not interested in hearing them." "Wow, Nelly," Bella said. "You know, I know you're super negative, but you weren't always like this. And even for you to say things like that, that's kind of disrespectful to our faith in God, and disrespectful towards God. That is not the kind of people we were raised to be. So why are you talking like that? Why are you talking like someone who never believed in the Lord and someone who never even went to church?"

"What are you talking about, Bella? I'm not talking any kind of way." "Yeah, you are. Yeah, you are," Bella replied. "And I guess you just can't hear yourself, but it's not good. I think a lot of the problems come from how you see others outside of the family, and how you see the rest of us." She thought for a minute, hummm, "No, maybe it's how you see yourself. Maybe, if you took a good look in the mirror sometimes and really started to ask yourself, 'Why am I the way I am? Why am I treating people like they don't matter?' Because you use people and throw them away, kind of like you did with Samuel, and kind of like you did with Mama and Dad and the rest of us." Nelly glared at her sister, mouth hanging open. "I didn't throw anybody away," Nelly said. "I just don't have time to deal with all this foolishness and drama when I've got a whole life and a whole career ahead of me. That's what's important to me, my career and my child, and nothing else." "Bella replied, "That's unfortunate that you think that way. I know that a lot of people think that way. They act and believe that they are the only ones that matter, regardless of anyone else's feelings or life issues. Only how they are treated matters, not how they treat others. In case you didn't know, this is called being selfish. Sis, you need to change. I don't know if the Lord needs to visit you in your sleep like the Grinch. No, wait, sorry, it was Scrooge. Yeah, you need a ghost of your past and future as Scrooge did. Although the only ghost we believe in is the Holy Ghost, maybe the Holy Ghost of our Lord and Savior will touch your spirit, my sister, and really wake you up to see how you're treating everybody. Oh, yeah, that will be really good. Because I tell you what, if I didn't stay in this room, you wouldn't have anybody staying in here with you. Nobody wants to deal with you. I don't even understand how Samuel put up with you as long as he did. He tried. That man is a saint, and unfortunately, he was given a really raw deal. And you know you're wrong. You know you're so wrong. You think because you're some powerful attorney that you can talk everybody into your way of thinking, and that includes your husband, oh, I mean ex-husband. And let me tell you now, the things you're doing concerning Samuel and not giving him shared custody with Jennesis, it's going to backfire on you. It's going to come back and bite you in the butt. It may not happen right away, but when Jennesis is old enough to make her own decisions, I promise you, her decision probably won't be to stay with you."

Nelly stood up, pointing in Bella's direction. "You need to mind your own business and keep my daughter's name out of your mouth," Nelly snapped. "Better yet, good night. I'm tired of talking to all of you." Nelly jumped into the bed and immediately turned over, ignoring her sister.

Bella turned and walked into the bathroom and shut the door. The conversation was done. Bella came out of the bathroom, picked up her phone, and texted Daniel, "Good night, my sweets." At the same time, he was texting her. "Good night, my love, rest well in Jesus." She put her phone down, got on her knees, and prayed before going to bed.

'Boy, what a long night it's been, what a long day it has been, Jesus, please keep me, I didn't see this happening today.' Myra thought as she sat on the side of her bed. '*All this came out in one day, and this is only the first day. So many hurt feelings. So many things have been uncovered already. Thoughts continued to drift through her mind. I can't believe what happened with Ester. I pray Faith is okay.*

Father, I definitely didn't want her to find out like this. It's been in my heart so long to share my true heart with her, how it happened, and how she was given away. I wanted both Ester and me to share it with her, not just me alone; it wasn't my place, it was her parents' to decide. I wanted us to love her and let her know how wanted and necessary she is in this family. But she is turning out to be the breaker. She is turning out to be the breaker in this family for generations, and that's a good thing. So many things need to be cleared up. My grandchildren do not need to be walking in things that happened generations ago. It has to be broken. Decisions I made, decisions Edward made, so much wrong, and so bad, and not living for Jesus, nor even trying. But at least he turned his life around before it ended. That matters more than anything. He transitioned in the right direction.' She chuckled softly and said quietly, "That makes my heart sing, Lord, knowing he's resting in You." "I want that for all my family. Show me how to be that for them. Show me, Lord, what to do. There are so many hurts and pains. How can I make it better? Oh God, I pray for Nelly. Her heart is so hard. I know something happened to put her in this place. Let it come out this weekend." "Thank You, God, for this time. For the food, and for the fellowship. Even though it turned into something I didn't expect, I'm still grateful. I will be forever. You, Oh Lord, are in control, Amen.'

The sun peeked through the blinds and right into the eyes of Bella. Bella looked up, stretched a little bit, grabbed her phone to check the time, and then said to herself, "My goodness, it's already time for me to get up." Bella raised up, closed her eyes, and said a quick prayer, just thankful that she was here to see another day. She quietly got out of bed, went over to her suitcase, and pulled out her running clothes. She went back into the bathroom and got dressed. All the while, Nelly was covered up from head to toe under the covers, asleep, and Bella didn't want to wake her up. Before Bella got dressed, she texted Daniel and asked him if he was ready to go.

Bella quietly walked out of the room, down the hall, and out the front door, where Daniel was already sitting on the front porch waiting for her. "Hey, baby. Good morning." "Good morning, my man. How are you doing today? How did you sleep?" "Like a rock. I was so tired." "Yeah, it took me a little bit longer to get to sleep, but I'm good now, and always glad to see you when I wake up in the morning." "Glad to see you too, my sweet girl. Are you ready? Let's go." "Wait, did you already stretch? Because I need to stretch a little bit before we start running." "All right, go ahead," Daniel said.

"Go ahead and get stretched a little bit, and then we'll walk first before we start running." "All right, sounds great." The two of them started off on their journey.

"But seek first the kingdom of God and His righteousness,
and all these things shall be added to you."
(Mathew 6:33, NKJV)

Chapter 9.

BROKEN

Yet for Such a Time as This

Myra came out of her room and went straight into the kitchen. She put on some coffee, quietly trying not to wake everybody up, even though she saw that Bella and Daniel were already out and about getting their workout in.

Myra walked over to the coffee pot, grabbed it, took it to the sink, and started filling it with water. Then she returned it to the coffee maker, measured out the coffee, and got it started.

As soon as she finished, Faith came into the room. "Good morning, Aunt Myra." "Good morning, sweet girl. How are you? Did you sleep well? I know last night was so heavy, and there was so much that we shared."

"Yes, Ma'am. I slept the best that I possibly could." "Faith, listen. I'm so sorry. That is not how I wanted you to find out. My dear girl, I'm so sorry. I prayed and prayed for so very long. I even fantasized in my mind about how Edward and I would tell you. I wanted to share with you how much you are loved. "I knew that I was so young and wouldn't be able to take care of you and give you the truly blessed life that my girl deserved. So, when my sister, well, when your mother, Ester, came to me and said that she would like to raise you as her own daughter, and Raymond too, I allowed her to. "Before they got married, he had a situation, if you wanted to call it that, so he already had two children, the twins, and of course, you know this. I think Ester was desperate at that time.

She found out she might not be able to have children, and I think she wanted to secure her relationship. I allowed her to take you and raise you as her own. "I knew that even if she raised you, I would still see you all the time. I made sure of it. Plus, I was still a teenager myself, and my sister was much older. After Edward and I got married, and we began to have children, my first was a beautiful girl, Nelly. Oh, my sweet Nelly. She sure was a sweet girl. And you two were so close in age, you, of course, being older, but she looked up to you like a big sister, a playmate. "And I held that secret deep inside, that you really were sisters."

"Aunt Myra," Faith said gently, "maybe we can talk about this in private another time. I know everyone is going to start coming in, and I don't want to deal with the looks and questions."

"You're right," Myra replied. "We can wait until another time. For now, I just want to say again, I'm sorry. Will you forgive me?" "Aunt Myra, there's nothing for me to forgive you for," Faith said. "I understand completely.

When I overheard my parents talking years ago, it settled in my heart. "I loved you as my aunt, and when I realized you were my mom, it made sense, even though they never told me. You were the one who showered me with love, took me to church, taught me about Jesus, and helped me receive Him as my Savior. I'm grateful for that. "Now my cousins are really my siblings, and I hope they'll still accept me. I love them already, and they love me; that makes David my brother, too. But at this point, family is what matters most. That matters to God, too." "Yes, dear," Myra said softly. "You are absolutely right." "I prayed so much, too," Faith replied. "Let's pray that from here on, it just gets better." "Amen," Myra said. "Now go get yourself a cup of coffee. I'm going to wash up and get ready."

"You know what I'd like to do today? Faith said, Maybe go shopping, and perhaps the ladies will want to come." "We can ask them," Myra replied. "Bella and Daniel are already out exercising. Essie and Ezra aren't up yet, and we haven't seen Nelly. We'll see." "Yeah," Faith smiled. "That's how it works the day after a holiday." "You're right," Myra said. "Let me get ready, and I'll fix some food if anyone's hungry." "Yes, ma'am." Faith was in the kitchen, sitting at the kitchen table, drinking her coffee, on her phone, and just thinking about everything that took place the night before when Arrya walked into the kitchen.

"Good morning, Faith. How are you?" "Hey, Arrya. Good morning. How are you doing? Did you sleep well?" "Yeah, I slept pretty well. How about yourself?" "I'm well. I'm good, thank you so much. Get yourself some coffee." "No, I'm really good. That's more Zek's style than mine. I'll just take some juice, I think. Miss Myra does have some juice in here, doesn't she?" "Oh, Aunt Myra got everything in here. She got pineapple juice, I see cranberry juice, and she got some orange juice. Name a juice, and she probably has that too. "Thanks, Faith, but you know what I would really love to make? A smoothie instead. "I did bring some of my protein mix and stuff like that, because I knew she wouldn't have that kind of stuff, so I came prepared, just in case." Faith laughed and said, "You know what, knock yourself out. I'm not going to be in your way. Aunt Myra just went to get washed up and dressed. Then she's going to come back and start breakfast, so you probably should go ahead and get the smoothie together before she comes back." "Yeah, you're right, I don't want to be in her way when she's trying to put a meal together. Right at that moment, Zek walked into the kitchen. "Good morning," he belted out under his breath. "Good morning yourself," Faith replied. "How are you? Sleep well?" Arrya kept her head down, preparing her smoothie, ignoring her husband. "Yep, slept just fine. How about yourself?" "I'm good, thank you. Your mom's getting dressed, and she's going to come back and get breakfast started, but coffee is ready if you want some." Zek kind of looked over at his wife and gave her a half nod to say good morning. Arrya nodded back, but kept her lips sealed for now. Right at that moment, Bella and Daniel entered the house. "Great morning, everyone," Bella said as she went into the living room to stretch. "Hey, good morning, everyone," Daniel said. "Hope everyone slept well." "Hey, Daniel. Good morning, you early birds," Faith answered back. "We've been out walking and running. The air is so crisp, especially around Lake Misty. It is so beautiful. We should all try to go on a lake walk later." "That'd be great," Faith said. "We can finish chatting and catching up." "Hey, Bella," Faith added, "Aunt Myra is getting dressed and coming back to make breakfast, but she thought maybe we ladies might be interested in going shopping today. You know, it's one of those busy shopping days." Arrya spoke up. "You know what, I think I'm going to skip if Zek wants to go do something with the kids, I think I'd rather do that than go shopping." Zek, hearing his name, responded immediately. "Yeah, well, I don't really want to go anywhere, but if we do, we need to be back by three o'clock." Arrya nodded. "If we go anywhere, I thought maybe we could just take the kids out and see what's around here. They'll probably have a good time with you; they always do when you spend time with them." Arrya went to make her smoothie and walked out of the room before Zek could answer. After the conversation he and Arrya had the night prior, Zek felt it necessary to agree with what she wanted to do. She was absolutely right about him, his attitude, lack of love, harsh toned and how he viewed their life together. She was right, and she deserved better, he knew that.

Myra came back into the room. "Good morning, everyone. I see everybody's up bright and early." "Good morning," echoed back to her. Myra loved sweat suits, and her kids loved spoiling her with new ones, especially Michael. "Everyone hungry? I can go ahead and put some food on. Zek, Daniel, I hope you all got some coffee." Arrya popped back into the kitchen, bringing her glass to rinse out. "Good morning, Miss Myra. I made a quick smoothie, and now I'm going to get out of your way," Arrya said.

"No worries, my dear. I'm glad you brought what you needed." "Mama, how did you sleep?" Zek asked. "Well, I believe I slept pretty well, despite it all. God is good, and He got me back up this morning, especially after last night. My eyes have been opened to a lot of things, but I'm well, and I thank the Lord that I'm feeling good and still here to see this day." "How about you, son? Did you sleep okay?" "Yeah, Ma, I did. I'm good." "All right then. Bella and Daniel, are you both doing okay?" "Yeah, Mama, we're okay," Bella replied. "Bella, would you like to help me whip up some breakfast?" "Mama, whatever you need. I'm your girl." Bella got up with her cup of coffee and walked over to help her mother. "Bella, my dear, you're my sidekick today," Myra chuckled. "Mama, I'll always be your sidekick in the kitchen and out. You know, I know, how to throw down in the kitchen, just like you taught me. Plus, I told everyone already, they know, I'm still your favorite." Everyone within earshot busted out laughing, especially after what had happened the night before. "Yes, my beautiful daughter," Myra said, smiling. "You know what you're doing in the kitchen. Daniel will never starve." Daniel perked up. "I know that's right. Thank the Lord." Myra thought to herself, *If only it could be like this all the time. If only.* "All right, I'm going to sit outside and rest for a little bit and have my coffee. Make sure everyone is up, please, and especially the babies. Make sure to feed the babies, especially the boys." "Yes, ma'am," was heard in unison. The kitchen was full of joy and laughter, with minds nowhere focused on what had taken place the evening before, as the rest of the family floated into the kitchen, waking up as they smelled the food, like an instant alarm clock for their stomachs. Myra took her drink and went to sit on the front porch. Bella stepped outside with her mother. "Mama, isn't it such a beautiful day today?" "Yes, it is." "Daniel and I did our laps. We were running and walking. It was great being out in the early morning hours with all of nature." Yes, my dear, I love to sit out here, think, and talk with the Lord. Yes, Mama, me too. They sat in silence, as voices and laughter carried out into the outside atmosphere.

"Mama, where are you?" Essie called out to Myra. "Where are you guys going anyway? What kind of shopping is around here?" "Myra replied, well, there's one of those outlet malls, not far from here. They have all kinds of stores. There is a Nike store, got all kinds of stuff up there. So, we're just going to go out there and see what they've got left. They also got some really great purse stores out there, too, and you know how the girls like to look at purses.

We're just going to have a great day, just going out there, spending time with each other, maybe not even buying anything." "Yeah, that sounds good. You know what, Mama?" Bella said, "the girls might want to come with us." "Yeah, Eliana and Jennesis. They might want to come shopping with us. Let's go find out if they want to come, because I don't want to just leave them here with all the guys and boys and nothing but sports and games all weekend, if they want to come out with us." "You know what, you are right, Jennesis is getting older and I believe she will want to join us. She's a little preteen, and she loves looking at that stuff for her hair, purses, and all the other girly stuff. I think she'll have a great time with us and especially with her cousin." "Yes, that'd be great. Too bad Nelly's not coming, because she could be spending time with her daughter, but that's neither here nor there. We're not going to worry about that." "Nope." "Well, you never know. Why don't you go see if Nelly wants to go with us? Don't assume that she doesn't want to go, at least let her know that we're planning on Jennesis with us, says Myra. "Okay, Bella replied. "Well, I don't see why it's necessary, after all, her daddy's downstairs. He'll let her mother know." "I know, I know. Myra rolled her eyes, please don't start nothing, go and let Nelly know that Jennesis is going to be coming with us, if Jennesis says she wants to come." "Yes, ma'am."

Everyone turned to their own respective rooms. Bella went to check with Jennesis and Eliana to see if they wanted to come, and of course, the girls wanted to go with the women. Then Bella went back to her room to see Nelly. Nelly was just walking out of the bathroom. "Good morning." "Good morning. Well, good afternoon to you," Bella replied to Nelly. Nelly said back. "It is not afternoon yet." "Well, it might as well be, because we've been up early. We did everything you could possibly do this morning, and now you're finally up when we're getting ready to leave." "What do you mean, getting ready to leave? Where are you going?" "Well, I was coming in here to see if you were even up. We, ladies, want to go shopping. We're going to the outlet, Mama said it isn't far from here.

The guys are all just going to hang out here, clean up the kitchen, and watch sports. Did you want to come with us, or did you want to stay here?" "I think I'm going to pass and stay here. Nelly crossed her arms as if she were defiant and standing her ground. "I've got work to catch up on, and I can sit up here on my laptop and get some done." Some of us don't get to just sit around talking about our feelings all day." Bella tilted her head.

“Nobody’s sitting around, Nelly. We just… we got some real family breakthrough last night, nothing but love and peace, it wouldn’t hurt you to get some too, if you join us for some womanly fellowship.” Nelly scoffed. “Peace doesn’t pay bills, Bella.” Bella smiled sadly. “No, but it sure does get you much joy, and we know that’s worth more than anything money can get you.” Nelly rolled her eyes, turning toward her vanity mirror. “Save the sermon. I’m fine right here.”

Bella nodded slowly. “Alright, sis. I love you, though.” “Yeah,” Nelly muttered, “I know.” “Is Jennesis going with you?” “Yeah, actually, I was going to let you know that Mama thought that Jennesis and Eliana would like to come with us instead of staying here with all the guys doing nothing but watching the games.” “All right, that’s fine. Jennesis loves shopping anyway. Let me give her my card so you don’t have to worry about her.” She’ll be fine, sis, we got her.” “No, it’s ok, she’ll have her own money. You all won’t have to worry about her.” “All right then. It’s great to have the life of Jennesis, isn’t it?” Nelly shot Bella a nasty little stare, turned her head, but didn’t respond back, as she walked out of the room to find Jennesis, and give her the credit card, and to make sure she was ok with going shopping with her grandma and their aunts.

When Bella left the room, she stopped in the hallway for a moment, leaning against the wall. Myra had just come from the kitchen and saw the look on her daughter's face. "She ain't coming', is she?" Myra asked quietly. Bella quietly mouthed the word "no" to her mother and walked away.

As the women, Myra, her girls, and her granddaughters, returned from shopping. They were laughing as they came through the house and inside. Nelly was in the living room working, or where she had been working, but now she was talking to Aunt Ester, having a private little conversation. As they came in the door, Myra said, "Oh, hey, Ester! I'm so glad you came back. I was wondering when you were going to come over today." "Yes, well, after yesterday and everything, I definitely wanted to come back past here. I also wanted to talk to Faith, but I got here and, lo and behold, Faith was gone." "We were shopping and having a great time," Faith spoke up. "Yep, we had a great time. Despite everything that occurred last night, it was still such a blessing to be able to go out and just enjoy the day with family. The girls had a wonderful time as well. Eliana, Jennesis, what do you think? You guys had a great time with us, did you not?" "Yes, Aunt Faith, we sure did!" "Wonderful. I'm so glad you did." "Well, Mama, I would love to talk to you if you're ready to have a conversation with me," Faith said. "Yes.

I would rather have your dad up here, too, but you know what? Can we just do this a little bit later? Right now, I've just been relaxing here talking with Nelly, and I don't want any more drama today. If you can wait, that would be just great." Faith said, "You know what, Mom? It's not a problem at all. We can talk another time. Let me go ahead and relax, take off my shoes, and sit down for a little bit. We did so much walking today." "Yes, we did," said Bella. "But you know what? It was so much fun just being with you ladies, being with my sisters. I don't always get to see you, with everyone always working so hard, everyone so busy, having different things on a schedule. It was really nice to be able to spend time with Essie, Faith, and Mama, and the girls too. I don't get to see the girls that often, so it was great being with them." Essie added, "Yes, Eliana loves being with Jennesis. I wish she could see her more, but I know Nelly works long hours and she's not always able to make that happen." Myra said, "I would love to maybe keep Jennesis and Eliana some weekends, just have the girls stay over here with me. Especially now, with me being by myself, there are a lot of weekends when I'm not really busy. Maybe they can go to church with me." "Oh, Mama," Bella said, "I think that would be a great idea. I know both of those little ladies would love being with you, because they just love their grandma and aunties."

At that point, Nelly got up from her chair in the living room and came into the room. "Well, Mom, if you think you want to be dealing with Jennesis on the weekends, and tie up every weekend with the girls, babysitting..." Myra spoke up gently. "It's not really babysitting. They're turning into beautiful young ladies, both of them, and I love spending time with them. This way, I can pour into these young ladies and not allow the world to continue pouring into them." "Mama, I don't want to hear about all the world stuff," Nelly replied.

Myra said calmly. "We need to have a conversation. Maybe after dinner, we girls can all go sit around the fire this time and just talk. After all, the guys are probably going to still be downstairs watching the game." "All right, that's fine. We can do that." "Well, let me go ahead and prepare dinner and get everything ready. After that, we can clean up, and then all of us ladies, including you, Nelly, I think you should come around the fire and talk with us as well." Nelly didn't say anything. She just nodded her head a little, almost like, '*Oh, here we go. I guess I'm going to get pulled into this again.*' "Yeah, I guess I can come in there with you ladies." "All right, sounds like a plan. Let's go ahead and start pulling everything out for dinner."

"Train up a child in the way he should go, and when he is old he will not depart from it."
(Proverbs 22:6, NKJV)

Chapter 10.

CLEANSING OF OUR SOULS

Essie went downstairs to let her brothers, her husband, and her uncle know that dinner was going to be ready soon. She walked down the steps. "Hey, guys, we're back." Essie walked over and put her arms around her husband's neck, kissing him on the cheek. "Hey, y'all. Have a good time?" "Yes, we sure did. How about you guys? I know there are lots of games on today. Which y'all been watching?" "Oh, it's been cool. We did watch the Bears and Eagles this afternoon, but now we've just been watching all college basketball." "Yeah, there's a lot of college basketball on, so it's been great watching all that and catching up. And then tomorrow, oh man, there are a lot of games on tomorrow, especially the Ohio State and Michigan game. Can't wait to watch that either." "Man, you guys and all these games. My goodness gracious, you have a lot to watch." "There are a lot of heavy hitters, and it's cool to be able to sit here and hang out with my brothers and watch the game and everything like that, you know, like no nagging." Essie laughed and said, "Now, when do I ever ask you about watching games?

You know I've got plenty of stuff to do myself, whether it's in the house, whether it's away from the house, whether it's reading, studying, or working. I can always find something to do other than watch a game. But at the same time, I don't mind sitting and watching games with Ezra. We get to talk about other things, and sometimes I'll actually really be watching the game, and I'll ask him questions, and he doesn't even get upset, you know, because I'm taking his attention away from the game. And I appreciate that." Then Samuel spoke up. "Man, yeah, that's cool. That's cool. If Essie wants to sit and watch the game with you and spend time with you like that, oh man, that's really nice." Essie smiled and said, "Now, I don't say I do it all the time, just here and there. But if I've got something to do and that's what he wants to do so badly, it's all good. I know where he is. He's right here in my house, in our house." "Yeah," Ezra replied, "you're right about that." "Well, you know what?" Essie said as she rose to go back upstairs. "I'm going to go upstairs and help Mama get everything ready and pulled out. I'll let you guys know when everything is ready. Have y'all been checking on the boys since Ya'll been down here playing, or have y'all just let them stay on those games all day long?" "No, the boys are good. They came out here and watched the games." "Hey guys," Samuel said, getting everyone's attention. "It's been great watching with you all again. I'm so glad Miss Myra invited me to be a part of your holiday weekend, your family weekend. I missed you guys. You know, it was cool. It was like having brothers around. "You know, David, just like you, I didn't grow up in a big family. It was just my mom and me, too, so I get it. You know, wanting to have family around, especially brothers and sisters, too. This weekend's been great." "Yeah, it's been great having both you and Daniel here," Mike said. "You know, it's great that now Zek is here, and even Josiah. We're all here together. Essie is always here, she's solid, and you, too, Uncle Ray. Uncle Ray, it's great that you're here with us as well. You know, since I know you and my Pops didn't always get along." Raymond sat up, staring out the window. "Well, that's water under the bridge now. Ain't nothing much I can do about that now." Then Mike spoke up. "You know what, Uncle Ray? I don't know what went on between you and my dad, but I tell you what, even though my dad is gone, whatever unforgiveness or whatever you're holding against him, I think you still need to release it. Not releasing it will still make you question things, and not to mention even make comments that maybe you shouldn't be saying, because you're still holding something against him. Obviously, it doesn't matter to him because he's no longer with us. Pops is better than all of us. He's really good. But you, you're still going to deal with the consequences of holding unforgiveness and holding things against people. Even whatever you're holding against the rest of us, because sometimes you act like you don't want to be around us, like we did something to you. We were kids, and you're our family. So I'm just saying. That's all I wanted to say." David noticed how the environment was changing from relaxed game watching to the seriousness of the family and the festering wounds that still existed. "I'm glad, no, not just glad, but extremely grateful that Miss Myra invited me to be here with you all this weekend. You just don't know," he said, shaking his head. "You fellas just don't know how nervous I was, and even how afraid I was that I would discover that I was never really wanted, not even by you all. I was more than a little bit afraid. "This was the dream I had as a child. The only dream I ever had was being a part of a family. And not just any family, this family, with all of my brothers and sisters, with my father here, and even Miss Myra, and despite how it happened, I believe in my heart, God honored my desires. I was petrified of the rejection. Rejection that I felt all of my young life. Rejection that I tried to make up for it in other ways. Making sure I'm the man I'm supposed to be, treating people right, and making sure that as long as I was living my life right, living a God-led life, then why would I be rejected? Still, to come face to face with it, man, I tell you. I wouldn't want to have to redo yesterday again. Yet I'm glad it's over, at least that part, and I'm sitting here with you all." The guys nodded in agreement with David's words. "The fact that I was illegitimate, and illegitimate in a bad way, you know what my mom did and everything like that. And even now, my mom still refuses to even talk about it or repent about it. I've talked to my pastor about what happened, my upbringing, and how it made me feel, and my mom's part in it all. I even asked her if she would like to go talk to someone at the church, and she said no, she's good. And she is so far from good. I'm just praying that she will turn to the Lord before it's too late."

"Yeah, man, none of us know the day, nor the hour, and yet people continuously play around with their lives as if it's a big joke and they're going to live forever. So many believe or say things like they're just going to live their life how they want, and when they die, that's just it, they're dead. I think in my head, you just don't understand. Yes, your physical body is gone, but your spirit must go somewhere, just two choices, Mike concluded."

The rest of the guys nodded their heads, acknowledging both David and Mike's words. "Yeah, man, you're right, they will go somewhere, and right now, while they are still living, they have a decision to make, one that will change life for the good, if only they understood. "Mike, you know what? You are such a good guy, and you're a good, solid man to have in our lives. A guy who loves the Lord, a guy who lives his life serving others. You know, the stuff you do, I know you and Faith are doing something with the church, right?" "Yeah, man. Faith and I both teach Bible study to new believers. You know, on campuses and away from… well, we teach new believers that come into the church. We teach new believers that we just met, and they get to know us, and they want to know more about the Lord and studying the Bible, and that's what we do.

But also, I'm a part of an inner healing ministry. I truly do understand because of what I went through. "Fellas, I was going to take my life. I didn't want to be here anymore. I was so ashamed. The enemy had me thinking that my shame and my guilt, that everything was my fault. That nobody wanted to be around me, that my family didn't want me, that no one would love me, that I was damaged goods. You know, and then on top of that, the way I was living my life, I was trying to hurt and harm myself. I was trying to live up to that thought, that belief in my head. I stayed in that place of shame for so long.

"So, I understand the rejection. I get how it feels to believe that you are rejected. And those are just tricks of the enemy.

That's how he works in our minds. Mike turned his conversation towards his brother, "Josiah, that's what's happening with you." "Man, leave me out of this conversation. I told all of you yesterday that I'm not trying to hear all this." "Josiah, there comes a time in your life where you've got to deal with the things that you have done, the things that you have said, and how you treat other people. What about your daughter, Lai-Joy? Why aren't you trying to go see her?" "I can't just go see her. She doesn't even live in the same town as I do, man. I got a job. I got to work. And what do I look like, just taking off and not getting paid for it? And on top of that, her mom ain't trying to let me come see her or be in her life. We're done. All she wants is money, and I ain't trying to call her.

Why bother?" "Joey, you're holding on to a ton of unforgiveness and a lot of accusations in your heart. Man, you've got to let it go. It's bondage, and that bondage is holding you to her, whether you like it or not. On top of that, man, there's so much stuff we can get into when I'm talking about inner healing, the soul ties. The soul ties you established with her when you guys came together, when you fornicated. Ya'll weren't married. There was no marriage covenant, but a bond was definitely established. You, Bro, are dealing with soul ties. "You're angry, you're bitter, and you hate everybody, including the world.

Man, you don't like your family, nor yourself, and we all know you don't even want to be here. You see all this bad, this negative happening, and you don't want to change. "Joey, how do you see your life? Do you want every day to be like the roller coaster that it has been for you?" "I told you, Mike, I'm not trying to deal with this stuff. I don't want to hear it. I don't want to talk about it. There ain't nothing about me that needs to change. I do what I have to do for myself, and I look out for mine. I take care of her, all she needs." Mike replied, "Oh, my brother, that's where you're wrong. Whether it's a little boy or a little girl, they need both their parents, their mother and their father. They need a true father figure in their life, and even more, one who loves God and who serves God.

Ez spoke up, "Joey, I understand that your life hasn't been easy. I get it! We all got stuff. But when you submit and surrender to the Lord Jesus Christ, those are decisions that you have to make. No one can do it for you, and I pray you make the right decision. "I know you look at me and think that Essie and I got it going on, that we don't have any issues or never had any issues, and that is crazy, thinking of anyone like that. You don't know what we've been through, especially all the issues and the anxiety that she has been dealing with over losing our business. "She had to go talk to someone. It was the best thing that we both did, but she did it first on her own. She allowed herself to get stuck in comparison syndrome, always comparing herself to her sister, and I'm not talking about Bella. She was always feeling less than compared to Nelly, thinking that she did not live up to her sister's standards in every aspect of life. "How crazy is that? She couldn't see her own worth in who God created her to be. She believed the lies, and it began to affect every part of our lives and our marriage. Since our finances were affected, especially losing the business, she took that as her personal defeat or failure. "Essie even believed that we shouldn't be married anymore, because I could do better. That I could find someone who is better financially, that way I'd be happy, as if that is what mattered to me more than loving her and her being my wife. "I had to realize that I fueled her belief because of how I always spoke about money and finances, not realizing I was making her absorb hard and bad decisions that not only she made, but I made too. Yet, she only saw it as her mistake. Maybe I did silently blame her, and if I was doing it, she felt it all. "And I'm so sorry for ever, ever making her feel that way. I didn't even realize I was holding things against her in my heart, and I had to repent to God for that. Even though I didn't say anything to her, I did have some resentment in my heart about the money. Your sister believed that stuff, just like you, Josiah.

You believe all the lies that you hear in your head, and you don't try to change. You don't cast it down. And we all really get it. At this point, what I'm saying is foreign to you, and you don't understand what I'm talking about. But you would if you stopped living your life out in the world and surrendered and received the salvation the Lord has for you." Josiah said nothing but continued to listen to his brother-in-law. "I asked her, and we went to counseling together. She started seeking God about these things, these thoughts. We got into our Bible together, studying and praying together, and now, man, she studies all the time, with or without me. My seeking and gaining more understanding, for her and our family, and she had to do the same thing, from the right source and not the world's point of view." "I hear you."

Josiah stood up and held his hands behind his head. He turned to face Ezra and said, "I get it, too. It feels like I'm angry all the time. I had been doing nothing but chasing after being like Zek, my big brother, for so long. Yep, I've been angry at the world, and yeah, I blame my Pops. "Now what? What am I to do? He's gone. I can't get the time back. I can't even talk to him. Now what do I do? What do I do, Mike? How can my life change when I can't get out of this hellhole I dug myself into? I got nothing but guilt and pain. He's gone. Pops left me. What am I going to do now?"

Josiah lowered his body to the floor, sobbing, tears hitting the wood tile, as the brothers got down on the floor with him, Mike putting his arm around his baby brother. "Hey, bro, listen. It's okay. You've got to get it out. You've held on to this anger, this bitterness, for far too long, bro. It's time to let it all go. It's time to give it to Jesus. I'm telling you, it's the best change. It's the best start that you can have."

Josiah wiped his tears. "I can't do anything about it now. I used to say stuff like I hated my dad. I couldn't stand him. I wished he would just leave Mom. I knew she wasn't happy. She tried to be when he was around, but she had more peace when he was at work, or just out of the house." Josiah lifted his head to David. "Man, I'm sorry, David. I acted as a fool towards you last night and didn't know half of what you had been through, or the life you lived, and here you are, my family. I'm sorry."

"It's okay, Josiah," replied David. "I get it. Like we've said already, we all had a lot of heavy baggage piling up and up, and it wasn't anything good. It wasn't anything that we wanted, but it looks like all of it needed to be unpacked. "And once we opened up that luggage, we saw the things that didn't need to be in it, and we saw the things that needed to be discussed, discarded, uncovered, and changed for good.

"I had some of the same contents in my bags, with the same attitude. The hurt, the pain, all of it. And yet what did we do? We did nothing, nothing but drag the luggage from relationship to relationship, hurting others and never healing along the way.

"When that battered and bruised luggage bust open, all the filth, the bad, the unhealed wounds, the anger, it all bleeds out on someone that didn't deserve it, all because we stay in pride and refuse to surrender and get the help that we need to heal, spiritually and emotionally." David looked over at Ez and smiled. "Yeah, I had to ask for help too."

"We can apply that luggage to our situations that we find ourselves in. That's how I looked at it. I had someone explain it to me like that, and when Dee explained it to me like luggage, it made so much sense."

Mike smiled. "Man, I love that example. You're right. It does make a lot of sense, and it helps. "Let me make it simple. There is something called fruit. Not the kind we eat, but it depicts a person's actions. All the fussing and cussing, like what we hear you do, Uncle Raymond, you and Aunt Ester, even what you say to each other. "I guess this is just as easy for not only Josiah, but any of us, to think that you don't have a relationship with the Lord. Unfortunately, a lot of people think that just because they go to church, they must have a relationship with God. They think they're saved and living right. "They must be better than everyone else, right? It's okay. I get it. Let me continue.

"There are a whole lot of people sitting up in church. You hear statements about living one way on Sunday and a whole other life Monday through Friday. Partying on Saturday, back at church on Sunday. Am I right? That's what you think, Uncle Raymond? Josiah? You get what I'm saying. "They talk differently. They act differently. They treat people differently. They do things that are not biblical, that are not right. Oh, but come Sunday, 'Hallelujah, everybody. Good to see you. Praise the Lord!' You all know that good Christian talk, on Monday through Friday, or when no one is looking. However, what kind of fruit do we see on your tree? I hope you get what I'm saying. "Yeah, we know, Mike," David responded. Mike continued, "We know how to talk that talk, don't we? But God sees our hearts and sees everything. It's not serving anyone to be pretending, hurting, and broken, and more than anything, treating people horribly. "God first life, yet in reality, you're living, thinking, speaking, and believing the same way the world does, there is no difference, you're no different from the world and their way of doing life." "Amen," David said. "And you know what's happening in the world? That is nothing to be a part of. You are so right about that.

"Well, I need to eat, and I've heard enough," said Raymond. "Uncle Ray, you don't act as if you need, or are ready for, some real change in your life. It's not too late to change. As long as a person is still breathing on this earth, it's still possible to change while we still have time. "Time to repent. Time to make it right with folks. Time to forgive and ask for forgiveness. We still have a chance to call on Jesus and accept Him as our personal Savior, if you haven't done so." The room was quiet, and all eyes were on Raymond, including Josiah and Zek, who had been standing in the hallway watching and listening to everything that took place, including Josiah's confession about how he idolized his big brother. "Uncle Raymond, I'm talking to you.

This is important. This is life and death." "Enough, Michael, enough!" Raymond snapped. "Why can't you just let it be? Who do you think you are anyway? Huh? What makes you think you're better than me, than any of us here? You ain't nothing." Raymond angrily walked past Zek, bumping into him, glaring, and shaking his head. "I don't need you to save me," Raymond hollered. "I know the Lord for myself." "Well, I guess I missed all the fireworks," chuckled Zek. Mike said, shaking his head.

"Yeah, whatever, whatever." Mike turned and walked out of the room upstairs behind Raymond.

The guys heard footsteps coming out of one of the bedrooms. "Hey, what's up, guys? Daniel, where have you been, man? You were here one minute, then you left and never came back." "I was so tired after lunch. I went to the room to lie down and fell asleep. I didn't even wake up until Bella came back from shopping. She thought I was downstairs with you guys. "I was, but then I fell asleep. I slept well. Heck, it's almost time for dinner."

"Repay no one evil for evil. Have regard for good things in the sight of all men. If it is possible, as much as depends on you, live peaceably with all men. Beloved, do not avenge yourselves, but rather give place to wrath; for it is written, vengeance is Mine, I will repay, says the Lord."

(Romans 12:17-19, NJKV)

Chapter 11.

FIRE PIT REVELATION

Dinner was definitely better than it was on Thanksgiving Day. At one point, Myra looked around at the table. There were no big announcements. No crashing or accusations about the past. There wasn't any "you did this to me, kind of stuff taking place. Nothing like that. Just laughter and togetherness. What she saw was family. Her children, their spouses, her beautiful grandchildren, even her sister and brother-in-law. She silently thanked God that she was able to witness this beautiful time of togetherness. Family. *'This is the way it should always be," she thought to herself. "Still, I know there are some unresolved issues, but my prayer is that by the time this weekend is over, everything will be on the table. All the hurts, all the pain, just like we did last night. I'm praying that we will continue."*

Right now, it feels good just to see everyone laughing, smiling, joking, eating, and having a good time together. After all the eating was done, everyone took turns helping out, even the guys, cleaning up the kitchen and putting everything away. Bella said, "I know you guys are going to go back downstairs and finish watching TV, but can you at least make sure you keep an eye on the boys down there? And you, Jennesis and Eliana, you guys can go to your room and watch TV if you like." "Oh, sure, I think that's fine," Nelly said. "Is it okay if she gets on her laptop?" "Yeah, that sounds fine. That's why she got it, Nelly replied. "All right, I'm just asking," Bella said. "I just want to make sure everything is okay, because you are her mother." "Not a problem at all, Nelly winked at her daughter. "Okay. Well, all right, ladies, why don't we go outside and sit around the fire like we said we were going to do, asked Myra to the women. "Faith responded first, all right, sounds like a plan!" Nelly spoke up. "What's this about a fire?" "Well, we said we were going to sit around the fire and just have a girls' campfire chat," Faith said. "There are still a lot of things we need to talk about and get off our chest."

"Oh boy, here we go again," Nelly replied. "I really thought all this was over, throwing her arms up in the air, and landing loudly on her legs." "No, my dear," said Myra. "There are still some things we need to clear up, even some things with you and me." "All right, fine." Everyone walked off to their respective rooms to get their jackets and sweaters. "Well, first of all, who's going to get the fire started?" Essie asked. "You know what? I'll go ahead and try to get it started," she said. "And if I can't, we'll get one of the guys to come out here and help us."

The ladies began walking down to the fire pit and began pulling up the chairs, just as Michael and Daniel appeared. "Mama, I'll go get the fire started for you ladies if you'd like." Of course, Michael. I appreciate your help." "I don't mind helping with it either," David chimed in. "Myra laughed, absolutely the more the merrier." Sure enough, the guys were able to get the fire pit started. After all, it was a real fire pit, and ready to go.

As the ladies got their chairs and sat down, Myra looked up at the stars and said, "This is a beautiful, clear night. A little bit nippy out here, but it sure is beautiful." "Yes, it is," Ester said. "And I enjoyed my day here with you. After last night, I wasn't too sure how today would turn out, but we had a pretty good time. I'm glad Raymond and I came back." "Mom, I'm glad you came back, too," Faith said. "There are still a lot of things we need to discuss. I just want you to know I'm not holding anything against you and Dad. I understand how it may have looked. "You know I love Aunt Myra, and yes, Aunt Myra really is my birth mother, but you raised me, so you are my mom, and you will always be my mom. I love Aunt Myra, and I know she loves me, but I'm not trying to replace you with her. I just want you to understand that." "I do understand, Faith," Ester replied. "And I'm glad you said something. It makes me feel better. "I can honestly say there were times when I was negative, maybe even mean-spirited. I can admit it. I was jealous. I was jealous of the kind of woman you are, Myra. You're not like me at all, and especially after all you went through. You still have so much love in your heart, something I know.... I don't always show, or to be honest, even have for most. "Ester continued, I do love God, but I know something is missing with my walk. If I have a walk, I know I'm lacking, and it's something that needs to change.

Myra, and even you, Faith, the way you seek Him is how I need to seek Him." Faith nodded. "It's not just about having the 'Christian identity or having to walk around telling people you're a Christian and go to church. A lot of people do that, and that's where their faith stops. That's where their belief ends; it's more like checking boxes than being surrendered and desiring a true relationship with God.

"It's about seeking God and going deeper in His Word. Getting to that place where it becomes who you are, who we are. It's becoming more like Jesus, each and every day." "Yes," Ester said. “Ester,” said Myra, “We want to be pleasing to God. We want to do His will for our lives and for others. We want to live for Him, and He through us, as we crucify our flesh daily, and take up our cross.” “I appreciate the woman of God you’ve grown into, Faith. You went through a lot. I went through things that you don’t even know about. I’ve never shared some of them. Ester shared,” The girls looked at each other but stayed silent.

“Yes,” Faith continued. “You all don’t know this, but I got married to run away from life, and the sexual trauma that I went through. I met this smooth-talking guy who told me everything I wanted to hear. I thought he loved me. He knew what I went through, even the abortion, so I thought he was behind me, I thought I made a great decision. This man was a narcissist through and through. He daily gaslit me; he despised me. He made me despise and hate myself. He put me down. He was verbally and mentally abusive and even tried to physically hurt me. He had other women friends, even those in the church, and at his job, and he put those friendships over our marriage. I was left out all the time, just beating myself up, and so embarrassed over yet another mistake that I made. I ran back to Mom and Daddy’s house, embarrassed. He had me thinking I was nothing. He had me afraid to go to school, afraid to pursue my dreams.

"That was one of the biggest mistakes I ever made. And when I left that marriage as a Christian, I felt bad.

People made me feel like, 'What kind of Christian leaves a marriage?' Maybe I judged myself too harshly. "He was a womanizer, an adulterer. For all I know, he has children all over the country. Yet I tried to stick it out because I thought I was supposed to." Myra spoke up. "I believe the Lord understood why you had to leave. He was dangerous. He didn't love you. He loved himself." "Yes, honey, he loved himself," Ester agreed, as she reached over and grabbed Faith's hand.

"And I know my daughters, especially you, Nelly, didn't understand why I stayed with Edward. He wasn't abusive, and our situations were different. One thing is for sure: he did love me, yet he didn't respect our marriage vows like she should have. He didn't see family as his responsibility. He saw taking care of his own fleshly needs as a priority for his life. You know, I loved your father, but he didn't cherish me, and by his actions, he didn't even cherish the family God gave him. He cared about himself, and what he liked, the gambling, drinking, partying, sports, the grumbling and complaining about politics as if complaining and not praying would change anything. Now, this was when he was younger, yes, he changed for the better once he got older, but the damage to our family was already done, and there were no attempts to repair the broken, our broken family, not the right way.

I remember an incident where he didn't even bother to protect and defend me when another man, with whom he was playing cards, disrespected me. You think he said anything, but no, he sat there with a beer in his hand, looking down, and said not one word to stand up for me, not one word. I hadn't done anything wrong. I thought it was an adult conversation, and I spoke my opinion about something, and that man did everything but tell me to shut my mouth; no one was talking to me, and Edward just sat there. I was so embarrassed, afraid, and hurt, I went and sat down looking and feeling like a complete fool, in my eyes. That's how I saw myself in the eyes of everyone there. Now, he's got nothing to work on and nothing to run away from. Yes, financially, he took care of the home, but during that time of our lives, that is where it stopped, because it was all about his wants and his desires. I was too young and innocent, and I mean worldly innocent, to even understand all of this. I just wanted him to be happy, and I thought I did all I was supposed to do. Now I come to understand that I made him an idol in my life.

I know it may sound crazy, but I looked to him more than I looked to God. Yes, he stepped out, and yes, we had a child. He got trapped by a Jezebel he should have stayed away from. When you play with fire, you get burned. He got burned badly. Unfortunately, he didn't just get burned; I got burned too. I felt like a joke, a big fat joke. I thought everyone knew my situation, even if they didn't. And Lucy didn't care who knew. She thought she was taking my husband, so she told everybody."

"Mama, why are you bringing this up?" Nelly asked. "I need to bring it up, Nelly," Myra replied. "Because it was you who saw it first and brought your brother into that mess of a situation." "Mama, you act like we did something wrong," Nelly said. "We didn't. It was Daddy. He shouldn't have been over there. Why does it sound like you think I did something wrong?" Myra stood up. "Now calm down. What I'm saying is, please help me understand why you act the way you do toward me. You act as if you hate me. You always have. I've cried out to God, asking why my own daughter hates me so much. How can you hate me when I love you with all my heart? I only ever want good for you, yet you look at me with contempt, like I'm the bad parent, like I stepped out, like I mistreated your father. And yet you know very little of the truth. At that time, it was a truth I didn't even know fully for myself. "Still, you blamed me. That

I'm the one who's what, spending up all the money your daddy brought home, hanging out at bars and not living right, seeing other people.

Those were not my actions, have never been, and even now, you don't treat me well. You don't think of me well, and it breaks my heart, the thought that my own daughter hates me." No words were spoken after Myra's emotional and painful outburst to Nelly. Her sisters, aunt, and cousin all sat quietly, Bella shaking her head, and not a word spoken. Nelly, put her head down. Nelly's spirit was heavily convicted, because she knew her mother was telling her right, telling the truth. She walked around accusing her mother of everything except for being a child of God, and that is exactly what her mother is. "Mama, listen, I can explain."

"Yes, you absolutely do need to explain. But Nelly, before you explain anything, let me tell you this. I love you. I love all you children. I love all of you, and I loved my husband with all my heart. And I was a good wife, and I was a good mother to you all. I did all I could do. I don't know why he did what he did, and I couldn't continue to blame myself, because that's what I did. I blamed myself for him being tempted by Lucy, for him stepping out into sin, choosing to live a lifestyle after worldly values that were not of God. I didn't deserve what he did. Desiring to go out every single weekend drinking and doing lord knows what, because it wasn't just Lucy, there were others too." Myra shook her head, thinking about all those years of her life. "When you put yourself in those atmospheres, that's what you get. You get the Jezebels of the world, waiting in the shadows, sent out by the enemy for destruction. I believe that with all my heart.

Demons are sent to take out marriages and to destroy families. I believe he had a target on his back, and I believe that target hit him, and he fell right into it. He had that woman believing that they were going to be a family. He allowed it. When he came back to the Lord, he shared all of this with me. You know, he cared more about materialistic things, and that's what the enemy offered him. Listen, that target, that open door he walked in, unleashed that curse on the lives of you, his children, and grandchildren. There is a consequence for everything we do. He fell into that trap, and for what, a quick thrill…

That's all he was focused on. He wasn't focused on us, on me as his wife. He wasn't focused on the kids. He wasn't focused on the fact that you need to be serving God, to live a Godly life, and leading our family for generations to do the same. She had him twisted up, and he allowed it. He allowed it because he should never have been in that situation in the first place. And I feel horrible, always afraid, walking on eggshells, thinking, '*Any day now he's going to come home and tell me he's leaving. And then what am I going to do? I hadn't worked in years. I had all the babies, so I'm trying to raise you right, take care of you. What am I going to do if he walks out?* This is why I say, and I know it to be true, I made that man an IDOL in my heart. Do you all understand why I say this?" "Yes, ma'am, we do, we do, Mama said. "And I believed he would, every day. I just tried to be kind and nice-hearted, and I just prayed to the Lord. I prayed and prayed. And I didn't even say anything to him, but I did give my ultimatum. It was either her or it was us. "And I didn't want to stay. Oh, it hurt my heart. That woman thought she had him, that my husband would soon be her husband. Oh yeah, she told me. It hurt me to the core of my being. There were so many times I dreamed of where I could go. How far could I go on my own with my children, and was I willing in my heart to leave? I needed badly to know I could leave. You will never understand just how hurt I was. How rejected and unloved, and used up, I felt. So, after finding out, I went to him, and he didn't even try to deny it. I really think he was tired of the lies, of trying to live a double life, and keep it all hidden away. He confirmed it. He broke down. He told me what a horrible mistake it was. However,

David was now here, and I told him, '*This has nothing to do with David.'* David didn't cause the issue. You, dear, you and that Jezebel, and the adulterous sin you're involved in, that's what caused this issue. It was a sin and heart and soul issue, spirit of lust." Myra paused, "Well, I didn't mean to go on and on, but you need to hear this, you need to know it all, you understand, Nelly?"

Shaking her head, then closing her eyes and bringing her hands to both sides of her head, resting her elbows on her legs. "I went on to tell him that he can't hold your son to any type of standard, or blame your son, or think that having another son has to stop you from being the father you are to all your children. You have to be a father to them all. David deserves to have a father just like Hezekiah, just like Josiah, and just like Michael. They all need to have a father in their life, just like you, Nelsa, just like you, Essobella, all of you. You all need to have a father in your life, and just like you, Annabella. "And I told him that. So, no, if he wanted to remain in the marriage, I would do my best to remain in the marriage. And I'm going to be honest; it took me a while. It took me a little time to forgive him. I forgave him. I have forgiven him. "But my God, it hurt me so much. It made me think from that point on in my life that I was not good enough for anybody. I didn't know who I was. I didn't think I could accomplish anything, more or less raise you all the way you're supposed to be raised.

I doubted and second-guessed everything I did. I didn't think that I had a purpose for my life, except to take care of my family. The rest was lost on me. And in time, I started to forget just how much it hurt me, what it felt like to hurt inside. The thoughts, in time, I captured the thoughts and took them to the Lord. But at first and for a long time, I didn't know how to do that. I had to go to the Lord, I had to surrender, and I looked at my life, that if this was all that was left, if I only had Jesus, then I had all I needed. I came to a point in my life where I took a stand. I was not going to tolerate it anymore. I don't deserve to be mistreated by anybody, my husband, and especially my children.

Mistreated by my children because they think that I was not good enough for their father, who trampled on our vows, our covenant. I had to believe the Word of God for myself, regardless of what others thought of me, or what they said, or even believed about me and my decisions. I had to press into the Lord every single day. And every time those nasty thoughts tried to come in my mind, the thoughts of everything, I learned how to just give them to God.

I prayed, 'Oh, Holy Spirit, touch my head. Lord, let me forget. God, You're a good God. You love me. God, I know You see what happens. Lord, oh God, I know You see what happened. God, but Father, help me. Help me to love him again the way he's supposed to be loved. Help me, God, to be a good wife. Help me, Lord. I surrender to you, and I forgive Lord, please forgive me, if there's anything I lacked, anything I didn't do, show me, God, how to be a better daughter to you, Lord. Show me, here I am for you, Lord, and only for you, Lord.

"And Nelly, that's what my life looked like. I didn't do anything to harm your dad. I didn't deserve the treatment from you and Zek. I didn't deserve the attitude you had with me. I didn't deserve the negative thoughts you had or even still have of me. I didn't deserve it all. Yet I took it because I love you, and I know neither of you truly understood, and yet, I also didn't know what you had been through, and for that, I'm sorry. I apologize to you, and I ask for your forgiveness. I wish more than anything that you would have trusted me enough to come to me, to cry on my shoulder, so that I could cover you with love and warmth and protection. I could have protected your sweet and tender heart and helped you understand what you saw with the truth. I hate that you and Zek held down this secret for so long, and what that did to both of you, my dear sweet girl." Nelly finally said, “Mama, I am so sorry. Mom, you have to understand, it rocked my whole world when I saw Daddy knocking on Miss Lucy’s door. I just stood there frozen. Because Miss Lucy had stopped coming around, she wasn’t really your friend anyway. I saw how she used to look at you, and I also saw how she was looking at Daddy. She wasn’t really your friend, Mom. You know, I was always smart, so I saw right through her. Then Zek and I, standing there, saw David come. Oh my God, we were so hurt. Mama, Zek cried, we both did. He cried so hard because he saw Daddy holding David. Zek kept saying, ‘He got another son, so he doesn’t want me. He got another son.’ And it hurt Zek, and it hurt me, and we didn’t know what to do. We didn’t know what to do, Mama.” Tears streamed down Nelly’s face, as well as the faces of her sisters and her mother. “Mama, we were so afraid to tell you, because we thought that if we told you, you would make our Daddy leave. And we didn’t want Daddy to leave. We didn’t know what to do. “So, we swore to each other. We swore to each other that we wouldn’t tell anybody. We wouldn’t tell! I said I wouldn’t tell Bella. I said, “We’re not going to tell Essie. I was so young. I was a baby. We said, ‘We’re not going to tell Michael. Michael’s too young. He’s not going to understand anyway.’ And all these years, Zek and I kept it to ourselves, and I know it hurt us. I know it did.

And I see now. I just wanted to be so good. I wanted to be better, the best. I wanted to be so good, Mama. I wanted to be so smart. It's almost like I wanted to show you, Mama, that I was better than you. That I was the smartest in the whole family. Yeah, I wanted to be the smart one, Mama. I wanted to be the one who had all the money that had it going on." She leaned back in her chair, and suddenly breaking down.

"Oh God, it was me. It was all me. It was my fault that Samuel left. I didn't want anyone to know at all, and what I had really done that caused it all." All eyes were on Nelly, probing as they looked at each other, anticipating what Nelly was going to say next. "Samuel loves children. That's why he became a teacher. He loves children. He always wished that he had brothers and sisters like we did, that we would have a big family like this. But that is not what I ever wanted. And when we found out that I was pregnant again, even after Jennesis," Nelly, paused as she thought about mentally where she was when it all happened… "oh man…Jennesis was finally in school. She didn't need daycare. I was able to work late. I was able to grind. I was able to do all I needed to do to keep moving up the ladder. I hustled every single day, even after being married to Samuel. I wasn't about to give it all up. College and then law school—there was no stopping me. There was no stopping me! I used the trials. I used all the pain inside of me from growing up and knowing what I knew to push me harder and harder and harder. I didn't care about anybody's feelings, even Sam's. I didn't care about the fact that he wanted to have another child. He was so happy, and I was so angry. Another child did not fit into my plans, and I didn't give Sammy a choice about it at all.

"I went to that abortion clinic and did what I had to do, and I lied! I lied to them, but of course, that was what they were there for. They couldn't care less about what I told them, I know that now. I told them he was gone, or he was deployed, or we were broken up, whatever I came up with that exited out of my mouth. As I said, they didn't care anyway. I told them, but what I didn't do was tell Sammy, not until it was all over and too late." Samuel was beyond upset.

He was so hurt. He was in so much pain. I had never seen him so angry. He was crying. He asked me, "How could you kill our baby?" You know what I said? I said, "It wasn't a baby. It was just some cells." I couldn't even look at him. I was so ashamed. I kept my head down, and to be honest, I didn't want to hear anything he had to say. It was done. It was over, and it wasn't going to happen again. Again, and this time I shouted at him, "It was not a baby. What are you talking about? I had to do what I had to do for my career. I don't have time to raise another baby. I have meetings to attend to, and cases and people to represent. I'm trying to make partner." Yeah, it was bad. It was pretty bad.

My God, Sammy was so upset. He packed his bags that night, saying he had to get away from me, get away as if I was this evil person." Nelly stopped and gurgled a little. "Well, I guess he was right, I was and am evil to do what I did."

"Daughter, Myra interjected, you are far from evil." Nelly nodded in agreement as she accepted what her mother said, and a tear ran down her face. "He said he needed to get far away from me, seek God, and pray. Sammy couldn't even look at me. About a week went by, and when he finally came back, he asked me for a divorce. Well, no wait, let me back up. He asked me for a divorce because I refused to go to any type of counseling. I wasn't talking to anybody. I didn't need to talk to anybody. He did. He does, so he went on his own. And even with that, I still refused to go. I continued with my career. I made sure that I stayed at work late at night, so I never had to come home. He took care of Jennesis. He is a good dad, can't deny that. And I think that's why, if I'm honest with you, my anger with Sammy is because he divorced me.

It's almost like rejection all over again. I felt that he rejected me, and I wasn't even looking at my own actions that caused everything. The way I was. How I acted. How I treated him. Not allowing him to be the man of the house. Always letting him know that I made more money than him, so I made the rules, and I made the decisions. He was so gracious all the time and didn't argue with me. I decided how Jennesis was going to be raised. I chose the school she was going to go to. I didn't allow him to have any choice because I would let him know that I ran this house. And he tried his best. He tried his best, and I was horrible. I was so horrible to him. God, help me, please. I don't want to be this person anymore. God, help me. Please help me, God. Help me, Jesus. I am so sorry."

Nelly cried out, crunched over in her chair, weeping uncontrollably, as her sisters and mothers ran to comfort and love her. "Help me, Mama, I'm so sorry. Just saying everything out loud, when it comes out loud, I sound like a monster. I drank Kool-Aid! I believed the lies! I never looked at it like killing a baby, but it was, and I did it. That's what I did." Nelly sat up in her chair, blowing her nose and wiping her eyes, as her sister still knelt beside her. "When he asked for a divorce, oh God, I was so angry. I was furious! How could he throw me away? Here again, once again, I was being thrown away. I wasn't good enough. I wasn't good enough, just like I thought you weren't good enough for Daddy.

Crazy, cause look what I did, I threw our child away, and still I was only thinking about myself, and blaming Sammy for ending our marriage, when in reality, I'm the one who ended it that day, and that bad decision changed everything." Nelly breathed out, blew her nose, wiping the tears. Essie leaned over her sister, hugging her so tightly. Nelly lifted her head, "Mama, I made you feel like you weren't good enough, and I'm so sorry. I'm so sorry, Mama. Please forgive me. Forgive me for all these years. Please forgive me." Nelly cried out. Forgive me, God, for all the things I did. Forgive me, God. Forgive me for having an abortion. Forgive me for throwing my family away. Forgive me for dishonoring my husband. Forgive me for serving my job first. Forgive me for serving money first. Forgive me for putting everything before You. I didn't know. I didn't understand. God, forgive me. Please forgive me, Jesus. I am so sorry.

Cousin Faith ran over and joined her sisters and aunt surrounding and loving on Nelly. "Oh, cousin, it's okay. Please know that God hears you. You did right, you did the right thing, cousin. You've asked, and He has heard you. He sees your heart, and He forgives you. You just have to trust and be honest with the Lord. "When you ask for forgiveness, there are bonds that are going to need to be broken, cousin. I know there's so much you don't understand, but there's so much I will explain to you. "There are so many things that happen in our lives growing up, and there are so many things that I pray I can help you understand; everyone in our family understands." I thought I knew better, but I was desperate, and I believed the lies too. It is easy to close out our hearts and allow the beliefs of the world to make us think that we're not doing anything wrong. But my sister we did, and we're still responsible. Even in our ignorance, we must repent and break the covenant bonds we established.

In the distance, Arrya was watching the women from the front porch, hesitating about approaching, she watched how they were loving on each other, yet she didn't know what was being shared. She hesitated to go any further, uncertain about joining the women who loved and cared for her deeply. Standing at the edge of the night, she gazed out into the starry sky, her thoughts swirling in her head, as she watched their love and warmth radiate from the fire pit below.

Memories of her life and marriage weighed heavily on her heart. She recalled the moments of betrayal, the absence of tenderness and concern from her husband, the wounds that her friends and family had witnessed, yet helped her endure and keep moving forward. These women had been her anchors. She watched them at the fire pit, and Arrya felt torn between the ache of fearing her marriage's end and the horrible guilt that entertaining such thoughts seemed wrong, especially as she wanted to trust God with her marriage. The weekend, with its honesty and revelations, felt like a turning point for the family, yet she needs it to be a turning point for her and Zek, for their marriage.

If God didn't intervene, how much more can she and should she bear? Arrya wondered how much more she could bear. She closed her eyes for a moment, overwhelmed, searching for strength, preparing herself to join the group by the fire. As she lingered a little while longer, the gentle voices reminded her that she isn't alone, she is never alone, even in her grief and struggles. This thought gave her the courage she desperately wanted. She slowly started to walk towards the group around the fire, then stopped again to watch. She could make out that Nelly was speaking, and it sounded like she was also crying. She could then make out Faith, and she could tell by Faith's stance that she was speaking about the Lord. Faith was so passionate about the Word of God, knowing this made her hesitate, yet she yearned to be there with them, but she wasn't ready to share what was truly on her heart; only the Lord knew. He knows all things.

Arrya finally joined the women. "Hey, what's going on? Is everything ok, as she glanced around at all the tear-stained faces, and arms around each other. Myra spoke up first, "Arrya, please come join us, my dear. We wondered when you would be joining us. Please come stand beside Nelly and me." Arrya nodded and shot worried eyes over to Nelly. "Oh, Nelly, please, let us pray for you and with you," Arrya heard Faith say. The women all stood, came together, surrounding Nelly, ready to pray with her and over her. "Nelly, cousin, you have to repent not only your sins, but also for the agreement and covenant you came into when you had the abortion. I had to do the same thing once I found out and gained understanding. I repented, but I didn't know or understand about breaking agreements. The more I studied, received great leadership and counseling in our faith, I was taught what it meant by my actions, and I want you to now understand as well."

Nelly nodded as tears began to trickle down her face, and she closed her eyes and lowered her head. "Boy, how could I have been so stupid to believe that I had a right to do what I did?" Nelly, this world, this fallen world, will mislead even those who think they've got it going on. Satan is very subtle, and he is the father of lies," Faith declared and shot glances at her family gathered around. "Cousin, there are many more, said Faith. "I understand, and I'm very sorry for everything, my sins against God, and for what I did to Samuel and our family. I want to repent for having the abortion, and please, what else do I need to do? I am truly sorry. Nelly never looked up or even acknowledged, but began to speak. "I do repent. I am so sorry. "Nelly, you will need to renounce the covenant and break the agreement that you made with a demon." "What? I don't understand. I don't know who that is." I will show you in the bible and explain as well, but for now, this is what happens with abortion. Abortion is a blood sacrifice.

In the bible the Canaanites worshiped a false deity called Molech, and what they did was sacrifice their children to Molech. This is why I said you must come out of agreement with the demon Molech; it's still a blood sacrifice, this is the agreement I'm referring to, sweetie. So, repenting you will pray, and declare with your mouth, that you break the covenant, denounce the agreement with the demon Molech, in the Name of Jesus. You must repent and come out of agreement, break the covenant with the demon Molech." Faith explained. "Yes, I do. I do. Absolutely, I do." Ok, Nelly, are you ready?" Nelly nodded her head. Her sisters, her mother, her cousin, and her aunt all bowed their heads and began to worship the Lord and pray, and then Nelly began to pray, to repent and renounce as her cousin had explained, and ask God for forgiveness of her sins, breaking all covenants that had been made in her life.

Praise and thanksgiving rose in the air of the night sky to our Lord and Savior, Jesus Christ. “Amen was heard in unison. That’s all you have to do, my cousin. That’s what people don’t understand, even believers, they too must understand why this act is not of God, He is not pleased and we shouldn’t take part in it. But like so many women, and just like me, we didn’t know, we were ignorant of this and must make it right with the Lord. “Yes, sisters! We all love you,” Essie said and hugged Nelly, as everyone began to hug and love on each other. “Yes, we all love you, my dear said Myra.” “Nelly, you’re my oldest daughter that I actually raised. I love you with all my heart, all of my being. I regret so much of what has taken place in our lives, and in your life. I wish that we had been closer, that you could have come and talked to me.

We all make mistakes and I would not have been mad at you. I just want to love you and be there for you if given a chance. “Please know there’s no guilt. There’s no condemnation. The devil wants you to feel condemned, but there is no condemnation in Christ Jesus. Jesus loves you. He hears you. He hears your prayers. He sees your heart. He accepts you. He forgives you." "That's right," Faith interrupted. "He forgives her. And not only does He forgive her, but He doesn't remember. And you broke the covenant as well. Nelly, the Lord says in the Word of God that He throws it as far as the east is from the west, so He's not going to keep bringing it up. "What happens is, we keep bringing it up. We continue to listen to the lies of the enemy, that we're broken, unwanted, not good enough, and that we're not forgiven. We don't forgive ourselves.

You must forgive yourself. You have to tell yourself every day, 'I forgive myself, and remember God loves you'. Bella walks over to her sister, "We all have to forgive ourselves, because when we don't forgive ourselves, we allow the enemy to keep throwing these things, our past sins, back in our face and condemning us. And then what do we do? We concentrate and ponder on those thoughts in our heads as if we're acting them out again, as if that's still us. "And God says, 'No.' He's redeemed us. He loves us. He's forgiven us. We asked, and we received. Faith began to minister to her family even more. "The enemy doesn't want us to know that.

This is what happens when people don't know the Word of God, when they don't seek out the Word for themselves. They want someone else to tell them the Word instead of seeking it for themselves. "But when you seek the Word, you know that you are forgiven, that Jesus does love you. We surrender, we submit, and we grow closer to the Holy Spirit." Myra raised her arm as she went and sat down, as Faith continued. "The enemy's job is to steal, kill, and destroy. How does he destroy? He destroys with those subtle suggestions in your head. Oh, you know the suggestions. The ones you don't capture. The ones that say you're not good enough. The ones that say you can't do anything right. The ones that say you're too fat, too tall, too short, too skinny. The ones that say your hair isn't long enough. The ones that say your skin is messed up. The ones that say no one's going to love you, you're unlovable, the ones that even tell you that you will never get married. But I tell you what, Jesus loves you, and that's enough. "And you've got to love yourself," Myra added. You've got to forgive yourself. And you've got to know that no matter what, God has you, and you know what else, Nelly? We've got your back, too. We've got your back, too, my daughter." Bella walked over to Nelly, "I forgive you, my sister. I don't hold anything against you, or toward you; you must know this." "Nelly responded to her sister, "I don't hold anything against you, Bella, I don't hold anything against my Mama. I don't hold anything against any of you, and I ask for forgiveness from you all. I apologize for everything, and I do mean everything. I've been pretty terrible for a very long time. It's become my way of life and how I see life, like a big game that I have to win. Man, I have been the evilest person, and I accept what I did and how I acted towards you all, our entire family, and even my father." Nelly, remember, we all got work to do, no one is perfect, you bet we all mess up from time to time, and you will too, but honey, "you've got to forgive yourself." "Yes, Mama, I understand." Myra continued, "Now I want to share this with you. You need to talk to Samuel. You've got to apologize. You've got to ask for that forgiveness. "He's a good man. He'll forgive you. He's trying to move on with his life. And more than anything, he wants to be in his daughter's life. You've got to recognize that he needs to be in his daughter's life. He's her dad. He's a good man. He's a good father. And he was a good husband to you." "Yes, ma'am, you're absolutely right. You're right. He was a good father, and he is still a good father to Jennesis. And he was a good husband to me, but I didn't allow that. I was so hard, and I will always regret how I acted and what I did. I turned that man against me the way I did."

Myra said, "No, I don't think you did. I don't think your actions turned his heart, because he knows what unforgiveness can do. He knows the Word of God. He loves Jesus. See, he seeks after Jesus' heart, so he does understand. "Sammy is the bomb, he does understand," added Essie, and the sisters and Arrya all nodded in agreement. "Sweetheart, it may hurt to hear this, but what happened with your marriage hurt him. It hurt him to his core, and especially not to have his daughter around. That's why we invited him. We wanted him to be here this weekend. We knew he would be so blessed to be able to be here with Jennesis and the rest of the family. We've always loved him being here." "Yes, that's right. And Ez still keeps in touch with Sam even though you guys got divorced. He's still his friend, you know, and they still talk. They go hang out at the fitness center and play basketball. I like the fact that Samuel is around our family. "Because even when Ezra and I were having issues after the business closed down, and a lot of the issues were my issues, it was how I saw myself. It was me thinking that the business closed down because I wasn't able to handle the money the right way. I did the best I could. I felt so guilty. I felt so guilty. "And this is something that y'all don't know about. I never told anyone. Only Ezra knows. He's my husband, and I love him, and I appreciate him in my life. But I was so distraught over losing the business, losing all of our money, losing our livelihood, and taking care of Elijah and Eliana, that I actually took some pills." Everyone gasped. "What? You took pills? What do you mean, Myra shouted?" The Lord was truly looking out for me, because they didn't work. I got so sick to my stomach, and he had to take me to the emergency room. And after taking me to the emergency room, he told them that he thought I had taken too many pills because I wasn't feeling well, and I just didn't remember how many I had taken. So there wasn't a record of a suicide attempt. "But that wasn't really the truth. The truth was, I knew exactly what I was doing. I was just so tired. I was so tired, and I didn't want to weigh him down anymore. I didn't want him to have to go out and find another job or take a loan; I didn't know what we were going to do. "So, I thought the best thing to do would just be to end it." "Oh, my Lord, what is happening?" said Myra. "Oh, Essobella. Sweet Essobella. Oh my God, my Father, thank you for protecting Essie." "Mama, I'm so sorry. I never wanted you to know. I never wanted anybody to know. I especially didn't want Nelly to know." "What do you mean?" said Nelly. "Well, Nelly, Ezra told me that I look up to you, like I wanted to be like you. And because I looked up to you, it made me feel inadequate." "What?" said Bella. Ah, come on, no. Essie, oh my God. "Yeah, that's basically what Ezra told me, and he's right. I used to covet the things I saw Nelly doing and the things I saw Nelly getting. I wanted to be like my big sister. I wanted everyone to be proud of me. I wanted to be this big business owner who could do this, and do that, and we'd be rolling in money. And basically, the money was rolling right out of our hands. And I was so embarrassed, because after all, I was trying to emulate Nelly." "Wow," said Nelly. "Essie, I'm so sorry. I'm so sorry that I showed you a part of me that was not of God. I showed you a part of me that wasn't good. I've got so much baggage and things that need to be cleaned up, even still. "Now I see. I didn't see it before, but now I see. And I'm so sorry. I'm just being honest with you. That's what happened." Myra got up and turned, looking out at the lake from the fire. "Mama, you, okay?" "Yes, my dear. I'm okay. I'm so sorry that I didn't know. I'm so sorry that you didn't come to me, just like Nelly didn't think she could come to me. I'm so sorry that it felt like none of you could come to me. But I've always been here, wanting you to come to me. "Maybe I didn't show it.

Maybe.... you thought you couldn't come to me. But you could always come to me with anything. I'm not going to judge you. I would never judge you like that. Who am I to judge you? "I love the Lord, and I always want to share the Word of God with you. But my sharing the Word of God is not judgment.

Please understand that. It's just directing you to look to God for the answers you need in your life, to look to God for the forgiveness you need to ask for, and for all the things He has for you and who He's called you to be.

"Yes, ma'am, Mama, I love and appreciate you, I love and appreciate all of you." "Please know that you can always come to me. Please know that no matter what, I don't look at anybody with eyes of judgment. I want to look at you with eyes of love, because God has called us to love and to draw others to Him by sharing His Word and his love. Don't ever feel that you can't come talk to me. "See, I understand, because I held stuff inside when I was growing up, Ester and I both. Right, Ester?" "Absolutely, my sister, and everything that was shared tonight, Myra and I still have more that no one has ever known about how we grew up. No one except Raymond and Edward knew. Myra stressed to all of her girls, "All of you here, every single one of you, you don't have to hold these things inside, you are never alone, you hear me?" "We hear you, Mama." It was now Ester's time to stand up and share what's on her heart, as everyone was very quiet, yet meditating on everything that was shared that evening, around the fire pit, with the stars shining above brightly in the dark and beautiful sky, with the moon glowing and casting its light on the glistening lake and the women around it.

Myra is telling the truth. You know, it's hard to talk about it sometimes, and we never really talk about it. In fact, Myra and I don't even talk about it with each other. I guess sometimes it's a little bit too hard, even to realize the things that happened to us as we were growing up." "Your Mama, you didn't talk about it?" said Bella. "No, Bella, dear. That's because we didn't grow up having a family. We didn't grow up having two parents, not consistently in our home at one time. Heck, we didn't even have one parent to take care of us and love us. "My sister and I had to go live with relatives, and it wasn't easy living with them. They acted like we were a burden, yet they said we weren't. We didn't get treated like everybody else in the family. No, it was a little bit scary at times. Our father basically dumped us at our aunt's house shortly after our mother died. When he left, we never saw him again. My aunt was so angry, she fussed and cussed and smoked these long, thin cigarettes every day, that she wasn't getting anything for taking care of, but one day we would pay, she'd make sure she got what she thought she deserved. A hard frown began to appear on Ester's face. "I can still remember that smell lingering in the air. The house smelled like cigarettes and beer all the time. From the time we got there, Myra and I were responsible for cleaning every bit of that house.

Aunt Ruby did nothing but sit on the sofa smoking, drinking, and cussing. "We didn't get a lot to eat, and at times our Aunt Ruby was so hard on us. You know, we knew the family didn't have a lot of money, but they said they wanted us there, at first, because they thought it was going to be a payday taking care of us. It was her, her wicked husband, and her son, our cousin Cory. Their actions and the harshness did not match up with them telling us we were welcome to live there, after all, we had no one, and we were so young." "Yeah, there were times when Myra and I would go into the kitchen at night and sneak and try to get some food for us, because we would be so hungry. Lord, and if we got caught, it was going to be bad. It was going to be bad." "Yes, ma'am, it was. She wasn't playing with that belt, or whatever she could find to beat us, or should I say to hurt us with." "Can you imagine being beaten because you're hungry? Hate and contempt are what she had for us both; she was a bitter, hurting, and unhappy woman."

"I'm so sorry, I never, we…none of us never knew this, about how you were brought up," Mama. Faith declared to both her mother and her aunt. "We know Faith, and if it wasn't for this weekend, you'd probably never know. Ester and I would go to our graves with such horrible secrets, and for that I'm sorry, for never helping my family understand, and to know, when you see my faith, and love for you all, and wanting you to love and care for each other, this is why God took care of us both. The Word says, God will use what the devil meant for bad, and use it for our good, and we will absolutely always give Him Glory." Amen's and head nods are seen and heard around the campfire. Ester took her seat and continued speaking after Myra, "But everything was harsh to us. She would tell us, 'I ain't getting no money for taking care of y'all, but you can stay here.' And we knew, when we got old enough, we had to get out of there." "Yeah, and that's what happened when I got older. That's when I met your Uncle Raymond. It's not even that I actually thought I loved him, just like he said; however, I knew he was my way out. I knew he was going to be my way out, and then maybe I could get Myra out of that house too." "Yeah, but unfortunately, something happened." "Myra, yes, I was attacked. I was basically attacked by one of the boys who was friends with my cousin. I actually liked the boy, and I was a little bit too nice to him. I guess… I was too nice to him because he tricked me. He was much older than I was, and he kept telling me how beautiful I was and how nice he thought I was." Myra leaned her head back in her chair and closed her eyes. The memories hurt so much, but she wanted her family to understand her life, her secrets, the things she didn't want anyone to know. "He would rub my hands, and rub my arm with his finger, and say, '*Oh, you are so sweet and soft. You girl, so sweet, little one.*' And I thought I was a little bit grown; no one had ever called or told me I was pretty. When he said it, I actually felt pretty, that someone liked me. I thought somebody liked me. This boy actually likes me. "And I let him get too close, more than once. I didn't tell anybody. Definitely didn't tell your auntie. Couldn't let her know. But I think my cousin knew. Yeah, Cory knew, but he wasn't going to say anything; he knew that boy was up to. They were playing games; heck, I believe he put him up to it just for laughs, to laugh and make fun of me, because I was naïve. "And whenever his friend came over, if I was home, he would always kind of tiptoe down to our room to see me. And I let him come in, because after all, Auntie wasn't there. If she only knew, boy, I'd have been in so much trouble. Ester was 19, almost 20, and had already graduated from high school, finished community college, and was working, and attempting to finish her education. Ester had left the house after she graduated."

"I sure did, said Ester, I couldn't wait to get my behind out of that dark and wicked place, but I hated that I had to leave Myra, but after that last beating, she gave me…not to mention things that had happed when I was a little younger, I knew that when I graduated, I was gone, no one was going to touch me again, no one. On top of that, Aunt Ruby had already warned me that as soon as I graduated, she was kicking me out, and I could no longer live there. I was aware and more than ready to leave. But I knew Myra liked that boy; he was really cute, too old for her, and I didn't trust any of them. He was the kind girls liked. He was handsome, and he knew it. He had those really pretty eyes, those eyes that mesmerize you, and that's what happened to Myra; he was sneaky, too.

I wasn't coming around much, working and going to school. I had even started giving our aunt money to help with Myra so that she'd leave Myra alone. "So what happened was, when I found out I was pregnant, I was so scared, because I was so young. Ester was older. She had already moved out of the house." "Yes, honey. Sister got up out of there, and I didn't know what happened to Myra; she hadn't told me yet. But I had met Raymond. Unfortunately, Raymond was also with another woman, and then he discovered she was with child, or should I say, children. "I was upset, but I had to stay with him. It was already planted in my mind what I needed to do, because after all, I couldn't go back to the house, and I needed to get Myra out. So, we waited. We waited until Myra was almost showing. Then we packed her stuff. She was 16 years old, about to turn 17, so we were able to get her out. "I told Auntie, 'I'm going to take care of my little sister now, and I wouldn't be giving her any more money.'

Aunt Ruby didn't care. She just looked at us and said, '*You know it's expensive out there. I don't know what kind of money you got. This girl likes to eat, and look at her, she is getting fat too, so don't think you're coming back here, get out and stay out.'* "Yes, she sure said that. She said Myra was getting fat. She didn't know Myra was having a baby. And I had to accept that she just thought she was getting fat. "So, Myra came and stayed with Raymond and me. We weren't married yet, but my talking Myra into giving up Faith, for her good, is really how I got Raymond to marry me.

All mouths dropped open. Myra nodded her head yes, while Ester nodded, then shook her head, for how she had manipulated her sister to give up her baby and get Raymond to marry her. All of it was manipulation on Ester's part. "So yeah, I may not have loved him, but Raymond was going to be our way out. He said, 'I already have two babies coming, and now you want to take your sister's baby too, how am I supposed to do all that?' "I told Raymond, 'Don't worry about it. It's going to be my baby. You will have your babies. This is going to be my baby. You don't have to take care of her.' Raymond didn't care, or so it seemed.

He had made a mistake with that woman, but he was responsible for taking care of his children, and yes, he did also take good care of Faith, because we're married, and both legally adopted her. The sisters were so shocked at everything they were learning that night about their own mother and aunt and the hard life they lived through, depending on each other.

"And when she had you, Faith, you were so little. You were only about four pounds, a tiny little baby with little black curly hair, and beautiful gray/brown eyes. You were the prettiest little baby I ever saw, the sweetest little thing, with one deep little dimple in your right cheek." Oh, I used to just kiss that dimple. I knew the angel, your angel, put it there. He put the love of the Lord, right there, so that when you look in the mirror, you see God's love right there in your beautiful face, and remember how special you truly are." Faith broke down in tears, loudly sobbing. Essie, Bella, Nelly, and Arrya were all tearing up over the revelation of how Faith's journey, "Ssshhh sweet girl, could be heard. Myra whispered to Faith, as both she and Ester wrapped their arms around her. Ester dried Faith's tears, and Myra said, "sweetie, you were wanted, and you will ever be loved." "Oh, and Myra asked if she could name you, and she said she wanted your name to be 'Faith.' I said, 'Faith, that's a precious name.' That's how you got your beginnings. After Ester finished speaking, Myra said, Faith, your name was what I was standing on. I was standing on my faith in our Lord and Savior.

One thing I knew was that I loved the Lord, and even if I had never heard a human say they loved me, I knew I was loved by Him. I knew when I was young that Jesus loved me and died for me. It was faith, it was love, and when I found out I was having a girl, I asked the Lord, " Can I call her Faith Jesus? She will love you, Jesus. She will serve you, Jesus. Let her live for you, Lord. See, the enemy knew that, and he wanted to destroy our little Faith, he tired, but do you know our God never loses a battle, ever. "Yes, glory to God," Bella jumped up and down shouting, and her sisters all praised the Lord.

My darling girls, always trust God for all things and in all things, no matter what it may look like with what you see in your daily life, no matter what, you trust God. I know that I am forgiven. I've repented of my sins. I forgive others, including what happened to me while we lived in our aunt's house.

"Faith, you got your beginnings with both of us, because Myra stayed right there with me. Myra stayed with me when you were a little baby. She nursed you. She took care of you. I was still working and taking classes to try to get my degree. So she stayed and she was your mother in all senses of the word. She was a good mother to you, Faith." Myra raised her arm as if she were pointing up to God. "Only God could work that out like that. What does this sound like? Do you know who nursed Moses in the bible, when his mother and sister put him in the basket to save him, you know the story right?" They looked at each other, and Bella spoke up first. "Yes, Mama, it was his own mother. Pharaoh's daughter found him and his sister followed and watched. She asked Pharaoh's daughter if she should go find a woman, a Hebrew woman, to nurse him and she said yes, so she went and got her own mother, who gave birth to her baby brother, to take care of him. Wow, just look at God!"

"See, Myra said, He used what was meant for our bad for good. My good, and Ester's good, and definitely for sweet baby Faith." Shouts of joy and praise continued to ring out around the campfire. "Raymond was there, but Raymond still had to deal with trying to provide for Renissa and Randall. After all, those were his kids. But I told Raymond, 'Still, it's my girl.' And you know what? He acted like he didn't care." Then Faith spoke up. "I guess that's why I always felt a little distance from dad. It always felt like he wasn't really my dad, or he didn't want to be. But when I heard you and Dad arguing, and him mentioning that I was never his child, I didn't know what to say. "But it actually started making sense to me, because Aunt Myra acted as if she loved me. No, not acted like. I knew Aunt Myra loved me. And even Uncle Edward treated me better than Daddy at times, too." "Well," said Ester, "let me tell you about your Uncle Raymond and your Uncle Edward."

"Oh Lord, here we go," Myra said. "No, Myra, she needs to know. She needs to hear this. "Your Uncle Raymond was always jealous of your Uncle Edward. In the beginning, they worked together, Edward was younger than Raymond, and at one time, they were friends. Which is how Edward met Myra, at our home. Raymond had brought Edward home to have supper with us. He told Raymond that he wanted to marry Myra and let her have a fresh start. Raymond acted like he was jealous, which also affected how I started seeing and treating Myra, unjustly, totally unfairly, because she had never done one thing, not one thing, to deserve to ever be treated but with love and kindness. Raymond actually said, 'How is he going to come in and sweep her off her feet and start fresh, like some knight in shining armor, and now who's going to take care of this baby?' And I told him, 'Why are you worried about that?" "There's nothing you are doing for Myra anyway. Let her go and live her life. Let her start her life with her new husband. Let her be. We raised Faith as our own." "We formally did the adoption. We got the papers to make sure she was and is our girl, and Myra was okay with it." "Yes," Myra said softly, “I had to be okay with my sister rescuing me out of that house and allowing me to take care of Faith as she did, I felt I had to allow it and be ok with it.” “She allowed me to take care of you, Faith, from the beginning,” Myra said softly. “Ester allowed me to nurse you and actually be a mom to you, even for a little bit. It was hard to let go, Faith. Oh God, it was so hard at first.” I thought maybe Edward and I could just live next door, and I would still take care of you and still be a mom to you, even though I gave Ester my word that she was going to be your Mama, and that I was not going to interfere. I was just going to stay in my lane.” The ladies gathered around couldn’t believe all they were hearing from their own mother and aunt. “This is something that none of us ever knew,” Bella said quietly. “We didn’t know how hard you had it growing up. We didn’t know about you getting pregnant. We didn’t know about you and Aunt Ester not having enough food, the beatings, and all you endured. We didn’t know about any of that stuff. I’m so sorry. I’m so sorry that was the life you had.” “It’s okay,” Myra replied gently. “It was the life we had, but God is still good. We’re still here. We survived. We both have beautiful families and beautiful children who are doing so well, not perfect, but we’re very grateful, right, Ester?” “Right, Myra, we had to do what we had to do. We had to go through what we had to go through. But it doesn’t mean we were broken. It doesn't mean our upbringing broke us. It built us up. It helped us survive, and not just survive, but thrive. It taught us how to take care of our families and where our strength comes from. Myra continued, "So, you understand why, even when your daddy did what he did, how he allowed the devil to use Lucy to come into our lives and disrupt our marriage and our family with seduction, I still had to stay rooted in the Lord. I have lived with all kinds of hurt and pain. I had been so lost, so helpless, and had no one to turn to.

I was stagnant and didn't believe in myself or that I was worthy of doing anything worthwhile in the world. That horrible incident left me so broken, lost my identity, and unfounded courage. The last thing I wanted was for our family to break up and for my children to be without their father, a father who I knew loved them and took great care of them, regardless of what it looked like and the rocky path that our marriage landed on. That's not what God had for me. He is a good God. He sees the bad that happens to us, and still, we are never alone. It will all turn out for our good, and He will always receive glory from us, as we already said." "Faith nodded and said, even when bad things happen, He's still a good God. And I knew we were going to be okay." Myra stood and looked around. "So many secrets.

This is why we had to come here this weekend. Nothing can be healed if things are kept secret and not revealed.

Healing can't come without truth, without forgiveness, without things being brought to the light. "Sometimes, no, most times, the breaking has to come before the healing can take place. You know how when you get a scrape, and they say don't cover it up, let the air get to it?

"We need the refining, remaking, reshaping, and revealing, and the reconciliation, so the healing can take place. It's going to look ugly at first, but eventually it's going to smooth out. It's going to get better. In time, it will get better. But we've got to be here for each other." "Yes, ma'am," Essie said. "We absolutely do have to be here for each other. And I'm so glad my girls are here; my sisters, all my sisters are here, as she winked at Faith." Myra turned to Ester. "Ester, I want to ask you to forgive me." "Oh, Myra, I forgive you." "And I want you to please forgive me," Ester continued. "I haven't been a good big sister to you like I should have been. I started off that way, but I let the world and the things of the world, and even things Raymond would say and do, dictate how I behaved towards you." When he acted funny toward you and Edward, I let that affect me. And I know I acted wrong. I know I acted high and mighty. I know that's how y'all saw me. And I didn't care. I knew your girls looked at me that way, and I didn't care. I wanted to look like I always had it going on."

She sighed. "Yeah, I hate to tell you this, to both you, Aunt Ester, and Nelly, but we used to say, 'Nelly sure does act like Aunt Ester." Nelly looked up. "What?" Nelly said in shock. Bella and Essie started laughing. Faith and the others began to laugh as well. They all knew exactly what they meant. "We did," Bella said. "We used to wonder how Nelly was so much like Aunt Ester and how Faith was so much like Mama." Myra smiled. "Well, let me let you both know, I did have Nelly too. She came out of me just like the rest of you." Everyone burst out laughing. "Boy, we are one big family," Ester said. "Yes, we are," Myra replied. "And from now on, we're going to be a blessed family, walking in our blessings, treating each other the way we're supposed to treat each other. "And that includes our men, too. We need to support them, speak positively of them, encourage them, stand with them, and pray with them, as the head of the house; they need to be in the place God has called them to be in.

"We need Maddie, Luca, and Eli to see strong, God-fearing, God-loving men who love their families and take care of them. To become a firm foundation for our family and for their future families, because all of our families matter! "And we need Jennesis and Eliana to know that they are special, that God loves them, that they are beautiful and smart. We don't want the world to define them. They get their identity from Jesus. He calls them beautiful. He calls them unique. He calls them special. He calls them one of a kind. He calls them His own. "And we need to teach them that." "Amen," Faith said. "I love it. You are absolutely right." "Yes, my dear," Myra said. "And I thank you, because if it wasn't for you and Michael talking to me, praying with me, and pushing me to do this weekend, we never would have done it. "We would still be going on with our lives, not really supporting each other, not really being in each other's lives, and the truth hidden and never revealed.

"But this is the new 'now'. You just wait and see." "God is good, and He loves family. And He loves a family who loves each other even more. And we are going to be that family for each other, for generations to come. Amen." "Amen, Mama. I love you." "Well, girls, we've been out here long enough," Myra said, smiling. "And isn't it mighty funny that when there's a game on, doesn't nobody come looking for us? I'm sure hoping everything's okay, because not one of them men came out here to check on us, to make sure no animals came out of the woods or nothing like that." They all started laughing. "Yeah, you're right about that," Essie said.

"But you know what's even funnier? The kids didn't even come looking for us. If we were home, they'd be coming up here, wanting something, staying up late, and calling their friends. Tonight, they didn't even come looking for us." "Well, maybe we need to come here more often," Myra said. "I was thinking the same thing," Nelly added. "Maybe this is something we can do once or twice a year. It's nice coming up here for Thanksgiving, but maybe we can come in the summertime too, all of us. "And you don't have to worry. I'll pay for it. After all, that's what I've been driving my life to do, and it's a blessing to be able to do that for my family. It will be something I've never really done for anybody but me and Jennesis, of course. But that's going to change." "Amen, sister," Faith said. "We're glad, and we thank God for you." "Come on, ladies," Myra said. "Let's head back up there and see if they're still watching the game or if they've fallen asleep. I bet they're asleep, Bella shouted out, as the ladies all laughed." Yeah, you got to be right, I bet they ain't even up." Essie agreed. "Oh, shoot, let me tell you this, if Ezra were home, he'd be asleep. He can't stay up watching any game. I usually start recording it for him because he's going to fall asleep anyway, TV is always watching him. The guys, except Sammuel, don't know that's how he is." They all laughed.

"All right, my dears," Myra said. "Let's head back up." The women turned and walked back up the hill toward the house. It was a good evening. A wonderful evening. One that will never be forgotten. So much had been revealed. So much had been shared. So much had come out, things that needed to come out from all of them, so they believed. And they were better for it. They were all better for it. New days were on the horizon for this family, and God will get all the glory, every bit of it, for everything, and especially for bringing them together and keeping them together as one strong family unit.

"As far as the east is from the west, So far has He removed our transgressions from us."

(Psalm 103:12)

Chapter 12.

TRUTH REVEALED

As all the women started walking back up into the house, Bella said to Essie, "Pause for a minute. I need to talk to you about something." "Sure, sis. What's going on?" "Let's go sit on the front porch real fast. It won't take too long. I just… I started to say something when we were out there at the fire, but then I thought, well, maybe I should wait. I kind of know what I need to do. I know my answer, but I still need to get this off my chest." "Sis, what's going on? Is everything okay with you and Daniel? You're still getting married and everything, right?" "Yeah, yeah. You know, while we were talking tonight, and just how Nelly was saying about how Samuel… you know, how Samuel was only raised with his Mama, he didn't have any brothers and sisters, and how much he loved her family… well, Daniel was raised the same way. "His dad had other kids from a previous marriage and outside relationships, but Daniel was the only child between his two parents. So, when Daniel talks to me, and when he asked me to marry him, he talked about how he wanted a big family. "I told him, maybe we should just have like two, a couple of kids. I don't even know if I want three. Well… I found out that I may not even be able to have one. Essie stared at her sister, mouth open. "Did you just say you can't have children, Bella?" "Wait, let me finish, I haven't told Daniel. I'm afraid to tell him. I'm afraid that maybe he won't want to marry me. I'm so scared to tell him, but at the same time, I feel bad for keeping it from him." "Oh, Bella… oh, sis, I'm so sorry. Are you sure?" "Well, I mean, I guess there's fertility testing and things we can do, but my goodness, that stuff costs so much money. And even with insurance, from what I know, and I don't know everything, but I believe you still have to come up with thousands of dollars on your own. "As I said, I'm not sure and haven't discussed this with Daniel. I don't know how he's going to feel about it. I don't even know if he would want to adopt. I'm thinking he probably would, but I don't know. "I just don't know what to do right now, and I haven't spoken to anybody about it. Well, I have prayed about it, because I was like, Lord, I can't believe this is happening to me.' You see so many people having kids after kids after kids, whether they are married or not, actually more not married than married, and here I am, about to marry the love of my life, a man of God, who loves me, and loves family, and now I find out that I may not even be able to have any children."

“Oh, Bella… Bella, come on. Daniel loves you, sweetheart. He loves you with all his heart. I truly believe that. Number one, you should tell Daniel. He’ll be so hurt if you didn’t tell him, if you didn’t trust him with the information, and you’ve prayed, and now you must also trust our Lord. He is not at all taken by surprise by this. Your faith must stand for you in the Lord, and with whom He has given to be your husband. “Number two, I believe you will see that no matter what, whether you both have children, whether you adopt children, or whether you do fertility treatments, I believe no matter what, he will still love you, and he will still want to marry you, even if the decision is that it will just be the two of you, living life together as one with the Lord.”
“Well, I’m praying for that, but it’s a little scary.

Can you imagine how he’ll feel, knowing this, if he really starts thinking about it? I’m just really afraid. I guess it’s just those fears that like to pop up. Just like we talked about tonight, about how the enemy likes to get in your head. I literally feel like, ‘Man, I can’t even do this right. I can’t even just get pregnant and have a baby the way most women do.” “You know what, girl? You need to stop, stop now. You haven’t even tried, girl. Stop now and turn it all over to Jesus. You need to smack those thoughts down with the Word of God, take them captive, put the Word right on them, sis, and don't allow the enemy to gain a foothold in your mind.

There are a lot of women, and you'd be surprised, there are a lot of women who don't really desire to have kids. That shouldn't be looked at as if it's a big stigma. It's not to say they don't love children, but they may not believe that it's in them to be a mom, and that should be okay, especially if that's not what God has for them. Maybe it's to look after someone else's child when a parent dies, you just don't know, but you've got to tell him, and you've got to trust God, sis, you have to. We have to desire what God has for us. And if God has that for you, and it's in your future, then you'll do it, and you'll be fine. I believe in my heart that you should talk to him. Don't let this night go past without talking to him."

"Okay… yeah, I guess you're right. I guess you're right." Both sisters sat quietly, lost in their own thoughts. Bella finally spoke again, her voice soft and hesitant. "Essie, tonight has been amazing… I mean, it really made me realize how important our family is." She paused, searching for the right words. "And how surrendering to the Lord, really knowing Him for ourselves, is so much more vital than I realized." Essie nodded in agreement, the conversation flowing between the two sisters.

"Bella, and just having the desire to be fed by anyone without seeking the Lord for yourself isn't enough. Can you imagine how many people sit in church every week, believing they have a relationship with the Lord, yet never reading the Word of God for themselves, as well as checking what they are being taught." Bella considered the question, then replied, "I agree, sis. It's so easy to be fooled and misled when you don't have your own relationship and understanding." "Amen, my sister," Essie, her response donned in sincerity. As they continued sitting in the quiet, listening to nature all around them, both women reflected on their lives. Essie's mind drifted back to the moments when she felt completely broken by her marriage and finances. The ache of those days was still vivid; she remembered feeling hopeless, allowing the enemy's lies to seep in until she nearly gave up, believing she was worthless, and that her husband thought of her the same way.

The loneliness was suffocating, and she never shared the depth of her pain with her family, especially her mother. 'There's no way I could have told Mom what I was going through, not when she was struggling herself. I just didn't want to be a burden.' The quiet moment reminded Essie of her responsibilities, prompting her to rise. How things are quickly changing for their family, making her feel a little overwhelmed, yet hopeful at the same time.

Essie turned to Bella, "Hey sis, I'm going to go in and find Ez. Hey, can you do me a favor? When you go inside, can you tell Daniel that I'm waiting for him on the front porch? If he can come out here and just chill with me. But, please don't tell him I want to talk to him, because I don't want him to get anxious. Just tell him I'm sitting out here waiting for him to share the beautiful evening stars with me, you know, something like that." "Oh boy… yes, girl, you know I got you." "All right. I love you, babe." The sisters hugged each other. "I love you too, sis. Thank you for listening to me. I really appreciate you. I appreciate everyone tonight. Boy, it was so eye-opening." "It really was, sis. And boy, wait till I share with Ez everything we talked about. After all, he is my husband, so I definitely have to share all this with him." "Yeah, you're right. I'm going to share with Daniel too, after I share with him our issue." They both chuckled a little. "Yeah. Let's pray for Nelly. Let's pray that she had such a great breakthrough this evening and that she won't go backwards. And let's also pray that she will talk to Samuel and turn a whole new leaf." "I agree. And you know what? All of us getting together with Faith and Michael, and even Mama, whether at Mama's house, or at Faith's or Michael's, just sitting together, going over the Bible, doing Bible study, that would be so good. "And remember, Bella, Michael is involved with Inner Healing. There's so much that he knows. He's deep in the Word. He loves God so much. He's been through so much. No one would understand the testimony Michael has. That's why he has such a heart for God's people, to see us all spiritually healed." "Yeah, Michael is amazing. I'm so glad he's my brother." "Bella, girl, he's my brother too. What are you talking about? He's our brother." "Yes, we love him, and we're grateful to have all of them. Even what's going on with Zek is amazing. Both Zek and Nelly had the same experience, and look what happened. Their view of life was twisted the same way. "And because they shared their thoughts, they fed off each other's emotions, bad emotions. It wasn't for good, plus they both made inner vows without even knowing what they were doing, and look how that wrapped their way of thinking." "Yeah, it's unfortunate. But you know what? From this point on, sis, I believe they'll be okay." I believe in time they will, if they both truly commit to the healing they need, and definitely the forgiveness, and submit to our Lord and Savior."

"Amen sis." "Amen," Bella replied. "I believe our whole family will, but we'll have to keep everybody in prayer," Bella said. "Yeah, and check on each other. Do more than what we do now, more than we've ever done for each other, instead of just making assumptions. "Yeah, you're right. You're right. We will, we must. All right, well, can you please go in there and tell Daniel to come out? "I will, sis, and remember, trust God while you're sitting here. Go ahead and say a little prayer first, okay? Just stay calm and share with him what happened." "All right, I will, and thank you again, my sister." "Essie nodded and blew a kiss to her sister as she entered the house.

"There is therefore now no condemnation to those who are in Christ Jesus, who do not walk according to the flesh, but according to the Spirit."

(Romans 8:1, NKJV)

Chapter 13.

HEALING LIGHT OF FORGIVENESS

As the screen door closed behind her, the guys were already coming upstairs. She sees everyone coming upstairs, including Nelly and Samuel, and she says, "Hey, is Daniel still down there?" "Yeah, he's down there." Okay, thanks." Essie runs down the steps. "Hey, guys, she addressed everyone in the room. "Daniel, listen, Bella's outside on the porch looking at the beautiful stars, and she said to send you out there so she can spend some time with you." "You don't have to tell me twice. Let me go on up there and spend some time with my Bella. I ain't been with her all day, but either way it goes, it's still been a good day." "Yes, it absolutely has." Daniel went running up the steps to go outside.

Essie went over to Ezra. "Ezra, my dear, I missed you so much today, but boy, a lot has happened today. We could literally be up all night talking about it, but I'm so tired. Maybe we can chat about it tomorrow." "Yes, sweetheart, we sure can. It's been a good day. And yes, we were down here having some good talks too, especially earlier with Michael and David. I'm glad I got to know him. I didn't know he could be so nice." They both started laughing. Ok, so Ez, we'll start tonight and finish tomorrow. Ez smiled at his wife, " You just can't resist, alright, I'm all ears for you, my dear, kissing her on the forehead, wrapping his arms around her, as she nestled her head in his chest.

"Therefore, as the elect of God, holy and beloved, put on tender mercies, kindness, humility, meekness, longsuffering; 13 bearing with one another, and forgiving one another, if anyone has a complaint against another; even as Christ forgave you, so you also must do."
(Colossians 3:12-13, NKJV)

Nelsa's Regret

Nelly, looking behind, turned her head back to Samuel. "Hey Sammy, I need to talk." Samuel looks at his ex-wife kind of sideways, not quite sure what she wants to talk about, but hoping it wouldn't be really bad, like most of their conversations, and especially when it deals with Jennesis.

"Yeah… yeah, sure. What do you want to talk about?"

"Hey, well, let's go back outside and have a little bit of privacy, if you don't mind." "All right, cool." They both walk outside, but when they get outside, they see that Bella is already sitting on the porch.

"Oh, hey, Bella. I didn't know you were still out here." "Yeah, I'm waiting for Daniel to come out here." "You going to be out here for a minute?"

"Well, not sure how long." "No problem, no problem." Then Nelly said, "Hey, Sam, let's walk back down to the fire pit where we were tonight." Samuel looked back at Bella and shrugged as if to ask her what was happening. Bella had a slight smile on her face, waving to Samuel. "Good night, you two."

"All right, cool." Nelly and Sam begin to walk down to the fire pit. As they were walking down, both were silent. Once, they made it down to the fire pit and sat opposite each other. Nelly, looking down at her hands, took in a deep breath and said out loud, "Father, please be with me. Listen, Sam, I just want to tell you, number one, I am extremely sorry I am. I'm sorry for everything. I'm sorry for how I treated you. I'm sorry for how I trampled on our marriage. I'm sorry for not loving you and respecting you the way I was supposed to, as my husband, the father of our child, and the man of our home.

Samuel stared at his ex-wife with his hands clasped and turned in front of him with his elbows on his knees. He began to shake his head in disbelief at what he was hearing coming out of Nelly's mouth.

"Tonight," Nelly continued, "I had a whole revelation with my mom and sisters. I came clean. I came clean about everything, Sammy. I told them everything. I repented of my sins. I asked God to forgive me for everything, and I do mean everything." "Okay… well, that sounds good. I don't know what to say. You kind of took me by surprise. I didn't know you were going to come at me like that. I thought maybe you wanted to tell me I had to leave or couldn't see Jennesis." "No, no, Sam. That's what

I'm trying to say. I'm wrong, and I've been wrong. I've always been wrong. I am so very sorry. I was a monster to you. When I think of what I did, if you never forgave me, I'd understand. I now see just how bad it is, no, I was. Even down to us getting married, I think I went into it with the wrong motives. I went into it like, *'Oh man, Sam is this big handsome guy, and everybody's going to envy me.'* I kind of looked at it like what marrying you would give me, or how wonderful it would make me look to everyone else. That is all I ever thought about Sammy, and I'm sorry. I didn't go into it submitting to God.

I didn't do that." Sam said, "Yeah, I know you didn't understand that. And I know when we were young and got married, my faith wasn't where it is now. I wasn't submitted to the Lord like I am now. So yeah, Nelly, I understand better now how marriage is supposed to be, the covenant we were supposed to have with the Lord, and I knew that wasn't us."

"Well, Sam, that's what I'm trying to say. I absolutely did not know, and I did not want to know. I didn't even care. It was all about me. I was selfish, opinionated, and mean-spirited. These are all the true and ugly attributes I brought to our table." "Well, don't forget to mention you're beautiful, because you are a beautiful woman, Nelly." Nelly, surprised by her ex-husband's compliment, started to blush and even giggle a little. "Well, thanks, Sammy. I appreciate you saying that, but people can be beautiful on the outside and ugly on the inside. Dark on the inside. Hateful on the inside. The inside needs Jesus so the outside can truly shine. I never shone for real like I'm supposed to. I didn't have Jesus on the inside of me, and that is what you deserved: a woman who loves the Lord, and loves the person and position I am supposed to be at for what I am to do in this life. And tonight, man… I truly surrendered my heart to the Lord. I had to. I broke down.

My Mama talked to me. She explained everything, and I told her everything. "Even about why I had the abortion. It was selfishness. Me not wanting to be a mom again. Me not wanting to gain weight. Me not want to take care of another child. Me, not caring how you felt. It wasn't about you. It was all about me, my career, and money." "Yeah… yeah. I'm sorry that's how it was," Sam said. "I'm sorry again. I'm even more sorry for how I acted, putting everybody against you, or at least that is what I tried to do, and I'm so glad it didn't work. My family loves you, so they weren't having it. Saying I would sue you. Using the law against you. I was wrong. "I used what I knew to keep you from Jennesis. And knowing the man of God you are, it doesn't even make sense why I did that. I knew it would hurt you, so I did it anyway." Samuel stood up and walked closer to the lake, and stood there, shaking his head, looking at the ground, hands on his hips. "Sam, I'm sorry. I had to be honest with myself tonight. I didn't like what I saw, but I didn't stop. I was chasing the world and being spiteful and hateful. Who wants to be that way?

Yet that's how I was. "I want you to spend as much time with Jennesis as you want. I even want her to come live with you in the summertime. We can work it out. We're in the same school district. It won't mess anything up." "Nelly, do you know how long I waited to hear these words? Waited and waited. I couldn't understand, and I asked God, I asked the Lord. I said, 'God, Your Word tells me that You bless the righteous with favor. God, I am the righteous of God through Christ Jesus, and because I am the righteous of God through Christ Jesus, please bless me with having my daughter in my life.' "It hurt me so much not to at least see her. It hurt me what you did. It hurt me how we lived. It hurt me to know that you did not love me as your husband, and for the man that I was and still am. And not only did you not love me, but you didn't respect me. Nothing hurt me more than you keeping my daughter away from me, just to spite me, just to try to hurt me, as if I wasn't already hurting enough, that twisted the knife, and the pain cut deep. "Here I was, trying to be the best I could be, and I couldn't even raise my own daughter. "I'm so sorry, Sammy.

I'm so sorry. And I hurt Jennesis too. I hurt my little girl, our daughter, I hurt her. She loves you, and she heard me say things, mean things, about you, and it's wrong. I also owe her an apology for all I did. It's wrong for any woman to talk badly about a father to her kids, especially when he's a good man, and especially when he loves his children, and especially when he does the best he can for them, and what is being said is all lies. "There's so much of that in the world today, and I fell into the same basket. It didn't matter if you were a good father and a great man; I only saw the pain that I wanted to cause you. I wanted you to hurt as I hurt, and it didn't matter that it hurt our daughter. What is wrong with me? Oh my gosh, I can't believe what I fell into, that I fell into those lies, and spewed them out so effortlessly to anyone who would listen.

"And I'm so sorry, Sammy, please forgive me. From this point on, it will not be this way again. You are her father. You're a good dad. If you want her to stay with you, she can do that. I owe that much to you. I owe that much to Jennesis." "Thank you so much, Nelly. Thank you so much. You don't know how blessed I feel tonight, how honored I am, how much I owe the Lord. I'm so grateful that God heard my prayers, that He honored my faith. Now I'll be able to have my daughter in my life, and I thank you. Tell you what, you don't have to worry that Nelly is gone, and Nelsa's back. Samuel raised his arms up to the sky, "Thank you, Lord, thank you, Lord!" he shouted! "Well, I think I need to be pinched, this is really happening for me, for us." Nelly reached over and gave his arm a hard pinch, and they both laughed. "All right, all right," Nelly laughed. "It shall be all right."

"All glory to God, all glories to our gracious Father, Samuel again raised his hands as they walked back up to the house.

"Let all bitterness, wrath, anger, clamor, and evil speaking be put away from you, with all malice. And be kind to one another, tenderhearted, forgiving one another, even as God in Christ forgave you."

(Ephesians 4:31-32, NKJV)

Cleansing of Our Souls

"Oh, you wait. You ain't seen nice until you hear what happened with my sister. Man, just ask Zek and Nelly. It's all good. We give God the glory." "I'm telling you, you're not going to believe everything I have to share with you. Our family is truly blessed to have each other. I'm so grateful hearts are changing, attitudes are readjusting, and the way we see and support each other is changing. We're actually doing what we're supposed to do, and I give God all the glory for that."

"My dear, I love you so much. I love your heart. I love everything about you."

"I love you too. Thank you for loving me, especially through the hard times, especially after all the things that happened. You know it was hard for us. It was hard for me, because I thought you didn't want to be married to me anymore. "I thought you were so upset over the money. The way you talk sometimes…it's like it's almost an idol you. You equate everything to it, and when I made a mistake, I just knew in my spirit that you were going to hate me. It's like you didn't think I cared or wanted to do better, because I never spoke about it like you. You always seemed so down, and you relate everything single thing to money and finances. And when we argued, you actually said those words. When you said them, I grabbed hold of them. I kept thinking, "One day he's not going to be here. He's going to leave." "And then what am I going to do? How am I going to live? My mama told us that is what she thought our father would do one day, that she always felt like she was walking on eggshells with him, even after all the bad he did. She was still there trying to make life easy for him. Anyway, I just thought that was interesting because that is how I felt, too. I thought to myself, I'm going to have to start over with the kids and just everything." "Man, Essie, I'm so sorry. I'm so sorry. That's not how a man of God, a husband, and a father should act or make you feel. I should never make you feel less than the amazing woman of God that you are. "I'm so proud of you. I don't want you to feel anxious. I don't want you to feel less than or afraid. You're not less than anyone.

We all make mistakes. No one is perfect. I messed up too. "I'm sorry for making you feel like losing the money, losing the business, for running our credit up, and starting over was your fault. It's not your fault, it's something that happened, and the enemy took the opportunity to use it for bad. I'm sorry I ever made you feel that way." "Ez, I appreciate you saying that. I truly do. And I'm also sorry, because I actually told my mom tonight… boy, I thought my mom was about to jump in the lake after hearing everything from all of us. I told her about the pills."

"Oh my God, you actually told your Mama about the pills?"

"Well, Essie, I didn't tell anybody about that part. I just told her what your brothers said about how you looked up to your sister, Nelly. They were kind of shaking their heads like, 'What in the world?' But I sure didn't tell them about the pills. "And even though you told your mom, I'm not going to talk about it anymore or to anyone else. You're good, and we're good. Right?" "Amen." "Yes. Let's go gather these kids up and see what they've been doing. They need to be asleep." "Well, you know the boys ain't sleeping now. Jennesis… well, I don't know. Jennesis and Eliana have been quiet all evening. They've been in that room doing what girls do, doing their nails and watching girly stuff. They've been having a good time." "Yeah, it would be nice for Jennesis and Eliana to share more time, because they're the only two girl cousins in the family. The boys always have their time together." "Yeah, the boys do. They do sports together. They hang out. They do a little more than the girls. So, it would be nice to get those two together more often, especially with Mama. "Mama even volunteered. She said she'd love to have both girls come over on the weekends. Now that she's alone, she misses the company. That would be great, especially if she's taking them to church." "Even though we go to the same church, just being with their grandmother, who they love so much, and who has so much wisdom, would be good for them." "I agree. And after today, I think Nelly would agree too and allow Jennesis to spend that extra quality time with Grandma." "Yeah, she sure should. That's the best place for Jennesis to be, with Grandma Myra." I agree, and they turned to go find their children to check on the boys and find out what they were up to.

"Husbands, love your wives, just as Christ also loved the church and gave Himself for her, that He might sanctify and cleanse her with the washing of water by the word."

(Ephesians 5:25-26, NKJV)

Bella's Faith Walk

As Daniel walked out the front door over to his fiancée, who was sitting on the porch in one of the rocking chairs, he said, "Hey, my sweet girl, you warm enough?" "Hey, honey bunny. I am. This is a nice, thick blanket, so come over here and join me. How have you been? How are you?" Daniel sat on the lounger with his fiancée as she made room for him and placed the blanket over them both. "I'm good. I'm good. It's been a truly, truly interesting day today. It's been a full day today." "Yeah, I would agree with you. I would agree with you. Spending time this weekend with your family has been really eye-opening, really eye-opening. But at the same time, I think it's been a good thing for all of you. All of you." "Daniel, that's why I want to talk to you. I have something I need to share with you that I haven't shared with you. First off, I want to start by apologizing for holding it in this long, because I didn't know how to share this with you. To be honest, I was afraid. I was scared.

It's not right for me not to share with you what I found out. "You know I had my GYN appointment last month, just an annual appointment. But I talked to my doctor, and I shared with her about you and me being engaged and starting a family and everything. She said she wanted to run some tests, if I was okay with it, because I was getting a little bit older. I told her, 'Sure, it's not a problem.' "Well, I got a phone call from her. It was from one of the nurses, and they said the doctor wanted me to come back in and talk to her." "All right. Well, what did she say? Everything okay? You're okay?" "Well, Daniel, I might be okay, but I'm not sure. We're just going to have to really pray about it, because she said she didn't know if I was going to be able to have children." Daniel was quiet and stunned, and jumped to his feet in shock. "You're telling me the doctor shared with you that you may not be able to have children?"

"There's a little bit more to it than that, as far as the testing and stuff. There's more that needs to happen, but so far, that's where we are." "So, Bella, let me get this straight. This was a month ago, and you didn't tell me? Why would you be afraid to tell me? Why would you not share something like this with me, honey?"

"Daniel, just like I said, I was afraid." "Bella, you have nothing to be afraid of. I love you. We're going to be married. We share this. This is not something you have to carry by yourself, my dear. You don't ever have to carry this by yourself.

That's why I'm here. I'm here as your husband, soon-to-be husband. That's my role. But I want you to know, you don't have to be afraid to share these kinds of things with me." "Daniel, I love and appreciate you so much. I was afraid because I know you want kids. I know you want a family. You talked about it all the time. Because you didn't have a big family, and I did. I know how it is. I can't imagine if I didn't have my brothers and sisters in my life. But I know you never really got that experience until now with my family." "Listen, Bella, whether we have our own kids, whether we adopt, as long as we stay open and honest with each other, however God does it for us, we will praise Him. We will honor what He gives us to do. We will be the best parents. We will love our children, even if we have to adopt or foster, it's going to be okay, honey." "Thank you so much for making me feel so much better. And you know, there are fertility treatments and stuff. There's so much we have to learn if we cross that road. But we're not there yet. God can do miracles.

I really prayed about it. I believe God can do a miracle. I believe this is what He has for us." "Amen. I believe it too. When you and I put our hearts together, and our prayers, and join with the Holy Spirit, you best believe God can do miracles."

"Well, speaking of that, I was asked today if we've set a date yet. When do you think we should get married?" "Well, I'm not sure I want a big wedding. Maybe we can just do something at our church, with our pastor and our immediate family. We can have a small ceremony and then maybe a dinner at a restaurant."

"I agree. You should still wear a beautiful wedding dress. I can't wait to see you."

"I can do the dress. I just don't think we need to spend all the money. Our marriage is for God and us." "Then we can save money and go on a nice honeymoon." "Yes, just me and you." "I love you, Bella." "I love you too." "I apologize again." "Let that be the last thing you keep from me." "Yes, sir." Ester and Raymond got in their car to head back to the hotel.

Ester said to Raymond, "You know, Raymond, I'm glad we came up here this weekend." "Well, I guess it was all right," Raymond said. "I just chilled down there with the guys, watching the game, got a good old nap in. But as long as you had a good time, I guess it was good." "I guess we've got to come back over here tomorrow. Can we go home?" Raymond asked.

"No, Raymond," Ester replied. "We're coming back tomorrow. We're going to come back up here, and we're going to have a good time with the family, especially because Faith is up here." "Yeah, all right," Raymond said. "We'll come back again tomorrow." "Yes, thank you for bringing me up here," Ester said. "And also thank you for just spending time with the family. We had to do a lot of talking, but Faith, we still have to talk. You, Faith, and Faith have to talk.

There are some things we need to clear up." "I don't think I need to clear anything up," Raymond said. "Yes, Raymond, you do need to clear some things up," Ester replied. "And I think you owe Faith an apology, just like I owe Faith a huge apology. And even though tonight we were talking about it, we still didn't talk about it the way we should and the way we need to, you know, to let her know just how much she was wanted, and how much we loved her. So I would like for both of us to talk with her." "All right," Raymond said. "Whatever you want is fine with me." "Yep, that's what I want," Ester said. "Thank you so much."

"The Lord is good to those who wait for Him,
To the soul who seeks Him."
(Lamentations 3:25, NKJV)

Chapter 14.

POWER OF FORGIVENESS

More Grace

It was early in the morning. Zek tiptoed down the steps to his brother's room, knocked on the door, and then entered the room. Josiah and Michael were both fast asleep. Mike woke up when he heard someone coming in.

"Hey man, what's up?" "What's up? Good morning, good morning." "Sorry to be disturbing you guys so early, but I want to go ahead and just, you know, talk. Have a chat with you early before everything gets going, and everyone else is around." "All right, man, all right," Mike said. "Sure, come on. Just, you know, let me go on up here. Joey, wake up," Mike said to Josiah. "Man, why so early, Zek?" Josiah said. "Man, why do you have to come in here so early? Why can't we talk about this later?" "No, I really need to get this off my heart, and we really need to have a talk. Listen, y'all know this weekend has changed a lot for me, and for my family, and for all of us. Not just my personal family, all of us. There were so many things that we were all holding on to. I know I'm speaking for everybody, but I believe I can speak for everybody, because I know myself that there was so much in my heart, so much ugliness, so much, so much that needed to come out, and so much forgiveness that I needed to ask for." "All right, yeah, man, but you got to keep going down this lane?" Josiah said. "I told you, I'm so sick and tired of hearing this, and I can't even believe that I came here this weekend just to hear this." "Joe, listen. You know you're the main one, man. You have got to change. The life you're chasing is not for you. It's not going to do anything but kill you. It's not going to be good. And here we are all trying to do our best, and I know because that's where I was. I had so much bitterness in my heart.

You've got to change, man. And I'm here just to tell you and ask for your forgiveness, because I believe that I helped lead you astray. I filled your ears, your head, with so much foolishness, so much negativity, so many things that I should not have been saying out of my mouth, and I did. Out of my own foolishness, out of my own ignorance, believing all kinds of lies, listening to things that weren't right. And every time something went wrong, I was blaming anybody but myself, especially my wife. I blamed her for so much, and she's a good woman. She had nothing to do with my bad attitude. Even with the things that we suffered through at work, and then Mom, I treated them all badly.

My attitude sucked, not only to Pops, but to Mom too, and Mom didn't deserve that. Not at all." Michael spoke up. "Zek, you are so right, and man, I forgive you. We all forgive you, and we're glad that you manned up enough to understand, you know, that the life God really has for you was not headed down a good road, especially trying to leave your family. It was not good, and you weren't seeking after God. But man, I'm so glad you are now. I'm so glad that you had a complete 180 turnaround." "Yeah, Mike, I'm glad I did, too. Listen, Joey, listen up. I'm trying to talk to you. You've got to make a change, man. I'm asking you to forgive me." "All right, fine. I forgive you, if that's what you want to hear. I forgive you. Why you got to start this stuff so early, man?" "Because it's important. I got to get this off my chest. I want to make sure I have a clear conscience that I'm doing everything that I'm supposed to do, and I've done everything I'm supposed to do, making sure you understand that it was wrong. And I pray you come around, dear Joe. I pray you come around too. We're family, we love you. We care about you.

The stuff in the past is in the past. We can get past all that. We don't have to concentrate on the bad and the things of the past.

You can start fresh, and you can start now." "You know what, all this change in one weekend? I don't for one minute believe it, you're hard, and you can't change that fast, so I'll talk to y'all later. I'm going to the bathroom, and I hope you're out of here by the time I come back out." Josiah got up and walked out of the room to escape his brothers, leaving Michael and Zek sitting there on the bed. Zek said to Michael, "I don't know what else to say." "You said enough," Michael replied. "And you really said all you can say. You said the right things to him, but at the end of the day, he's a grown man, and he has to make the decision for himself; no one can do it for him.

He will have to live with the consequences and the decisions that he is making and has made for his own life. There is nothing else we can do but keep praying for him. The one thing God gave us all is free will, and because of that, I think many times people don't really have an understanding of what that means. They are quick to ask why this happened or why that happened, or to blame God for any and everything that goes wrong in their life, not understanding that we have free will. "Zek, you have free will. You have the free will to live your life the way you want. You have free will to accept Jesus Christ as your personal Savior or to ignore Him. It is your free will. It is your choice. God does not go around hitting people over the head and making them serve Him and surrender to Him and His will. That is not how it works, man. But I tell you what. God loves us, He loves you, and He sees you and is pleased with you now. There is no work we could do to make God love us any more than He already loves us. He is our strength. There is nothing more we can do. He already loves you. But yes, it pleases the Father to know that you have changed your mind, to change your life, and follow Him, to accept the Lord as your Savior." "Well, you know what," Zek said, "maybe we need to talk about that later with the whole family. Maybe we all need to have a total rededication." "All right?" "Yeah, all right, bro, I'm down for it, and I bet everybody else is down for it too." Then he looked back toward the bathroom door, then toward the door leading out of the room, and said, "Well, everyone except Josiah." "But you know what, Zek," Mike continued, "he will be okay, because he has us praying for him. And as a family, we will come together in prayer, lifting him up to the Lord.

This will be a hard lesson for him, but I believe he will come around. The seeds have been sown and watered, and that is all we can do." "All right, man. I hear you. Well, I am going to go ahead upstairs and let y'all get ready." "I will see you when you come up." "All right, man. Talk to you later." Zek turned around and went back upstairs. He walked up into the kitchen and saw that it was not his Mama up there. Instead, he saw that Faith and Essie were in there having a conversation. "Good morning, my sisters." "Good morning, Zek. How did you sleep?" "You know what? I slept really well for the first time in a long time. I prayed before I went to sleep." Both Faith and Essie looked up and stared at him, and then at each other.

"Sis, you can close your mouth before you catch a gnat." Both of them busted out laughing, "My brother, Zek, I'm sorry, you sort of caught us off guard, but you have to know we are more than happy, we are all truly rejoicing over your heart change, truly we are. Ditto that, cousin, that we definitely do," reiterated Faith. "Well, I thanked God this morning. I am just saying, I have changed a lot, and I do want to change, man, I keep thinking about how I am, or was, and sometimes, I can't even believe how much grief I gave to everyone, and especially my own family, and even more so, my wife. I know it's going to take even more time; I do get that. I know better now, I always knew, but obviously I didn't care, if it wasn't about me, let me just be real with you, it had to be about me and my way, and I get that." Both ladies nodded their heads in agreement with Zek. "It had been a long time since I prayed and did all that. But you know what? I have to trust God. I have to do what I have to do. I guess I kind of copied what I see Arrya doing. She prays at night. She prays in the morning. She talks to the Lord while she is putting her makeup on. She is singing and praising God all the time. Even when I was making her mad, she was still giving God glory and praise. That is kind of how I want to be. I want to know how God knows God. "Look at me," he said, laughing at himself. "Here I am trying to emulate my wife, the one who has been trying to show me the way all this time. And here I was just making life hard for her, even ridiculing her." Right at that moment, Arrya came into the room. "Making life hard for who?" They all turned around. "Hey, good morning." "Good morning." "I hear my name," Arrya said. "Well, I think your ears must have been burning," Zek said.

"Yeah, I was talking about you. I was just saying how I am now trying to emulate you and all the things I have been seeing you do all this time, all these years. Praising God in the morning, praising God at night, praying at night, reading your Bible, the things that I should have been doing, but the things I was kicking to the curb because I did not think it was for me. I did not think God cared about me. I did not think He loved me. I thought that because I walked away, He walked away from me too." "No, sweetheart," Arrya said. "God does not operate the way man operates. God loves you, and He was just waiting for you to come back. He knew you would. That is what His Word says, and I knew you would too. You are a smart man." They all started laughing. "You want some coffee, sis?" "Yeah, coffee sounds good. Where is Mama Myra?" "Oh, she is still in her room. She was resting. It seems like she had a lot on her mind after everything that had taken place this weekend, so we did not wake her up." "Yeah, let her sleep. She was still lying in bed. Just do for her the way she does for us and the way she has been doing for us every morning and every day, trying to make sure we all have everything, from coffee to food and cleaning up, always checking on everybody. "You know what? That woman has a heart of gold. She loves us all, and she wants good for all of us." "Yes, she does," Zek said. "That is how Mama has always lived. She has been that way since I was a little kid. That is why it hurt me so bad when I knew what I knew. It hurt me so badly because I knew she was not like that, and I did not understand why Pops wanted to hurt her so badly. It was almost like, why would you hurt Mama? After all, she loves you. She loves all of us. Why would you not want to be a family with her? There was so much I did not understand as a kid. I wish I had gone to either my mom or my dad. It did not have to be both, but I wish I had been strong enough to go to one of them and tell them what I knew. Maybe then the foolishness would have stopped. "Maybe they would have talked to each other and talked to Nelly and me. Maybe things would have been different for us, how we saw ourselves and how we treated other people. We always treated each other well because we had that little secret, or so we thought. Because we knew what everyone else did not know, we thought we had power over them. That is how we looked at it. We thought we had the superpower of knowledge of how people really were. "But anyway, I am glad it is all out now." "Yeah, Nelly had a whole change too," Faith said. "And I am sure there is a lot on her mind as well over everything that has taken place, especially between her and your Mama. They really had a conversation and got everything out in the open. "And as we talked about, everything that happened this weekend is what truly needed to happen for this family to be restored the way God wants it restored, being there for each other and back to our God and Great Father." "Yeah, you are right," Zek said. "You are right. I get it." "You get it." As the family continued chatting and enjoying each other's company, Bella walked into the kitchen. "Good morning, everyone. Man, y'all are up here early this morning. Hey Bella, good morning." "Good morning, good morning everybody." "What y'all in here talking about? It sounds like a serious conversation, because that's all we've been doing, having serious conversations." They all kind of laughed in agreement. "Yeah, we sure have." "Yeah, we were just talking and kind of going over some of the things that came out and some of the things that we learned." "Yeah, it's been kind of tough, but it's definitely been necessary." "Yeah, you're right." "Well, you know what? I'm going to go ahead back, get showered, get dressed, and come back in here. I'll give you guys a hand with some breakfast." "All right, sounds good." "I think we should just do a light breakfast today. We've done so much and so much eating and everything like that. I tell you what, I know Mama Myra likes being in this kitchen fixing food and making sure everybody has everything, but I don't want to be in this kitchen all morning trying to prepare food for everybody." "Oh, I hear you. We can just get what we get. The kids can get cereal. The rest of us will be okay. We can get some toast and coffee. Either way it goes, we'll be all right." "Sounds good, sounds good."

"Love suffers long and is kind; love does not envy; love does not parade itself, is not puffed up; does not behave rudely, does not seek its own, is not provoked, thinks no evil; does not rejoice in iniquity, but rejoices in the truth; bears all things, believes all things, hopes all things, endures all things."

(1Corinthians 13:4-7, NKJV)

Bonded with Love

Nelly quietly knocked on the door to Jennesis and Eliana's room. "Jen, sweetheart, are you awake?" "Good morning, Mommy. Yes, I'm awake a little bit, sweetheart." "Can I come into the room and talk to you for a minute?" "Sure, Mommy. Eliana's still asleep, but it will be okay because she sleeps really hard. She won't even wake up when I try to get her up." "No problem. We'll talk very quietly so we won't wake her up." "Okay, Mommy." "Jen, listen. I really want to talk to you, my sweetheart. I want to apologize to you, and I want to ask you for your forgiveness over all these years, over how I treated your daddy, and how I even treated you by not allowing you to see your daddy. He loves you, Jen, and I'm so sorry that I took my feelings out on Daddy and our breakup on you. I was trying to hurt him by not allowing him to see you." "Mommy, it's okay. I know that you were hurting, and I know that you were really upset because you talked really meanly about Daddy. But I knew it wasn't true, because I know I have the best daddy there is in the whole world, well, next to Uncle Ezra. I think he's probably pretty cool too." Nelly smiled. "Yeah, I think Uncle Ezra is pretty cool as well." "But Mommy, my dad loves me, and I love him. He always tells me how smart I am, how much he loves me, how good I am in school, and how pretty I am. Daddy even tells me I'm pretty, just like Mommy." "Oh, he does? He says that?" "Yes, Mommy. Daddy thinks you're so pretty. He still thinks you're pretty, even though you're not married to him. And he tells me I'm pretty, just like you. He also tells me I'm smart like you, too." "Oh, girl, my sweet girl. You're smart like both of us, because your daddy is really smart and he's a great teacher, and as for pretty, you are absolutely beautiful, inside and outside.

This is what I want to ask you. "I told your dad last night that I apologized to him, too. I told him that if you want to stay with him, you can. I do work long hours, but I'm going to start changing that. I put this job and everything that comes with it before everything. I put it before you, I put it before him and our marriage, and I even put it before serving God. "I just wanted to do what I wanted to do, and sweetheart, I was so wrong about so many things…so many things. I'm not even going to say I didn't understand. I just didn't want to know about it. I figured if you don't talk to me about it, then I don't have to act as if I know about it, and I don't have to change. But I do need to change."

"Yes, ma'am," Jennesis said softly. "Listen, you, me, and your dad are going to have a conversation when we get back. We'll figure out what it is that you want to do. You can talk to us. You can think about it. Do you want to stay with Dad? He teaches at the school, and he can keep you, get you to school, and be there after school more than I can. Or do you want to just stay with your dad on the weekends?" "Well, Mommy, what I would like to do on the weekends is go and be with Grandma Myra. She said that Ellie and I can come stay with her on the weekends if you let us, and then we can go to church with her."

"Mommy, can I tell you something? When you're not home, I call Grandma Myra on the phone. I love talking to her because she prays with me on the phone. Then she'll ask me, 'Sweetheart, go get your Bible.' I go get my Bible, the one she gave me for Christmas. "Then she'll say, 'All right, girl, all right sweetheart, I want you to open up to the book of Psalms,' and she'll tell me which one to go to. Then I'll read one verse, and she'll read another verse. After she reads it, she explains to me what it means, because sometimes when I read in the Bible, I don't always understand. "But Grandma is so smart about the Bible. She helps me understand it. Then I'm like, 'Oh, okay.' Like Daniel, when he was in the lion's den, I didn't understand. I said, 'Grandma Myra, how can he be in the lion's den and the lions didn't eat him?' Stuff like that. "Grandma helps me understand the Bible. I love hearing about Jesus. I love hearing about God. And something that she and I did, she asked me if I wanted Jesus in my life, and I told her, 'Yes ma'am, I want Jesus in my life.' Then she prayed for me. "Mommy…I'm already good because I already have Jesus in my life. And if something happened to me, Mommy, guess where I would be?"

Nelly looked at her daughter and said softly, "Wow. Wow. I never asked you. I never even thought that you wanted to know more. I didn't even think to say, Ok, so you can absolutely go to church with Grandma Myra." Thank you, mommy. "I didn't even ask you if you wanted to go to church with your dad, considering he goes to church too." "Yeah, I could have been calling Daddy, but I actually like talking to Grandma Myra about the Bible. Even though I'm sure Daddy can help me too, it's just more fun with Grandma. And she's a girl like me."

Nelly smiled. "That is so cute. All right. Well, I'm not upset, and I'm not mad, because those are things that I should have done. It was my responsibility to make sure that you had the knowledge of God in your life, and I didn't do that. So to be honest, I let you down, and I'm sorry… I'm sorry about so much, and I love you, Jen, and you know what? I'm also very grateful.

I'm grateful you have a Grandma Myra who loves you with all her heart and who loves Jesus with all her heart. She loves us all, and you know He loves us all too. And I know He loves me, even though I've been horrible, so horrible. But I know that I can ask forgiveness. And when you ask forgiveness, you have to change. You can't keep trying to do the same things and think you're going to keep getting forgiven like that, because that means you're not even trying, and that means you're not for real. "But I'm for real, because this has been really hard on all of us, and I'm sorry again."

Jennesis raised and gave her mother a big hug. "Oh, Mommy, I love you so much. I love you so much. Mommy, please stay just like you are right now, because I know you love me, Mom, and I know you're going to do the best that you can. And I know that you're not going to be mean to my daddy anymore. Daddy was always so sad, Mommy. I don't like seeing him sad. But I think he's going to be okay now. Mommy, I think he's going to be okay because you're being nice, and you both can talk with each other. "And Mommy, he's going to be so happy because he gets to see me. He tells me all the time that I'm his only little girl and how much he wanted me and how much he loves me, and he thanks God for me."

"Yes, sweetheart. Your daddy wanted lots of children, and that's my fault too. That's me being selfish, and I'm sorry. But I'm not like that anymore. I'm not going to be like that anymore. And I pray that one day, your dad and our relationship will get better and better. "Even if it's not with me, I pray that he finds someone who truly loves him naturally from their heart. And if they truly love him, I know they will truly love you too and take good care of you."

"Yes, Mommy, that would be so good for him. I want him to be happy, too. And Mom, I want you to be happy too. You both have to be happy. We all have to be happy." "Yes, sweetheart. It's important. It really is important. "So anyway, sweetheart, go ahead and get up and get ready. You can go have some breakfast if you want, maybe some cereal or whatever you want, because I don't know who's in the kitchen right now cooking. It might be Grandma Myra, but I can hear voices, and I didn't hear Grandma's voice, so it's probably your aunties. But they're okay." "Yes, ma'am." "All right, go ahead and wake up your cousin so she can get ready too, and you both can go to the kitchen when you're ready." "All right. Yes ma'am. I love you, Mommy." "Love you too, my big girl." Nelly closed the door and walked out of the room. She stood there alone against the door with her head down as tears began to run down her face.

"Oh Father, please forgive me. I am so sorry. What was I doing to my daughter? God, how can I say I love my daughter when I was keeping her father from her? "I thank You that her heart wasn't hardened. I thank You, Lord, for sending my own mother to intervene, to call her, to check on her, and to be there for her granddaughter, to pray for her, to teach her the importance of loving others. All the things that I wasn't teaching her, all the things that I wasn't even showing her. I was showing her the opposite, and that was so horrible of me, and I'm so sorry. "But I'm grateful, God. I'm grateful that she has a praying grandmother who's been praying for all of us, Lord, all this time. Father, I feel so much better, and I thank You." Nelly walked down the hall to her own room so that she could go ahead and start getting ready.

"Blessed be the God and Father of our Lord Jesus Christ, who has blessed us with every spiritual blessing in the heavenly places in Christ, just as He chose us in Him before the foundation of the world, that we should be holy and without blame before Him in love."

(Ephesians 1:3-4, NKJV)

Chapter 15.

FAMILY RESTORATION

One knock on the door, and in walked Ester and Raymond. "Good morning, Mom," said Faith. "Good morning, dear. How are you this morning?" "I'm well. How are you?" "I'm good. I'm getting better every day now." "Hey, Dad. How are you?" "I'm fine. I'm good." "You don't sound like you're good. You sound kind of rough. Is everything okay?" "Yes, babe, your daddy's fine. He will be fine."

Ester saw her nieces and nephews in the kitchen, "Good morning, everybody." "Good morning, Aunt Esther and Uncle Raymond rang back to her."

"You know what, Mama? I'm glad you and Dad are here. I would like to have a conversation with both of you out on the porch. Come and get some coffee, and maybe the three of us can go sit out on the porch and chat for a little bit." "All right, all right. That sounds fine." Raymond did not look like he wanted to go out there, but he really had no choice in the matter. Ester went into the kitchen and made two cups of coffee, one for him and one for herself. Then all three of them went out to the front porch and sat down. “Mama, I’m glad that you and Dad were here this entire weekend. I’m sorry that the information exploded as it did.” Ester said, “I’m sorry as well, but at the same time I’m glad that everything has come out, especially about how you came about. I’m glad all of it came out. It needed to. I literally feel healing in my soul. I feel like a huge weight has lifted off my shoulders. “For so long, I walked around with my head up in the air, thinking I was better than everybody. I didn’t want anybody to know my secret. I didn’t mind everybody knowing, not even your dad, you know, the part he played in it. But you know what? I’m glad it’s out now.” “Yes, ma’am, so am I. Daddy, I want to tell you something. I forgive you.” “What do you mean you forgive me? Let’s play no games.” “You know, when I was a young girl, you took me to that bar, and you had that lady who was supposed to be watching me. And you know that man, that bad man, tried to hurt me. It left me in a bad place. You were there drinking, and you weren’t watching me. You said that the lady was going to watch me, but she didn’t care. As soon as some men started talking to her and making her giggle, she turned her back. Anybody could have taken me. They could have snatched me. “And I know that you feel a certain way about it. I know you feel guilty about it. I know it in my spirit." "It was my fault?" said Raymond. "I ain't done nothing wrong." "Raymond, you need to listen to her," Ester said. "Yes, Dad, it was your fault. You were the adult. I was a child. Number one, you should never have taken me into the bar in the first place. But number two, because you did take me into the bar, you should have been watching me. You should have been watching me."

"She's absolutely right," Ester said. "And I told you that after it happened. You should never have taken her in there, and you should have been watching her." "What happened to me shaped my life and shaped how I thought about myself," Faith continued. "I was so scared and so timid. Those things should never happen to any child. But when it does happen, there are things that still need to be broken off in a person's life. "These are things I didn't know about before, but I know about them now. I know about repentance. I know about forgiveness. I know about renunciation. I know about things that need to happen even in a child's life. It didn't happen in mine. Maybe if it had, I wouldn't have gotten into a lot of the situations that I did, allowing myself to be fooled and taken advantage of, and more than once. Believing someone really cared for me, lies of the enemy to trick and hurt me, that's what that was, evil lies, and I believed it because I didn't know any better, unfortunately. "I didn't know who I was. I was trying to be everything to everybody, trying to please everybody, trying to make everybody happy, trying to make everybody think and believe that I'm just a friendly girl, everybody's friend. Meanwhile, I was dying on the inside because I didn't know who I was. I didn't believe anybody liked me. I didn't believe I was good enough for anyone or anything, including any man in my life, which made me pick the wrong man. You know how that ended up. "So yes, it affected my life in a bad way. But I needed to say this because I never said it to you. I walked around on eggshells trying to make sure I wasn't disturbing your peace, yet I never had any peace. I afforded you the opportunity to have peace in your life that no one gave me, and I was a child. I should have had that peace. I should have had that safety, and you were not that for me."

Raymond sat in the chair with his head down. Finally, he looked up at his daughter. "Faith, I am sorry. You're right. Your Mama is right. I should never have taken you in there. I had no business going in there myself. That was a different time in my life. But what happened was a decision I made in my life, and I didn't know what to do about it. I didn't know how to change it. I couldn't change it. I couldn't make it not 'happen.' "I thought that if I just didn't talk about it, it would go away, and you would grow out of it, and you wouldn't remember anything. But that didn't happen, did it? And I'm sorry. "And on top of that, I had Raynisa and Randall, and I didn't even allow them to come around you much, and they were your brother and your sister. Maybe if I had done right by them too and allowed you all to grow up as one big family, then maybe things would have been better for you, and you would not have felt like the only child."

"Daddy, I love Raynisa and Randall, and I know Mama does too. But you never allowed them to come around us, and I always thought that you loved them more than me. It seems to be a theme in this family this weekend, where none of us kids thought we were good enough or enough for our parents, or that we thought we weren't loved, that they loved everybody else but us. And I'm telling you now that it's a trick of the enemy, that rejection and all that shame that he likes to get into our minds, get into our families, and get into our generations.

I'm sure you are aware of this; maybe you're not. I certainly never heard it taught in a church about generational curses and how to break those things. But I know it now, being in ministry and being associated with the type of ministry I am in, I've learned these things. I've learned about deliverance. Michael is in Inner Healing. Do you know how important that is? We all need this in our family. There are things that have happened that we need deliverance from. There are soul wounds and deep wounds that need to be healed. This was a good start this weekend, but there's more that needs to happen." "Yes, you're right," Ester said. Just then, Ezra walked down to the porch. "Good morning, family. How y'all doing? I didn't know y'all were sitting out here. I came out here just to get some alone time before everybody else came out here." "Well, we're done talking," Ester replied. "We were just having a private family conversation, the three of us, some things we needed to clear up. But yeah, we're done out here if you want to sit." "In fact, I'm going to go back in the house and get myself some more coffee and get ready, because I'd like to go have a conversation with Myra."

"Yes, Mom," Faith said. "Myra was still asleep, but she's probably up now because it's been a while." "All right. Well, I'm going to go ahead back in the house and see about Myra, because I'd like to have a conversation with her as well." Faith, Ester, and Raymond walked into the house just as Essie walked out onto the porch to join her husband. "Well, I guess it's our turn now just to sit out here and look at the beautiful lake and everything, just take it all in. It's just a beautiful morning." "Yes, my dear. I can't believe the whole weekend is almost over." "Yes, but it sure was a good one. I mean, if you want to call everything that happened good. But I'm going to call it good." "How about necessary?" "Yes, I think necessary is a great word. We'll call it necessary." "Well, hopefully the kids are up now. There's no way I feel like cooking breakfast this morning. If Mama wasn't in the kitchen cooking breakfast, you sure weren't going to get me in there, and Faith up in there cooking either. Coffee and cereal, maybe some toast. That's about all we can muster up this morning." "That's no problem, honey. I'm always up for a good cup of coffee." "Yeah, me too. That is surely my thing." "I know it is your thing. That's what coffee drinkers do, crave their coffee fix." "All right now, ain't nobody asked you what coffee drinkers do, so you can stop making fun of me right now." "All right, all right," he laughed. "I guess I got my own little thing with the energy drinks anyway." "Yes, you absolutely do," she said, and started to laugh as well.

"Being confident of this very thing, that He who has begun a good work in you will complete it until the day of Jesus Christ."
(Philippians 1:6, NKJV)

Chapter 16.

HOPE ARRIVED

Esther went down the hall and knocked on Myra's door. "Myra, are you up?" "Yes, come on in. Come on in." "Good morning." "Good morning, sister. How are you feeling this morning?" "Well, I'm feeling a little better. I just wanted to take a little break this morning. I know Faith got up early and went in there to make the coffee, and I just felt like I wanted to stay in here, lying in the bed, reading the Bible, talking to the Lord, just me and the Lord, my own time this morning. After so much that has happened this weekend, I just needed that time alone." "Yes, my dear, I definitely understand. I want to share something with you. Faith, Raymond, and I just had a conversation on the front porch, and Faith actually confronted her daddy about what happened to her, how he took her into that bar and left her, and how that man tried to attack her. "And Raymond, you know, it almost angered me for a minute because he always acted like, and he literally said out of his mouth, 'It ain't my fault, that wasn't my fault,' like he wasn't accepting responsibility, just like he did all those years ago when it first happened.

Faith speaking about the incident, and him saying it wasn't his fault, took me back to all those years." "Oh my, I bet it did take you back. But you know, sister, that takes me back to what really happened to me all those years ago. "And you know, even though we shared so much about our lives and so much about what happened to us growing up, you know, we had to literally be dropped off at Aunt Ruby's house. She was our mother's sister, and after our Mama died, our father, Jackson, yes, Jackson was his name, he dropped us off on the front porch, rang the doorbell, and said, 'These are your sister's kids. I can't take it. I can't do anything with them. I can't do anything with raising no girls.' "And he left us. Left us and never came back. This was one of the worst days of our lives. I don't know what would have happened had we stayed and lived with our daddy, but I don't think it could have been any worse than having to live with Aunt Ruby and Uncle Leo. Oh my God, they were evil, just plain evil.

"I've not said his name in so many years. She was the meanest woman, just hateful, and he, all he did was drink." "Sister, he was a bad man. Yes, he was. The fact that he tried to lay his hands on you, sister. Why do you think I had to leave when I got old enough to leave? I had to get up out of there. That man kept trying to get after me. And when I did try to tell Aunt Ruby, she smacked me across my face and told me I was a liar. 'You liar! That's your uncle. That's your Uncle Leo. He's the one putting food on this table to feed you and a roof over your head. Who do you think you are talking about him like that? You better take them lies back, you little hussy.' That's what she called me. She called me a lying little hussy, as if she didn't know what kind of person he was." Too many people, in and out of that house, all the time. "I know you weren't, sister, a liar you are not, because he tried to do the same thing with me, and I was younger. I got into my own trouble. They had those sons, and I should never have let that boy come near my room. I should have never let him." "Yeah, you liked that old Peter, though. That's why you let him come into that room. And it happened because I was gone. But I should never have left you in that house. It was only long enough for me to get myself together. Because remember, I was chasing Raymond. I knew Raymond was going to do well, that he was going to have a good job and money. He was working for his father. Oh yes, he was going to have money. He was going to do well. And I just knew marrying Raymond would be good for me and you. I wanted it to be good for you, Myra. I wanted to make sure you were okay." "I know, sister. I know you did. I know. But you know what? You remember every night when we went to bed, we had to not only lock the door but remember we had to put the chair in front of the door too." "Yeah, because we never knew that old nasty Leo was going to try to come into our room in the middle of the night." "Oh yes, sister. Oh yes, I do. Oh God, it was the scariest part of living in that house. And you know, after you left me, I cried. I cried. I was so scared every day. I was scared when I came home from school. I did exactly what she said. She fed us oatmeal every day. I can't stand oatmeal to this day. As soon as I woke up, oatmeal again. Now and then I might get something else to eat. Maybe she would give me a piece of ham or sausage, or a piece of chicken, or whatever she was cooking. Oh yes, she was good for those chicken gizzards and liver." "Oh yes, it's almost like she was giving us a lesson. Man, that woman hated us." "She sure did. I know our Mama was nothing like her. We were young, but I remember Mama. She was beautiful. She was kindhearted. I don't know how she got up with Daddy."

"I don't understand that either. But I remember when she got sick. Oh, she was so sick. I remember telling her, 'Mama, it's going to be okay. It's going to be okay, Mama.' And she kept saying, 'I love you. Ya'll be good girls, okay? I love you. I love you.' And then she died. She just died. She left us. I cried so hard.

Why did she have to leave us? We have no one who loves us. I didn't believe anyone loved us or wanted to protect us. I can still remember going to church with our mother. She loved the Lord, and yet I don't understand how she was with a man like our daddy. At the time, we were so young, but I still didn't understand, because she was so loving to us. Remember, after she passed, how we tried to go back to the church she used to take us to, yet it was as if we had never been there. The judgmental looks of disapproval we received, I don't know if it was how we were dressed, or maybe our hair wasn't done the right way, I don't know, but what I do know is they knew who our mother was, and they knew who our father was, and what he was doing in those streets. "Yes, sister," added Ester, "That's it right there, they knew! They looked down on us, treated us like we had leprosy, and I have not forgotten that. I believe that is just another reason I tried so hard to look the part, to walk and talk the part. I had vowed that no one, and no man, would ever look down on me again, and I would never need anyone. Yes, yes, I said that deep in my soul." "Ester, it was from a place of great pain and loss, but you don't have to worry about that. God saw it all. He loves His children and wants good for us. He's a good God, and even in this world where there is so much hurt and pain, it's up to us to take care of others, to love on them, and show them the love of Christ and not act the way others do and mistreat people, we know better, sister." "Yes, you are so right, you're right, and I will do better myself, replied Ester. But I sure remember it like it was yesterday. I didn't understand everything that was happening mother was gone, and I didn't know what was going to happen to us. But I never thought that our own father would just drop us off on Aunt Ruby's front porch and just leave us." "Oh, my God. Even though it didn't work out the way we thought, with me getting pregnant by that old Peter, and then me having to pretend." "Yeah, she thought you were getting fat. Remember, she said she wasn't going to give you any more food, as if she was feeding you too much?" Myra shook her head, "Yes, I remember, she said I looked ugly and getting as big as a house. She told me that I needed to lose weight. She didn't know I was having a baby. I'm thankful that you were able to sneak me some food whenever we met up. And I'm so glad that you got me out of that house." "I had to. And I was so upset, sister, when Raymond told me that that girl… Raynisa and Randall's mother was having his babies, and he was going to have to support her. She trapped him, but I don't think she wanted him to marry her, at least that's what he said. He told me, 'Oh, I'm still going to marry you because I love you, that's what he told me. I'll still marry you." And I was stupid, but I was so desperate. I had to make sure we were taken care of. I told him, 'You can do what you want to do, and I ain't going to say nothing about you having those babies with another woman.

But I tell you what, Myra is coming to live with us." And he looked at me like, 'Why does Myra have to come live with us?' If she didn't get out of that house, Uncle Leo was going to rape her. Uncle Leo was going to hurt my sister because he tried to do that to me. And we can't have that. He understood. As soon as we got married, as soon as we got some place to live, oh, that was a great day. I packed you up and took you out of that house before Raymond got home. And Ruby just sat there at the kitchen table smoking her cigarettes, rolling her eyes. She couldn't care less. She wanted you gone anyway." "That's the last time we saw her, Myra declared. "Yes. After that, shortly after that, remember she died, heck, I think Leo may have had something to do with it, and he died too in jail. "Oh my goodness, the stuff that happened in our family. The lies, the secrets, the abuse, the evil, and all the nastiness.

Ester walked over, placing her hand on Myra's arm, "Sister, I am grateful. I'm grateful because I have God in my life. If it wasn't for the goodness of God, all these years taking care of us, I don't know where we would be. I'm so grateful now. I'm so sorry for everything. I know I told you yesterday, after all those years of living there in that house, we should have been able to have each other's backs. I should have had your back. You're my younger sister. I should have had your back. Instead, I got jealous because of the baby. I got jealous, and for that, I'm sorry. All I saw was that everybody could have babies but me. Raymond had his two kids, and you had Faith. Taking you in and you allowing me to have Faith made me feel like I was a real Mama. It made me feel like, hey, I got a baby too. But then I was scared. I was scared that one day you would tell Faith. I was scared that not only would you tell Faith, but that she would want to come live with you. Then, after you got married and started having all of those babies, oh my heart got even harder. All I had was Faith, and I couldn't lose her. I just could not lose Faith." "Esther, it's okay. I understand how hard and how hurtful you must have felt because you wanted to have and feel a baby in your womb, to feel a baby growing. I understand. But you know what? It's not just giving birth to a child that makes you a mother. It's loving your child. It's caring for your child. It's doing the best every day for your child. It's making sure they have everything they need. It's taking good care of them. It's treating them well. It's not abusing them. It's not despising them and treating them badly; it's making sure they are loved. That's a loving mother.

Esther nodded her head in agreement with her sister's words. "And you did that for Faith. I know some things that happened to her were horrible; it was bad the neglect with her dad, and it's horrible with the other attack that happened to her, which was at Raymond's hands. I know they shared everything with me. But I never told her I was her Mama. I never told her I gave birth to her. And you know why? Because you're her mother. You raised her. I may have given birth to her, but you raised her. "And you know what, sister? You raised a fine woman. You raised this beautiful girl who loves the Lord with all her heart. Oh, she loves Jesus mightily. She has such a powerful testimony. Sometimes when you go through the most, you have the biggest testimony. You love the hardest, and you want the best for others. Her testimonies have blessed so many and allowed them not to be afraid or ashamed, but to also turn to the Lord. What the enemy meant for her harm, as the Word of God says, God truly turned it around for her good, and we all will give Him all glory and praise. This is why Faith and Michael fought so hard for this weekend; they went through so much, and they knew just how much freedom and healing come when secrets are revealed. Nothing heals when it stays covered, and I will continue saying this as much as everyone needs to hear it." "I couldn't agree more, Myra. The others had their lives. They had their jobs. They had their education. Yes, they did well for themselves; they weren't all living for Jesus. And neither was Raymond and I. "But your sisters are just like Faith. I think seeing how much you love the Lord, and how much she loves the Lord, made me even more afraid that I was going to lose her, because I wasn't doing the necessary things. I wasn't like you. You two seemed like you were cut from the same cloth more than anyone knew. But I knew it. I saw it. "I saw how you looked at her sometimes, and I saw how she gazed at you. There was such love in her eyes, love and admiration. I didn't see her look at me like that, and I wanted her to look at me like that because I was her Mama. "But I know now that, nonetheless, she still loves me, and she loves her father. She has forgiven us for how we didn't do for her, especially Raymond. Oh, she told him today. That's what we were doing on the front porch. She told her daddy how she felt, finally. She told her daddy what he should have done, how he should never have taken her in that bar.

She said, 'I forgive you, Daddy.' "She forgave him. I think he was shocked. I know he didn't expect that. But she's not the kind of woman to hold things in her heart against people." "No, sister, she's not like that because she knows better. And she knows Jesus would not be pleased for any of us holding unforgiveness toward anybody else." "I know that now. She's a studied young woman of the Word of God. Faith loves the Word. She loves to have understanding of God's Word, and that's what she seeks to do." "Yes, she does, and we can all learn from her. We can all learn." "I'm going to go ahead and get ready, my dear." "All right. I'll see you when you come out. I'm going to go ahead back in the room with the rest of the family and finish sitting with them." "All right. I just wanted you to know that I love you." "I love you too, my sister. I love you for life."

"Do not sorrow, for the joy of the Lord is your strength."
(Nehemiah 8:10b, NKJV)

Hearts Transformed

As Ester left the room, and before Myra could get dressed, she heard light tapping on her door. "Who is it? "Mama, it's me, may I come in and speak with you? Is it very important?" Come in, Zek, come on in, son, she replied. "Mama…" Zek's voice trembled as he sat on the edge of the bed, his hands wringing together like a boy afraid of his own truth. "Mama, I don't even know how to start." Myra leaned forward, eyes soft and full of knowing. "Start where it hurts, baby. The truth always begins right there." He swallowed hard. "Mama, I've been carrying something heavy. For years. And I can't carry it anymore." Myra nodded slowly. "Then set it down, son. You can't heal from what you keep hid, son." He took a breath that shook his whole chest. "I know we already talked about this…what happened, but I need to confess out of my own mouth to you, Mama.

It was Nelly and me. We saw Daddy. We followed him one day, or should we go ahead, because Nelly already knew where he would be going, so we lay in wait for him to show up. Nelly had told me what she saw, and made me go and spy on Daddy, to see if it was really true, and Mama, we swore we'd never tell you because it hurt so badly. When he pulled up to that house… and that woman opened the door…" Zek's voice cracked. "There was a little boy. He ran out hollering, 'Daddy!' and Pops picked him up and hugged him tight. He called him 'my boy'." Zek bent over, his face buried in his hands. "Mama, I was supposed to be his boy. I hated Pops for so long, so long. I felt rejected and unwanted by my own father, who replaced me, Mama." Myra gasped softly, her heart folding in on itself. "Oh, Lord Jesus…"

"I just stood there," Zek said, his voice small and breaking. "It was like the world split into two. I couldn't breathe. Nelly was crying, she was turning red with anger, and I couldn't let you hurt like that, Mama. I couldn't. So, I just buried it. But it didn't go away, and instead what grew on the inside turned on you, on him, and on the whole family. It made me mean and hateful to everyone." He lifted his head, tears running down his face. "I started looking at Pops as if he were my enemy. Every time he smiled at me, I thought he was faking it, that he didn't really love me or see me as his boy anymore. Every time he prayed, I thought he was pretending. I hated him for what he did to me… and I hated you for staying with him. The voices in my head told me that God didn't care about any of us, 'Because if He did, He wouldn't have let it happen." Myra's hand reached out and found him. "Oh, my sweet boy. You've been carrying that pain like a cross you were never meant to bear." "I thought if I stayed mad, I'd be strong," Zek said quietly. "But it just made me bitter. I didn't want to be a husband, not really. I didn't want to be a father, 'Because I was scared, I'd turn out like him. And I stopped praying, Mama. I stopped believing." Myra drew him into her arms. "Zek, baby… the enemy has been whispering to you for a long time, telling you that you weren't loved, weren't enough, or wanted. But the truth is, you never stopped being loved by me, your daddy, and especially by God. The hurt didn't come from our Godly Father, son. It came from the brokenness of man, generational bad seed, and misaligned lust and lack of character.

But even in brokenness, grace can still find you, and it's in that grace where hope resides. It was forgiveness, rest, and love waiting. Zek clung to her like a child. "I want that grace again. I need God, Mama. I don't want to keep running. I want to come back. But I don't even know how." "You're already on your way," she said softly. "You came back the moment you opened your mouth and told the truth. Now let's pray, you and me. You don't need fancy words. Just speak from your heart. The Lord's been waiting on this moment longer than you have."

They bowed their heads. Myra's voice was low and trembling with power. She thanked God for her son, for sending our Lord and Savior Christ, His Son, for the boy who had finally laid down his hurt, pain, and his unforgiveness. She prayed for forgiveness to wash over him like rain, for peace to take root where bitterness once lived. Zek repeated after her, voice cracking, heart pouring out every word. When they finished, there was silence; the kind of silence filled only with love and grace. Then came a gentle knock on the door. It was Arrya. She stepped in quietly, eyes already red from listening at the door in the hallway. "Zek," she said, kneeling beside him, "are you alright?" He turned, tears still streaking his cheeks. "I'm sorry, Arrya. For everything. For how I talked to you, for how cold I've been. I was angry at my daddy, but I took it out on you. I was hurt, and I kept hurting the one person who loved me most, even having a child before we even got married, and I'm so sorry for everything."

Arrya took his hand and placed it over her heart. "You've been lost, Zek. But now you're found. I'm not perfect either, but I love you. I forgive you, Zek, and I believe the same God that healed you this morning is healing our marriage too." Zek nodded; emotions were thick in his throat. "I want to do right by you, by our kids, by Mama, by God. I want to live clean. I want to love again without all that hate and bitterness in me."

Myra stood, tears streaming down her face, but smiling widely. "That's the new man God's raisin' up in you, son. What the devil meant for evil, the Lord is already turning' for good." The three of them sat there, holding hands, as morning light streamed through the blinds, and they could hear the chatter from out in the living area.

This is the first real peace they'd felt in years, and there was no way they wanted to leave that space.

"And whenever you stand praying, if you have anything against anyone, forgive him, that your Father in heaven may also forgive you your trespasses."
(Mark 11:25, NKJV)

Chapter 17.

Sweet Day of Change

Arrya and Zek came out together, as Myra went into the bathroom to wash up and get dressed. Their faces, swollen red eyes, but smiles on their face as the peace of the Lord surrounded them like a blanket of protection. Michael looked up first. "Well look at y'all," he said softly, setting his coffee cup down. "I don't know what went on back there, but it looks like peace has finally walked in for good."

Zek let out a shaky laugh. "Yeah, peace walked in… and this time I let Him stay this time." Myra walked into the room. She could hear everyone talking and laughing and just having a great time, you know, the way families are supposed to.

"Good morning, everyone." "Good morning."

"Good morning, Grandma."

Myra smiled, that proud, trembling smile of a mother who'd prayed half her life for this very sight. "Ain't it something', when the Lord shows up in the middle of your mess?" "Sure is," Michael said, grinning now. "Been waiting to see that smile on your face, brother." Zek rubbed his eyes. "It's been a long time coming'. I had to lay some things down; things I should've let go years ago. But God is patient. He waited on me, even when I wasn't waiting on Him; instead, I was running." Faith had been standing near the doorway. She came closer, her voice gentle. "Sometimes we just gotta stop running from what hurt us. That's when grace finally catches up." Zek nodded, his throat thick. "Yeah, grace caught me this morning, and I ain't letting' it go again." Myra placed a hand on his shoulder. "You know what I saw in that room just now?" she said. "I saw a resurrected heart, full of love, humility, and now ready to seek after our Lord, and align your life with His Word, His Way, son.

The kind that doesn't come from the grave, but from the heart. The kind that says, old things are passed away, and all things are made new." The family went quiet for a moment, like the air itself was hanging, waiting for their release. Their breath, to exhale and then inhale the new. Everyone was there. What a joyful sight it was to see everyone in one room, everyone talking, laughing, having conversations, and enjoying each other's company. "Oh, I know the morning has already escaped us." "Yes, Mama, but that's okay. We're all here, and everyone's well." "You know what? I'm glad we're all here. Did everybody get something to eat? Is everybody okay?" "We're good. We're good, everyone. We got what we needed to get, and if not, there are still plenty of leftovers. We can fix some plates later before we all head out." "Well then, do you know what? Can we all gather together? Where are the kids? Make sure all the babies are here."

"All right, well, let's go ahead and get them. It's just the boys downstairs. They've been staying down there the whole time they've been here. Bring the boys up here." "Eliana and Jennesis, come over here with me, okay?" The girls came over there with their grandmother, and Bella ran downstairs to get the boys and tell them to come upstairs.

Once everyone was upstairs, she said, before she sat down, she noticed Michael and Faith were over in the corner having a private conversation. "Michael, Faith, everything okay?" "Yes, ma'am. Michael and I were just talking with each other and praying with each other this morning. We're just glad to see everyone here this morning together." "Yes, I couldn't agree with you more." "All right then, come on in here. I know we all want to talk, and we just want to go ahead and have one final conversation with us all together before everyone starts doing their own thing and heading home and going back to living your life." "Well, hopefully we won't all be living life the way we've been living it. That's for sure," said Zek. "Son, you are so right, and I am so very proud of you. Especially you," pointing to Michael and Faith. "I'm proud of all of you. But you too, I just want you to know again how much I love you and how grateful I am that you all came up here this weekend."

Everyone gathered around, and everybody was in attendance. David, Michael, Zek, Samuel, Ezra, Essobella, Arrya, Annabella, Daniel, Ester, Raymond, Myra, and Nelsa. Oh, not to mention Jennesis, Eliana, Elijah, Matthew, and Luca. The entire family was present, except Josiah, who still had not come up. Myra looked around. "You know, I don't see Josiah here. Is Josiah awake?" "Yes, ma'am, he's awake. I was down there talking with him and Mike this morning. I'll go down and get him." "All right, thanks, Zek. We'll wait until he comes back up here with Josiah, and then we'll go ahead and get started. Let's call this our 'First tomorrow'." You could hear footsteps coming up the steps.

Zek was the first one to appear, followed by quieter steps. Josiah. "Good morning, son. Glad you could join us." "Yeah, good morning. I'm here now. Y'all can go ahead and get started with y'all praying." "Well, we weren't really having a prayer meeting, but maybe we should have a prayer meeting. Either way, I'm still glad that you could join us this morning." Myra went on. "I just have something I want to say." "I'm glad everyone was here this weekend. This has been the best weekend of my life. All is well. All is well with my soul, and I am grateful for you kids. I'm grateful for you all. I'm grateful for every one of my family members who came this weekend. "I know we had some hard times. I know we had to talk about and say some things that no one wants to even admit, things no one even wants to reveal. And you babies in the room, I know you don't know what I'm talking about, but it's going to be okay." "Yes, ma'am." Myra went on to say, "Well, now, what I want to do is I would like to have Faith and Michael both speak, and then we will be praying. All right, Mike, you want to go ahead and start, and then your cousin can speak next?"

"I will let Faith go first, if that's okay." Faith nodded to Mike and to her aunt, stood up, and began to speak. "Mike and I knew that we really needed to have this gathering with everybody. It had been on Aunt Myra's heart for so long, and when she first mentioned it before Uncle Edward transitioned, unfortunately, we weren't able to move ahead before he passed away. "But we were blessed to be able to find this fine home, this big, beautiful home that was able to house all of us comfortably, right on this even prettier lake. Everything we needed was right here, provided for us. "I'm so very grateful. So much has happened in my life. There was so much heartache, so much pain, and so much that I had to overcome. And I was able to overcome because of my surrender and submission to the Lord Jesus Christ. Because of my surrender and my desire to just be in the presence of God every single day, to learn, to glean, and to grow closer to the Lord. "My entire life has changed for the better. That doesn't mean that it's been an easy road, but it has been one of seeking and following the voice of the Lord in my life. It has been one of obedience in my faith walk. "I know how it changed my life, and I knew it would change everyone else's life too. Right, Mike?" "Yeah, I agree with Faith. I went through some very hard, tumultuous times in my life. It was bad, and I did some things I'm never proud of. But here's the thing, I don't have any shame anymore. "The devil tried to shame me for so long. He tried to keep me chained to shame and guilt. Shame to share my story with anybody, and me not want anyone to know about my past life. I was afraid of how they would look at me.

You all know how church folks do. Sometimes they can be the worst ones when it comes to the judgment of others. And I'm not talking about righteous judgment according to the Word of God, but because they think they are perfect yet doing the same thing with the plank in their own eyes. "I didn't want anybody to know. I didn't want to share it. I didn't want to talk about it. Yet the more I didn't want to talk about it, the more guilty and shameful I began to feel. "When I started to walk in obedience…When I surrendered to the Lord, I found it easier to be healed and free than to stay buried in shame and guilt. The revelation I received was the breakthrough I had been praying for and desiring in my life. That only happened when I began to share, repent, forgive, and believe that there are people who will be blessed by my testimony and who truly loved me, as Mama and Pops did, and wanted the best for me regardless. "None of us deserve all Jesus did for us, but that right there shows you how much He loves us, even while we're stuck and smelly in our sin." "It only happens when you reveal those things that are in your heart, those things that we think are secret. But God knows everything. I don't know if y'all understand what I said.

God knows everything. There's nothing that you can hide. There's nothing that you can do. Even those things that you may not say out loud with your mouth, but they're in your head. God sees the condition of your heart. He knows what's in it, and He knows what we're going to do before we even do it. "I've learned so much as I'm walking with the Lord. There's so much I still have to learn. None of us will ever know everything. But I tell you what, I'm much better off than where I was years ago. "I would like for each of us to go around the room and at least say what we're grateful for. I know it's important, and Faith knows this, for us to keep and maintain a grateful heart for all things God has already done for us."

As Michael was speaking, Josiah was rolling his eyes and just looking back and forth like, "Why am I here? Mike looked over at him and said, "Joey, maybe we'll start with you." "Not me. I don't got nothing to say." "Well, bro, God woke you up this morning. Do you understand that you didn't have to wake up this morning? Your days on this earth could have ended last night in your sleep. Last night could have been the last day of your life. Everything done, too late to make amends, to forgive and ask for forgiveness. Do you have a clue where I'm coming from, Joey? "Yet here you are, blessed to be here with us all and to be living on this day. "Joey" waited for Josiah to acknowledge before he continued, "Do you understand? You're sitting here acting like there's nothing for you to be grateful for." Mike shook his head at the ungratefulness he saw in his younger brother. "All right, fine. I'm grateful I'm still alive. I'm still alive." He threw his arms up in the air, demonstrating his irritation. Is that what you want me to say?" "Well, it is a start. Maybe next time we're together, your heart will truly be changed, and the spirit behind your words will be true. Thank you for sharing, Joey.

Anybody else?" "I'll go next," said Zek. Then Zek cleared his throat. "There's something I need to say to everybody here." "I'm grateful for my family. I'm grateful for my wife Arrya, and I'm grateful for Maddie and Luca, our two boys. I'm grateful that my Mama is still here, and I was able to apologize to everybody, and ask for her forgiveness while I'm still alive." As he looked over at Josiah, he continued. "Yeah, I'm grateful for that, because I could be gone, and I could be living in eternity in hell because of those things that I've said and done and not accepting, truly accepting, the Lord Jesus Christ, as my Lord and Savior, and you know, really meaning it, y'all get me? So, I'm grateful for the turnaround. Amen." "Zeeeek," Zek's name can be heard shouting from the guys in the room, well, all except one.

While the clapping and praising God were happening, Bella jumped to her feet, "Ok, my next!" She stood up with Daniel sitting right beside her, smiling at his bride-to-be. "Well, let me first start by saying, I'm grateful for all of you. I'm grateful for my brothers and sisters, and I'm especially grateful for my sister cousin."

They all laughed a little bit. "I'm grateful for my Mama being the woman of God that she is, and that I've always known her to be. I'm grateful for my Mama not being afraid to face her own fears, to face the things that had tried to hold my mother down for so long. For her to face those secrets that she didn't want anybody to know about for so long. And I'm very grateful to have Daniel in my life. Bella stood silent, pondering what she would say next. "Daniel, he is such a good man, and we are going to go ahead and work on a date for the wedding. I just want you all to know that."

"Yes, about time, is heard by multiple family members. "I'm grateful for Daniel because there is something that I shared with him that I didn't share with everybody, well, except for Essie, and I just shared it with her. After our fireside meet up, I had to let it go and stop hiding my secret, because it wasn't doing anyone a favor, not me and definitely not Daniel." Bella took a deep breath and closed her eyes as Daniel squeezed her hands. "Go ahead, sweets. I'm right here with you."

Bella smiled and nodded her head. "Okay. Well, what I shared with Essie is that I may have a problem having babies, and Daniel wanted a big family. I was afraid to tell Daniel because I know he wants a big family. "But I'm grateful that Daniel loves me no matter what. Whether we have children or not, we will still do what we are supposed to do. If we have to adopt, or if we decide to foster, whatever it is that God has for us to do on this earth, that's what Daniel and I will do as long as we're doing it together." "Amen." Myra gets up and walks over to her daughter and gives her a big hug. "My sweet Bella, of course you will, you have the biggest heart, and you will love whom God gives you to love and take care of." "Yes, Mama, Bella is able to let out as tears begin to well up in her eyes. Sweetheart, you did fine, and it's ok, spoken as Daniel rose to his feet.

"Well, since Bella went, I'll go next," Daniel said. "Everything that Bella said, I'm grateful for her in my life, and I'm appreciative of this family, and for all of you opening your arms to me and welcoming me into your family. I promise to be the son-in-law, the brother-in-law, and the uncle for all of you. I love and appreciate you all." "Yes, we love you, Daniel, and welcome you to the family, early and forever," Bella hollered out. Everyone burst out laughing, definitely lightening the atmosphere of the room. "Well, can I go next?" asked David as he stood up. "Absolutely, son," answered Myra. "There's no way in the world I can sit here and not tell you how much I appreciate every single one of you, every single one of you, down to the babies who started calling me Uncle Davey. Man, they will never know how much it blessed me to hear them calling me Uncle Davey." Tears began to well up in David's eyes as he took the back of his hand to wipe them away. "Ya'll know how much that blessed me, to be called Uncle Davey, to know that I have nieces and nephews…I'm grateful that Miss Myra included me this weekend. She thought enough of me to want me here with you all. She knew my story. She knew who I was. Heck, she knows my mom, so she knows what I'm still dealing with. And she reached out and was gracious to allow me to come here this weekend, knowing it was going to be hard for all of y'all and me, and she still invited me, nonetheless.

"So now I'm grateful that I have a really big family that has welcomed me in. Just like what Daniel said, you opened your arms up, even though some of it was painful for some of you." He looked at Zek, and Zek was shaking his head, nodding up and down. Zek could not keep it in. "Yeah, you're right about that, man. But you know what? You're here now, and I couldn't be any happier to call you my brother." Everyone could not help but agree and laugh a little in agreement. David laughed too. "Man, yeah. I'm letting you all know, I ain't going nowhere. You guys are stuck with me. I'm going to be at Miss Myra's house every Sunday for dinner after church. And if she ain't cooking, it's okay. I will take her and whoever comes over out to eat. I just want to be in her presence. "I can't wait to come over, hang out, and watch football, basketball, car racing, you name the sport. I will be there with any of you that come over, so don't forget to invite your brother, please, I beg you, invite me. Oh, and include Bible study in there as well. And babysitting. Ya'll grown folks want to go out alone, Uncle Davey got your back. Heck, take a cruise, get out of town, I got them." The kids started screaming and laughing. "Uncle Davey! Uncle Davey! Uncle Davey!" and the whole family joined in with the laughter and shouts.

"Honestly, I'm grateful to have a family to call my own now. This is something I prayed for so long. I was a kid wanting so badly to have a family, wanting Pops to bring me over to meet you all. He never did, and it broke me for so long. I didn't know what it all meant, but I knew that I wanted to meet you all once I knew about you. I didn't know it was bad, what was done; I was just a kid who wanted to be wanted and loved. Everyone was now quiet, just watching David stare at the floor, not wanting to rush him to do or say anything. "Being broken, I tried to prove myself. I didn't understand who I was, so I thought that I always had to prove myself, to have to be the best at everything, until I met Jesus. And once that happened, I learned who I was in Him. Accepting the Lord as my Savior, as my Lord, will change everything about who I believe I am. My identity is in Jesus, and that blessed me, and that helped me, and it stopped me from believing I had to prove myself to anyone. I just had to be me.

And I'm grateful that y'all accepted me as I am. So that's my gratefulness." "Yay, that's a good one. That's a good one."

"Essie, you want to go ahead and go?" Essie rose to her feet, walking to stand near where her husband was sitting. "Yes. So y'all know Ezra and me. We've been around a whole circle, with us starting a business, losing the business, and now we're full circle back here again. I'm grateful for our family. I'm grateful for our sweet daughter Eliana and our handsome son Elijah. I'm grateful for Mama, and I'm grateful for Daddy, too. I wish we could have told him that…if only he were still here, but I pray that one day he will know when we all meet again. "I'm grateful for my sisters and my brothers. I'm grateful for my new brother. I'm grateful for all of you in our lives. And I'm grateful just for how Ezra loves and cares about me, and how I had to stop feeling guilty and blaming myself. "Just like Michael said, the enemy will keep you feeling helpless and inadequate. The lies in your head, let me tell you, you believe the lies in your head as if they are your own, especially when you start coming into agreement with them and speaking those lies out of your own mouth. I'm glad that's broken off of me, because I know who I am, and I know that I'm loved, loved very much and very well, I must say. I know that I'm necessary and purposed for such a time as this. I'm equipped, and I know that I'm supposed to be here. I'm supposed to be his wife. I'm supposed to be your sister. You're supposed to be my brothers. You're supposed to be my mom. And these babies are supposed to be my children, I was given to raise, for both of us to raise." Ez and Essie both nodded their heads in agreement. "And I'm grateful for the life that God has given me. God has given me one more day to get it done right." "All right, all right. Amen, Essie. Thank you." "No, thank you, Mike, Faith, and Mama, I'm blessed, we're all blessed to have you in our lives." "Aww, baby, thank you, my sweet girl. Heck, all my girls are sweet girls, and a beautiful, sweet niece, I love you and appreciate the woman of God you are, and my daughter." Essie walked over to her husband, grabbed his hand, and as she sat down, he stood up.

"Well, since my beautiful wife has spoken, I'll go next. Everything Essie said and even more. She is the best. She is my helpmeet. She is who God has blessed me with, and I'm grateful for her. I pray that I will spend every day for the rest of my life letting her know exactly how important she is in my life and how we will do our business, our life, and our ministry together for the Kingdom. "I love you, my dear." "I love you," Essie said back to Ezra. "And my children. Oh, can't forget Ellie and Eli. Oh boy, yeah, I love you too, little knuckleheads." "We love you too, Daddy, but you can't call us that." "All right, all right. I'm sorry. I love you too, blessed children of mine. Not knuckleheads. How about that?" "Yes, Daddy, that's so much better." "All right, all right. Well, thank you, Ez. All right, who's next? Who wants to go?" "Well, let's see. Samuel, would you like to go next?" "Absolutely. I'll go next. I wanted to give the family a chance to go, but hey, I'll go next." "Well, Samuel, you are family. Please remember that. You will always be family, Myra said and smiled. "You know what? I appreciate you saying that. I appreciate you reminding me; it blesses me to know that." Faith said, "Samuel, you will always be part of this family. Don't ever forget it." "Thank you so much, Faith," Nelly spoke up. "Sam, I ditto that, you will always be part of this family. Don't ever forget it." "Thank you so much, Nelly. Coming from you, it means a lot." "I bet it does, and well, it's the truth. And I'm sorry that I let you believe the opposite." "All right, amen. I accept that. "Well, I'm glad to be here this weekend. At first, I was so happy because the weekend for me meant that I was going to be here with my beautiful, sweet girl, Jennesis. But it turned out to be more than I ever imagined at this time, yet always prayed and believed for, and if you're praying and not believing, then what's the point, right?" All heads nodded, affirming his words. This weekend meant that not only was I going to be here with Jennesis, but we got to reconcile. Nelly and I got to talk. We have to forgive. We got to hear each other out. And that meant more to me than anything. Not to mention the fact that Miss Myra still considers me her handsome son-in-law. She told me that." Samuel smiled big nodding his head. "Ya'll must not know that I'm not lying." Everyone started laughing. "Well, she considers me family, and she asked me to come. And the fact that Jennesis was going to be here, even though I was really afraid of how Nelly was going to view me being here, I wanted to see Jennesis more than I cared about how upset Nelly might be." As he said that, Nelly could feel all eyes looking her way. "It's not that I wanted to upset her, but no matter what, I wanted to see Jennesis. And now we've worked through so much in such a short period of time. Who knew that so much change and so much restoration to our souls could come so fast?

"But I truly believe, and I can testify that when God is in the midst, anything could happen because He is in control. And anytime you think you are in control, you will be sorely surprised when you come to realize you are in control of nothing. God is in control. When you submit your cares, it's in His hands, fear and worry cannot stay." So yeah thank you all for being a part of my life thank you for welcoming me still as a member of this family and y'all got to know I am not going anywhere I was still be here and just like David said we going to be here when it comes to coming over to Miss Myra's on Sunday on a holidays on game day well actually game days at Zek's house not really in this Myra's house because she not having that but we're still going to be part of the family. Jennesis picks up on what her dad is saying and stands up and walks over to Samuel.

"Can I say what I'm for? "Yes, sweetheart, go ahead. "I'm grateful, and I'm happy that my daddy is here, but also I'm grateful that my mom and daddy are now talking to each other and they're talking nicely to each other, and they both love me, and I feel love from everybody, and I'm happy now. I'm not anxious about anything, and I'm not sad because I was always kind of sad. I missed my daddy so much, and I didn't like my mom saying anything about my daddy, especially because I knew it wasn't right, so I'm glad that my mom and dad are talking nicely to each other and allowing me to spend time with my dad. Or my mom, I know it will work out." All right, Jenny, my beautiful niece, that was beautiful." "Yes, my girl, it sure was, thank you, Uncle Mike and daddy, and everyone else, as kudos went around the room. Nelly gets up and walks over to her daughter and gives her a big hug and kisses on the top of her head. "You are such an amazing girl, I love you, Jenny, and I'm so glad I'm your mom." "I love you too, mommy, oh wait, I almost forgot to say that I'm grateful that my mom said I can spend the weekends with Grandma Myra, so I can go to church with her, and she will keep teaching me about the Bible." "Yes, love it, Jenny, maybe Miss Myra can teach us all, is heard coming from Nelly. Yes, Mommy, because Grandma Myra is teaching me not to be afraid, and she said don't look at what the crazy world is doing, we have to trust God, and she's teaching me about my words, watching, and the words that come out of my mouth, right Grandma Myra?" "That is exactly right, my dear," agreed Myra.

"What did Mama always say to us when we were young?" asked Bella. If we were saying things that aren't right, Mama would ask us, " Is that what you want to happen?" The family, knowing this was true, all smiled and agreed." "Bella, you are so right, and we all should have learned that lesson, if we didn't understand anything else, agreed Essie. Jennesis continued, "Well, yea grandma Myra will say to me, ' Is that how you want it, young lady, and I'll be like, ' No ma'am, I was just joking. Grandma Myra said, don't joke that way because your words are powerful. These are the things that Grandma Myra has been teaching me when we talk on the phone. Wait, I'm almost finished. Finally, I want to say that I love Grandma Myra, and Ellie, and I love everybody, and I just want everybody to be okay." Aww, and we all love you, Jenny!" Mommy, that's why

I knew you had to be careful about what you said about daddy, because grandma said words are powerful and we're not supposed to be nasty to each other. "Yes, sweetheart, you're right, I know I've said things I should not have said, and I will not do that again; I will do my best to watch what I say." "My dear, we have to watch what we allow to come into our thoughts. God's Word says." "For out of the abundance of the heart his mouth speaks." Yes, ma'am, I understand, more now than ever, Mama, thank you, replied Nelly. Thank you for loving Jenny enough to teach her what I should have been speaking and demonstrating to her, and that is an area that must get better.

"Wow, Miss Myra, and I agree with Nelly, that is pretty powerful and important to share with Jennesis. Thank you so much for teaching her about the Word of God, like you have been doing." "I love you all, and I will pray and help any of you understand God's word. You have to know that. We must all know, and not only that, but we must all understand God's Word as well. We have to have that desire in our spirit to want to know more and allow the Holy Spirit to operate in our lives." "Amen, Mama." "Arrya jumped to her feet, "I don't know if I should even try to go after Jennesis, she let us all know where we as parents need to step up our game, all of us, without even saying it like that," Arrya turned to Jennesis, "and for that, Jenny, I thank you, sweetheart. You are just as beautiful on the inside as you are on the outside." I agree, it is heard from both Samuel and Nelly at the same time, as everyone begins to clap for Jennesis. "Why don't we let the kids go downstairs and play while we continue to have this conversation? I can tell they are getting a little bit bored." I agree said Ez, and both he and Essie got up and helped all the boys go downstairs along with Jenesis and Ellie. "I was happy to come this weekend because I thought to myself if things didn't change, then my life, my marriage, was Zek was going to be over, so this weekend had to work for us, and I'm grateful because that was my prayer, and God answered it. I'm grateful that he heard my cries. God saw my tears, and I thank God that my husband is now walking a different walk and has committed to living a life after the Lord, because when you live for Jesus, you're taking into consideration your family as well. You're going to live life as you are led by the Holy Spirit and the Word of God. He may make mistakes; we all do, none of us is perfect. However, we have to know that we must stay and live a life of repentance and a life that is pleasing to the Lord. Some days, we wake up, and even in our gratefulness, we may not want to be bothered or engage in conversation; we have to understand how to step away and seek God and find our place and our peace in Him and take our cares and concerns to the Lord. I know I have to do a better job at that, because I normally don't; I normally shut down, all the way, and I don't want to talk, heck, I don't even want to look at you. I want to retreat into myself and into my head, which is not always a safe place. The safe place is in the Holy Spirit, because as the bible tells us, man's heart is wicked, it's not just wicked, what does it say, it says in the book of Jeremiah, that the heart is deceitful above all things, and desperately wicked; Who can know it? So, I say all this to say, I too need to do a better job on me, Arrya. I need to trust and put God first, and know that God has my husband, so that I can believe. Mama Myra, I love you, and I thank you for always loving me, treating me like one of your three, or should I say four daughters, and you ladies are and will always be my sisters, the sisters that I never had in my family. I love you all. I love being able to be here with you to feel your love, to feel your concern for me.

I love how you take care of our children, how when we're in your homes, I know Maddie and Luca are okay, and especially when Mama Myra is here with them, she takes great care of all of us." "That she does., that's how Mama is with everyone, and after all I had been through, having her in my life, as my mother and even dad, because he was still alive, and he was angry, very angry but not at me," Michael made sure she explained, "but over the hurt I experienced, he loved on me, and having a dad love on you, especially a dad like ours, that just didn't act like he regretted anything, had an answer for everything that sort of made him appear right, even when he wasn't, so thank you Mama, we all appreciate you." "Amen, thank you, Michael." Mama Myra your heart is so big, God blessed us all when he blessed you as our mother, Auntie, grandmother, mother in love, and we're grateful for you in our life, and we thank you for not, only opening these doors to us, but opening your heart, and opening your soul, and opening everything that was going to happen this weekend even though it was going to be painful, it was going to hurt but it was going to be necessary. I love you all, and I thank you, and I give special thanks to my husband Zek, thank you for stepping up to be the man that God has called you to be. For being willing to change and willing to be vulnerable in front of all of us. I love you, my dear, "I love you too, and I'm very sorry again." "Well, alright," Michael raised to take over the reins of the meeting, "I believe that's everyone, but Faith, Aunt Ester, and Uncle Raymond. "You haven't spoken either, Michael, Faith reminded him. "Oh, yeah, you're right, it has been so good, I actually forgot.

"Aunt Ester and Uncle Raymond would y'all like to speak?" Michael asked. Raymond motioned to Ester to go ahead and speak, as he didn't even want to get up. Well, Ester began, "I don't want to say too much, but I am happy that we came up here this weekend, Raymond and I know that I was not being open or even friendly when I first came. I had my guard up and just didn't know what to expect, and definitely didn't want anything to be said that would put me on the defensive. But that's what happens when you have secrets, always waiting for it to slip up, and what will you say, what will the plan be? I know I act like I didn't want to talk and didn't want me to bother, but I know that I was holding so much in, and still trying to be secretive, trying to not to let anything slip, but I'm glad everything is out. I'm glad that Myra and I got to share about our upbringing in what led to some of the secrets and things that happened to us, and nobody knew about it, so it's good that we finally got it out. I apologize for everything with Faith, and just how scared I was to let her know she wasn't our birth daughter, as if I was going to lose her. That was crazy fear, and fear like that brings all kinds of bad fruit along with it.

It was important for everyone to understand the situation we found ourselves in. I had to learn that our upbringing, Myra and I, wasn't our fault. We were children, and we were girls who wanted to be accepted, who wanted, no, deserved to be loved. How do parents not love their children? Children are a blessing, and sometimes, they don't come like we want. Bella, please understand that, my dear. Even if you aren't able to have a child naturally, can you see the love and trust God has for you to take another child and rear that child, teach His child, love His child? He expects that, and He knows you will do just that. He can trust you, dear. He can trust Daniel." Bella put her hands over her eyes as Daniel wrapped his arms around her shoulders.

"My sister, Myra. I'm deeply sorry, and from this point forward, I will be the sister I was supposed to be to you for so very long. Thank you for loving Faith the way you do. You really do love her like a daughter, because she is, she is the first daughter of our King, our mighty God, and he blessed you to bring her, a beautiful and healthy baby, into this world, already knowing the circumstances we would all face, yet knowing she was already loved and cared for. Thank you for standing and being the woman of God that you are, despite all opposition to your character and the good that you do. Your intentions are always good, even when we don't understand or see them. We don't always see them, because we don't want to. We are convicted by them, and that makes us look at our own hearts and ill intentions.

"Thank you, my sister, for coming here, both you and Raymond, more than me. I know Faith appreciated you being here and being a part of this family. Bella, one more thing I want to tell you. No matter what is said to you, go seek out whatever you need to do, and don't let them just tell you anything. Always get more than one or even two opinions. Do whatever test you need to do." "Thank you, Aunt Ester, and you don't have to worry, Daniel and I are already praying, and we have given it over to God, and we started studying to find the Scriptures that we will be speaking concerning the family we desire." "I just want you to be encouraged because I wasn't. I didn't do the things necessary, like what I'm saying to you, and it made me bitter. Bitter on the inside, and that bitterness turned to the outside and in, how I saw not only myself, but the world around me, and especially those closest to me. "Well, Ester, you know you are well forgiven by this family; there is no finger-pointing in here, we all have our faults, and that's what this weekend was all about, opening up and truly forgiving each other." "Yes, my sister, and I will keep letting you know how grateful for you in my life, Myra." As Ester stopped speaking, she looked over at her husband, still sitting in the chair, and as he spotted her glaring at him, he quickly turned his head as if he had lost something.

"Raymond, are you going to say anything? Ester said to her husband. "I mean, well, I guess I'm glad I'm here… yeah, kind of like what she said. I'll do better, and I'm kind of sorry for anything I said or done, and you know, so yeah, just kind of forgive me, forgive me, ok? "All right, Uncle Ray, we forgive you, but man, you've got to do better, too." "Yeah, Mike, I hear you, and I will do better. I might even go to church with one of y'all." "Well, Daddy, you can come with Mike or me, that we for sure would like to see happen," as they all chucked and agreed. Well, looks like we're bringing it all home, right, Mike? "Cousin sister Faith," "Yes," as everyone began to laugh again!!! "Well, just like Mama said at the beginning, I'm grateful that everybody came. I'm grateful that I didn't get any pushback, even if there was much discussion amongst us; everyone still showed up, and I appreciate it more than you can ever imagine. I feel like I got my family! We just got a family do-over, we've been blessed, and we have to recognize it because so many don't receive a chance like we just got. It's not just for us alone, but for our children, and future children, and even for those on the outside, to see us as an example of what family functioning in love, together in Christ, should look like. No one is perfect, and that is not what I'm saying, but what I am saying is that we can't give up, and we must stay connected to the only WAY, who is the

Way, Truth, and the Life! There's a lot we can't go back and redo, but we can start doing better from this day forward. We can love better; we can cherish each other's company. We can respect who each of us is. We can be there for each other, we can pray for each other, we can be the blessing to each other that we're supposed to be. Life really is shorter than what you think, and there are so many who won't get to see this day, who already have not seen this day that we're in right now, and yet here we all are. Please don't take it for granted, pops already isn't here with us, so let's do better. I love you all, every single one of you in this room. I love you all, I cherish our time together." I do as well, Myra added." Michael turned and looked at his mother, "Mama, thank you so much." "Son, you are welcome, and I thank you and Faith for everything, for all you did putting this together. I'm so grateful for both of you in my life. I mean, let's be clear, I'm grateful for all of you in my life, but these two right here, like Moses when his arms got heavy and his brother Aaron on one side and Hur on the other side, this is what they did for me. When all I could do was fall down to my knees and pray because I didn't know what else to do. I have one picking me up, the other one praying for me. One covering, the next covering everyone. This is what each of you did for me, and for our family. You never stopped, you never retreated, you never questioned what

God told you, or what your instructions were. You didn't allow what you saw with your eyes, or heard with your ear, to make you quit, and you covered each other, and blessed each other. Both of you offer up kind words, and you have a kind and loving spirit, so yes, kindness and love come from your heart. As a family, we must love each other the way God wants us to love all people, to pray and not just complain and talk about what they did, or what's not working, but help each other to see how, through God, all things are possible when you just believe. I didn't mean to butt in on Michael's time, but I just wanted you two to know how I feel about you, how I feel about each and every one of you." Michael turned and gave his mother a big hug, as each person began to rise to their feet, hugging Myra and then hugging each other as well. "Wow, this gratefulness discussion really did work today." Well, almost; the only one that remained in his seat was Josiah, shaking his head. He got up and walked out, going back down to his room. Now that everyone was on their feet, side conversations started to take place. Michael grabbed David's hand and pulled him in for a big brotherly hug. "David, I know we had never met prior to this gathering, Mom invited you, and we spoke on the phone. I was excited to meet you and know I had another brother." "Ah man, thank you, I looked forward to meeting you as well, meeting you all of you. I didn't remember seeing you at the funeral home, and to be honest, I was so torn up inside, I just wanted to escape, until Miss Myra stopped me. "Yeah, I'm grateful that my mom not only knew about you, but also had been praying for you, and wanted you to be part of our family. That's the kind of woman our Mama has always been. Yes, our father did not do right by her. He didn't treat her like he was supposed to, and mostly it did change as he got older, but there was a lot of damage done. He had an indiscretion in his marriage, something that should not have happened; your mother wasn't the first one. But you know, bro, God knew you'd be here. He knew how it would turn out despite the sin, and my brother, you are a great guy, and we're all grateful you're a part of our family.

Right then, Samuel came walking over to them both, grabbing them both, "my guys," Samuel, man, thank you, man, for coming." "Sam, I'm so glad to have met you, and I hope we can keep in touch, catch a game, shoot pool, whatever, man, just let me know. You can't have too many brothers in Christ, and I'm glad to have all of you. In one weekend, I went from just me to having five of you, five men, and four sisters to boot. Yeah, no one can tell me I'm not a blessed man." "Right you are David, we all feel the same about you, and Sam, let me just say, Mama always talks about you and she talks about how good of a man you are, and how you love Jennesis so much, and I'm glad you came I'm glad that you didn't allow the situation what was happening between you and Nelly, stop you from coming this weekend because had you not showed up what transpired, the healing the forgiveness, would not have happened. You would have been sitting at home still in the same situation." Bella approached Nelly, touching her arm, "Hey, Nelly, my sister, I know you and I never really got along, and I apologize for my part, because it takes two, and I said things and thought things that weren't nice, I ask you to forgive me, please." Nelly nodded her head towards her sister, "I do, Bella, I do, and I ask the same thing, for your forgiveness, and as I already told you all, I will do better, and you can call me to the carpet when I don't. I'm still a work in progress, just want to remind you all, just in case, old Nelly pops up, be patient with me." Everyone nodded, and Bella laughed. "You got it, my sister! I'm glad that you came. I know you were upset because you knew Sam was coming, but I'm glad you still came. Because you came, look what happened. Look at the goodness and the healing that was unleashed. Forgiveness, nothing but love. This is what love and forgiveness do for a family. Also, if you ever need me to take Jennesis, you just let me know; she is always welcome." "Absolutely, and hey, with her big heart, you know she'll be a pretty good babysitter. As the fellowshipping continued, Faith approached both Daniel and Bella, "Bella and Daniel you're like two peas in the same pod, always together you were going to be one beautiful couple, and I cannot wait to be at your wedding. Bella spoke up, "you definitely will be there, because Daniel and I would like you to officiate our wedding, if you would." "Glory to God, absolutely my sister cousin, yes, I'd love to do that for you. Thank you so much for asking me. I will do it for you." "We're grateful that you can do this for us." "As soon as you guys set the date, please let me know so I can go ahead and make sure that I'm prepared to do what I'm supposed to do for you." "You got it," Daniel replied. "I want to say to Zek and Arrya, y'all are going to be okay. I know you were fearful about coming this weekend, and I know just after what you just said about how you had stated that something had to change, or else this was it, and God honored your prayers. Arrya, it was your faith and your obedience. Obedience to the Word of God and to your marriage. The Lord loves us. He loves family and especially marriages between a man and a woman, as he created. I just wanted to tell you that." "Thank you, Daniel, we both appreciate your words." Ezra and Essie, and just like Bella and Daniel, now big brother Zek and Arrya, we're surrounded by love, so all of us singles are getting a great lesson, and it started with our Mama and her love, well...let me correct myself. It started from our Heavenly Father, who first loved us all, and who created marriage and our relationship with Him, as an example of how it is to be here on earth and why." "Amen, I couldn't agree with you more, Cousin Mike," Faith interjected. "Not to mention I love these kids, all of them calling me Miky or Uncle Mike," "Yeah, right Mike," David joined in, "I'm telling you, I'm loving Uncle Davey, just music to my ears, and it's cool having nieces and nephews, just cool." "Well, soon, it will make your wallet music when they see how easy it is to hit you up," laughed Ez. "Alright, I get it, and it's totally ok." Ez smacking David on the back, "man, I will not forget you said that." Everyone busted out laughing in the room. Well, family, "we must do more of what we did this weekend in the future. Maybe we'll even be able to go on some trips together. How awesome it would be for all of us to take a big family vacation together.

"Mama, that will be a wonderful idea," as everyone enthusiastically agreed. "Look," Nelly said, "I can use a vacation, but not just a weekend; I need more than a week.

"The LORD is near to those who have a broken heart, and saves such as have a contrite spirit. Many are the afflictions of the righteous, But the LORD delivers him out of them all.

(Psalm 34:18-19, NKJV)

Chapter 18.

BLOODLINE BREAKERS

Faith walked to the center of the room. "I've been listening here listening to everyone speak about their gratefulness, give their testimony, recap the whole weekend, and let me tell you, my heart is so full. I'm so full of joy. Look at what the Lord has done for our family. He is truly restoring our family! We still have some things that we need to work at, who doesn't? But when we commit to serving God, and we surrender our ways to him, it's not about us; it's about what he wants to do through us. What a great God we serve, and I'm so grateful to be part of this family. Mommy and Daddy, I love you both, and even though you didn't birth me, you still raised me, and I'm grateful to you both and admire my Aunt Myra, you're my only aunt on Mama's side, and I love you for life. I will always love you, and I thank you for allowing me to come into the world.

If you had made a different decision, I wouldn't even be here, for such a time as this. But God knew," as she looked at everyone in the room, "family, God knows what He is doing, He knows the beginning, and He already wrote the end. Aunt Myra, you have so much love in your heart. You're always ready to give and do for us, even if we can't do for ourselves. You give us the benefit of the doubt, and if we're acting ugly and speaking even uglier, you still forgive us. "Let's gather around and grab a hand. Faith and I would like to pray, and we would like to have you guys repeat after us as we renounce and break some things off of us and off of this generation and all of the things that may have been opened up because of our ancestors.

We're going to make sure that we break these things off of us, the hidden sins, the covenants that need to be broken off our family, that were made a long time ago, like idol worship, pride, strife, anger, jealousy, another big one, the spirit of fear, and the spirit of pride. Let's all grab hands. In fact, let's read a Bible verse?" Myra quickly asked, "Someone go and bring the kids back up here?" "No worries, I can do it." Daniel ran and called the kids to come back upstairs for prayer. "Uncle Mike, can I read the bible? I have my own bible up in my room?" "Okay, sweetheart, he said to Jennesis, "go get your Bible and come on back quickly." Jennesis ran as fast as she could to her room and grabbed her bible. Waiting for Jenny to come back, and when Jenny returned, Mike said, "Ok, let me see where the Lord is going to have us start.

"Jenesis, I want you to start with Psalm 23, and then I will end with Psalm 91, and in between we will all pray, Ya'll got that?" "Ok, Psalm 23, Jennesis began to flip pages looking for the chapter and then began to read the word of the Lord, with all the confidence God gave to her. Nelly and Samuel both exchange glances at the growth and love of God, their little girl, who is growing so fast.

"Psalm 23: The Lord is my shepherd, I shall not want he makes me to lie down and Green Pastures, he leads me beside the Still Waters, He restores my soul he leads me in the path of righteousness for his namesake yay though I walk through the valley of the shadow of death I will fear no evil for you are with me your rod and staff they comfort me you prepare a table before me and the presence of my enemies you anoint my head with oil my cup runs over surely goodness and mercy shall follow me all the days of my life and I will dwell in the house of the Lord forever and ever."

"That was Psalm 23!" "Amen, Jennesis, great job. Thank you so much for reading to the family." "My sweet girl," says Myra, "thank you, Jennesis." "You're welcome, Uncle Mike." Let's go ahead and break down this bondage in this family line." Michael begins to pray as he's praying, he's worshiping and seeking the Lord, and asking God to not only forgive them of their sins, as the family humbly comes before the Lord. As he is asking for forgiveness, and breaking covenants that were made by their ancestors.

The family begins to also pray and worship, and repent. Shouts, cries, weeping, and tears, breakthroughs were not being held back but ushered in to this family, so desperately seeking after God. After praying, Michael asked, "Who here wants to rededicate their life to the Lord?" Everyone raises their hand but Josiah. Zek says, "Mike, I'm ready to physically rededicate my life to God. I am, too; they all speak up. "Well, I think it's about time I did the same thing, says Ester. "What about you, Raymond?" "Well, I asked for forgiveness, but I guess I need the whole package deal." "Package deal, really, Dad." "What? You know what I mean," as he shrugs his shoulders. I want the whole package, and your mother and me, and I'm going to change Faith. I'm sorry, as I said before, please forgive me. So again, the whole package deal, after this weekend, everyone in this room needs the whole package deal, and especially that young fella over there with the long face," and as he said it, all eyes turned to

Josiah, who had refused to join in praying, in everything taking place. Even the little ones, let me talk to my nieces and nephews. "I know you all know about Jesus, right? "Yes, we do," they answered him.

"Uncle Mike, we pray all the time at home and in church, so we understand, and we love God, right, Luca? Yes, we love Jesus, and we know why He had to go to the cross. Yes, and some kids, they don't know, but we know, right, Mommy? "Yes, Arrya answered back. Uncle Mike, Eli, and I understand, and we already said yes in church, and we got baptized, but we can do it again, because we love Jesus too, yeah, we all do." Everyone in the room couldn't believe what they were witnessing. "May I say something, Uncle Mike, all of us kids, well, I prayed with them this weekend, and I talked to them about how we are to act, and treat each other, and I read my bible to them, and they all listened to me."

"Jennesis, girl, I think you are ready for ministry. Well, I'm so glad you told us this, and I'm so glad you all know what you know, but what I'm about to do is read it straight from the bible ok." Let's pray with the kids first. Zek and Arrya, you heard your sons, Ez and Essie, you heard Eli and Ellie, and Nelly and Sam, you both heard and witnessed your daughter as well." They have all agreed and said they want to accept Jesus as their Lord and their Savior, so let's all pray, and kids, you will repeat after me?" "We will all do this along with the kids." Before Michael could begin, Josiah stormed out of the room, "I don't have time for this. I don't need to do this. I just need to go live my life. I'm out of here. Josiah turns around and walks out the door, slamming it on the way out.

"What in the world, Myra says, clearly upset. What has gotten into Josiah that he's willing to turn his back on the Lord?" "Mama, do you want me to go after him?" asked Zek. "No, don't go after him. This has to be his decision, but what we're going to do after we pray is to pray for him and lift him up in prayer. When we all come together, and on one accord, praying God's Will for Josiah, we know God will do the rest. The seeds have already been planted in Josiah's life, so right now we're praying for the water to come, and God will receive the glory in all of this, you watch. Josiah's going to return to the Lord." Ok, let's continue. I'm going to read out of the Bible the Scriptures Romans 10:9-10 says, "When confessing the Lord Jesus Christ, and accepting Him, repenting and confessing that He is your Savior, I'm going to read, and please repeat after me, okay."

Michael begins to read the Word of God as the entire room repeats after him, each one verbally repeating and accepting Jesus as their Lord and Savior. All glory to God, a family in unison receiving salvation, and most re-dedicating their lives back to the Lord, well, all except Josiah, who had walked out of the room and onto the porch when the prayer began. As Josiah is walking to his car, his phone starts ringing. Looking down at his phone, he sees it's his daughter's mother calling, "Man, I don't have time for this!" His attitude already set to fire, he answers the phone, thinking it's probably about the money he owes her, that has to be it; other than that, she doesn't call. Joyous, what do you want? Why are you calling me? "Josiah just I have been trying to reach, something's wrong with Lai-Joy?

"What do you mean something's wrong with her?" He then heard Lai-Joy's mother say.

"She's very lethargic, I can't get her up, and I think I really need to take her to the hospital right now. I don't know what's wrong with her, but I'll let you know. "What did you do? He screamed at Joyous. "Did she fall? Did she hurt herself? It's all your fault; it's all your fault! You are always running the streets and not watching her." "No, no Josiah, something's wrong with her. She's been like this for days, just not herself. I know something's wrong with her, but I'll let you know. I just wanted to let you know that I got to take her to the emergency room, but I'll let you know what they tell me. I will tell you!" "Yeah, call me back! Call me back as soon as you can, all right!" Josiah hangs up the phone, and he stands there not knowing what to do. He didn't know if he should leave or go back in. "Naw man," he said out loud to himself, "I can't go back in there, can't have them trying to preach to me, trying to run my life, telling me how I need God! I don't need anybody!" Instead of going back inside to his family, he jumps in his car and speeds away. The family hears the tires screeching, and they look at each other. We need to pray now, let's pray, because Josiah needs Jesus more than he realizes. They bow their heads and begin to pray and intercede for Josiah and for their family.

"But may the God of all grace, who called us to His eternal glory by Christ Jesus, after you have suffered a while, perfect, establish, strengthen, and settle you."

(1 Peter 5:10, NKJV)

Chapter 19.

New Beginnings

Can you imagine the joy Myra had in her heart? Her children had finally come home, but not to a physical home. They were coming back to their spiritual home in Jesus. Yes, all is very well with Myra, now and forever.

The sting of words, attitudes, and unfair treatment demonstrates the state of the world. But God calls us not to act like the world, to demonstrate a heart of forgiveness, a heart of love and understanding, a heart that believes you can overcome the struggles when you surrender and seek the only living God. How can we do this? By demonstrating the love of God toward others, by readjusting our minds from a worldly perspective to a Kingdom mindset.

Many in the world turn their backs on the hurting, the helpless, the lost, and the challenged, those who may have had a misstep, even a big mistake. Yet people keep the bondage of their sin around their neck, never allowing them to receive forgiveness. However, Jesus has called us all to do our part in the world, and with the time that we still have on this earth, to share the love of Almighty God with a very hurting world.

With exposure, we can experience freedom when the hidden things or issues come to light. The enemy is strategic; he attacks our souls. His attacks begin in the mind. The attacks we face are often in our minds when the enemy begins planting thoughts, twisting our perspective, and causing chaos and confusion in the lives of believers. When we begin to speak and act on those very thoughts, we have now activated those beliefs and lies that were planted within our minds. When we come into agreement and begin to speak it out of our mouth, the reality of what we are saying has not been established in truth. "For we do not wrestle against flesh and blood, but against principalities, against powers, against the rulers of the darkness of this age, against spiritual hosts of wickedness in the heavenly places" (Ephesians 6:12, NKJV). After speaking it out and believing it, our actions align with our words and thoughts. Hopelessness, confusion, anger, you name it, it is now in full effect, playing on repeat.

Light must come to the dark areas of our lives. This is exposure, revealing the lies, secrets, the pain, the hurt, and the unforgiveness. Our healing will come when truth is revealed and uncovered in our lives. The accepted love of God heals and exposes lies, yet enables a person to not be afraid of the exposed memory, nor endure the pain of reliving or experiencing those past soul wounds, when we know the Holy Spirit is at work in our lives and when we are submitted to the Holy Spirit. "For the weapons of our warfare are not carnal but mighty in God for pulling down strongholds, casting down arguments and every high thing that exalts itself against the knowledge of God, bringing every thought into captivity to the obedience of Christ" (2 Corinthians 10:4–5, NKJV).

Forgiveness is not about believing a person is getting away with whatever has taken place. Forgiveness is less about them and more about your spiritual state and your relationship with Jesus. It is about our heart's posture and our peace of mind. It is for our good when we extend forgiveness. Unforgiveness, bitterness, anxiety, and shame can disintegrate into ashes when the sacrifice of forgiveness is extended, even in pain and trauma. Peace of mind, spirit, and soul, peace can then ascend.

Not forgiving is bondage. We will all remain in bondage to the situation and to the person who hurt us. This bondage can eat away at our souls and our peace. Start by offering the sacrifice of forgiveness, to offer and to receive the peace our hearts are yearning for. Forgiveness does not have to reopen a relationship that is over, but it will allow you to live again. If by chance, the person who caused the pain and hurt in your life has passed away, the closure needed can still be received when we forgive. God truly does see our hearts in the act of forgiving and not forgiving. When we accept Jesus as our Savior and ask for forgiveness, He will forgive. All the sin, hatred, and evil in the heart and deeds of man, yet Jesus still forgave us and went to the cross, demonstrating His full love for us. When God is allowed to come in and do the work in the lives of His children by the Holy Spirit. "Make allowance for each other's faults and forgive anyone who offends you. Remember, the Lord forgave you, so you must forgive others" (Colossians 3:13, NLT). Standing and believing the truth, the truth about yourself, and the truth of God's Word. "If we confess our sins, He is faithful and just to forgive us our sins and to cleanse us from all unrighteousness" (1 John 1:9, NKJV).

Well, what about repentance? Are you really sorry? Is there remorse in your soul? Do you desire to live right, to make amends to those who have been hurt by your words, actions, and deeds? Do you ever wonder how God feels when He sees the actions and the hearts of His children, treating people any way they desire, as if it is only about themselves? Selfishness is rampant in the world, only caring about self and desiring what others have, as if it makes them better. If you know the story of how Moses helped free the children of Israel, how not only did they wander and complain, but they also began to blame Moses for what they saw as a lack. Nothing but complaints and idol worship is how they showed God their gratefulness. How crazy is it that they wanted to go back and be slaves? We may look at it and shake our heads, but that is how we live today, not caring about others, and especially about our own actions, as if we are in right standing, yet God has seen and heard it all. 1 John 1:9 NKJV declares, "If we confess our sins, He is faithful and just to forgive us our sins and to cleanse us from all unrighteousness." He wants His children healed. He wants His children to walk in freedom, with joy and peace in their souls. Let us start with repentance and forgiveness. Surely, you must be tired of trying to live for the world and not for the Lord. "If My people who are called by My name will humble themselves, and pray and seek My face, and turn from their wicked ways, then I will hear from heaven, and will forgive their sin and heal their land" (2 Chronicles 7:14, NKJV). But God calls us not to act like the world, but to demonstrate a heart of forgiveness, a heart of love and understanding, a heart that believes you can overcome the struggles when you surrender and seek the only living God. How can we do this? By demonstrating the love of God toward others, by readjusting our minds from a worldly perspective to a Kingdom mindset.

"And he said to him, 'Son, you are always with me, and all that I have is yours. It was right that we should make merry and be glad, for your brother was dead and is alive again, and was lost and is found.

(Luke 15:31-32, NKJV)

Chapter 20.

GLORY

All glory belongs to God! The love of our Heavenly Father is demonstrated throughout this book. It's shown in each member, starting with Myra. The unconditional love that Myra has for her family demonstrates how Jesus loves us all. Even in our imperfections, our sin, our huge faults, He is still standing with His arms open wide, welcoming His children home. Myra James is an example of this for her family; she loves her family with all of her heart. Children whom she did her best to raise up in the fear and knowledge of our good, good Father. When her children slipped, some more than others, she continued to pray for the restoration and the reconciliation they needed. Myra trusted the Lord, and she had faith in the knowledge that God hears her prayers and sees her tears. Just like the prodigal son, who squandered the money his father gave him on riotous living, when he came to his senses and returned home, his daddy was waiting for him. His daddy ran to him, oh, the joy he must have felt!

The James family received a beautiful gift. They received the gift of that needed restoration for themselves and for their generations to come. And to God, we give all the glory and all the praise. He's calling you home, He is calling you to rest, He is waiting for you!

Prayer of Salvation

"Heavenly Father, I come to you as a sinner. I believe that your son Jesus, was the perfect sacrifice, and He died on the cross for my sins, and He was buried and rose again. I repent of my sins, I turn from my sins, and I ask for your forgiveness. Lord, I ask that you come into my life to be and be Lord over my life. Thank you for salvation and a new life in You.

"And it shall come to pass That whoever calls on the name of the Lord Shall be saved."

(Acts 2:21)

About the Author

Denise C. Herndon Harvey is a Christian author, speaker, and transformation coach with a passion for sharing God's grace, love, faith, and hope. She is the author of the children's books *Growing Up Sassafras: Where Is My Daddy?* and *Emergence of Me: Discovering My Identity and Courage Within*, and an Amazon bestselling contributing author in multi-author devotionals.

Her writing centers on faith, family restoration, and the power of God's love. Inspired by the hurt and hopelessness she has witnessed within families, Denise uses her voice to encourage healing, identity, and transformation through Christ.

Denise has been featured on television, radio, and podcasts, and her work has been showcased on the Disney Times Square digital billboard. She has participated in major literary events, including the Tucson Festival of Books, LA Times Book Fair, and international book fairs in Seoul, South Korea, and London. She has also been featured in various publications and literary platforms, including the Readers Magnet Festival of Storytellers and the New York Library Association Annual Conference and Trade Show.

She holds a master of arts in Human Services Counseling with a concentration in Family Advocacy and Public Policy from Liberty University. She also earned dual Bachelor of Science degrees in Psychology with concentrations in Christian Counseling and Crisis Counseling, along with a minor in Biblical Studies. Denise is a Certified Life Coach, with a certificate in grief coaching as well as Mental Health Coaching. She has also completed training and received a certificate in voice coaching.

Denise has been married to her husband, a retired Air Force veteran, for over 42 years. Together, they have two adult children and six grandchildren.

www.ingramcontent.com/pod-product-compliance
Lightning Source LLC
LaVergne TN
LVHW010558100826
845148LV00014B/2753

9798950585005